What people are saying about …

The Fresh Life Series

"I'm touched and blessed by Lenya and Penny's heart for His kingdom."

Kay Arthur, Bible teacher and
author of many best-selling Bible studies

"What a great way for women to learn to study the Bible: interesting stories, thought-provoking questions, and a life-changing approach to applying Scripture. Lenya and Penny provide a great method so women can succeed and grow spiritually in a short period of time. Kudos!"

Franklin Graham, president and CEO of Billy Graham
Evangelistic Association and Samaritan's Purse

"Skip and Lenya Heitzig have been friends of my wife, Cathe, and I for more than twenty years. Lenya loves to study God's Word and teach it to women in a way that is both exciting and accessible. I trust her latest book will be a blessing to you."

Greg Laurie, pastor and evangelist of Harvest Ministries

"Lenya and Penny's love for the Lord and knowledge of His Word uniquely equip them to help other women discover the pathway to God through these in-depth Bible studies."

Kay Smith, wife of Chuck Smith (Calvary Chapel)

"The Fresh Life Series is an insightful and in-depth look at God's Word. Through these Bible studies Lenya Heitzig and Penny Rose lead women to deeper intimacy with God."

K. P. Yohannan, president of Gospel for Asia

"Lenya and Penny have created another wonderful Bible study series that invites participants to spend time in God's Word and then see the Word come to fruition in their lives. What a blessing! These studies are perfect for small groups or personal daily devotions."

Robin Lee Hatcher, women's event speaker
and award-winning author

Live Faithfully

The Fresh Life Series

A
20-Minutes-a-Day
Study

Live Faithfully

A Study in the Book of James

Lenya Heitzig & Penny Rose

David C Cook®

transforming lives together

LIVE FAITHFULLY
Published by David C Cook
4050 Lee Vance View
Colorado Springs, CO 80918 U.S.A.

David C Cook Distribution Canada
55 Woodslee Avenue, Paris, Ontario, Canada N3L 3E5

David C Cook U.K., Kingsway Communications
Eastbourne, East Sussex BN23 6NT, England

Some names have been changed to protect privacy.

Some material and questions written by Kristi DuBay and Sharon Danneels.

LCCN 2012947819
ISBN 978-0-7814-0613-0
eISBN 978-1-4347-0596-9

© 2012 Lenya Heitzig and Penny Rose
Published in association with William K. Jensen Literary Agency, 119 Bampton Court, Eugene, OR 97404
First edition published as *Pathway to Living Faith* by Tyndale in 2002
© Lenya Heitzig and Penny Rose, ISBN 978-0-8423-7234-3

The Team: Terry Behimer, Karen Lee-Thorp, Amy Konyndyk, Caitlyn Carlson, Karen Athen
Cover Design: ThinkPen Design, Greg Jackson

Printed in the United States of America
First Edition 2012

1 2 3 4 5 6 7 8 9 10

082912

Contents

Introduction

What games did you play growing up? If you crave a good mystery, perhaps Clue appealed to you. Wordsmiths no doubt loved games that challenged verbal skills, such as Taboo, Outburst, or Boggle. Crossword puzzles and sudoku drew deep thinkers into their complex webs. And if you lacked access to board games and puzzles, perhaps your parents' closet provided all that you needed for a good old-fashioned game of "Grown Up." Dressing up in adult clothing and pretending to be an executive, librarian, or teacher filled your time with imagination.

The joke is told about a teacher who once asked her class what they wanted to become when they grew up. Kids shouted out, "President!" "A policeman!" "A professor!" One by one they answered until it was Betty's turn.

She said, "When I grow up, I want to be Possible."

"Possible? What do you mean?" asked the instructor.

"Mom often says that I'm impossible. So, when I'm a big girl I want to become possible."

Although we laugh at childish games, the truth is that as adults some of us still play games. For example:

- Instead of Sorry we play Be Sorry. The ultimate goal is to lay a guilt complex on others.
- Rather than playing Risk we take Unnecessary Risks, messing around with sex, drugs, and rock and roll.
- Monopoly morphs into Monopolize, where insecure people demand the time, attention, and emotional resources of others.

G. K. Chesterton once said, "The human race ... has been playing at children's games from the beginning and will likely do it till the end, which is a nuisance for the few people who grow up."[1] Instead of playing "make-believe," the apostle James challenges Christians to join the real world and Live Faithfully. The early church was caught up in playing games too. And James identifies some of the different players in this "Game of Life."

James 1 reveals Quitters: in hard times his brethren wanted to take their balls and go home. *Patience* turns Quitters into Conquerors: "Count it all joy when you fall into various trials, knowing that the testing of your faith produces patience" (James 1:2–3).

James 2 highlights Braggers: some members of the early church could talk a good game but had never left the bench or made a play. *Works* change braggers into those who behave: "You see then that a man is justified by works, and not by faith only" (James 2:24).

James 3 exposes Bullies: his audience was guilty of calling each other names. They hurled "sticks and stones" instead of blessings. *Taming the tongue* will convert bullies into blessers: "Out of the same mouth proceed blessing and cursing. My brethren, these things ought not to be so" (James 3:10).

James 4 shows Squabblers: these twelve tribes of Israel suffered from sibling rivalry, arguing over who'd get the biggest piece of pie. *Humility* transforms those who squabble into servants: "He gives more grace. Therefore He says: 'God resists the proud, but gives grace to the humble'" (James 4:6).

James 5 depicts Hoarders: they think that he who dies with the most toys wins. *Eternity* transforms hoarders into helpers: "Establish your hearts, for the coming of the Lord is at hand" (James 5:8).

Just as James challenged Jewish believers—his "brethren"—to grow up, the apostle Paul exhorted the Gentiles to become mature too. Paul wrote to the Corinthians, "When I was a child, I talked like a child, I thought like a child, I reasoned like a child. When I became a man, I put childish ways behind me" (1 Cor. 13:11 NIV).

It's true. There comes a day in each of our lives when childish things fall by the wayside. Donald Grey Barnhouse wrote, "A mature adult never has to give up anything ... but there are a lot of things that will *give him up*. They will go one by one. There will be no grief. It is the way childish occupations are abandoned."

For instance, I (Lenya) used to play with Barbies. I loved to make them new clothes and perform wedding ceremonies with Ken or Skipper. In my youth, it never occurred to me that Barbies were for babies. I didn't join Barbies Anonymous or throw them in the trash as a sign of independence and maturity. Instead, my older sister began to lose interest in the fun. And it wasn't as much fun playing with dolls all alone. She started reading Nancy Drew novels as an alternative. At night she'd retell the latest mystery to me as I fell asleep. Before I knew it, I had graduated from Barbies to books. I didn't give up

Barbies—rather, I grew up to the next level of maturity and left Barbies behind me.

Do you still play games with God or others? Isn't it time for you to move forward in maturity? It is our prayer that in studying James's epistle, "you may be mature and complete, not lacking anything" (James 1:4 NIV). Make-believe is not for true believers in Christ. Instead of exercising your imagination, "be doers of the word, and not hearers only" (v. 22).

LEARN ABOUT ...

Author:

James, the half-brother of Jesus.

Audience:

The Twelve Tribes Scattered Abroad. This refers to Jews living outside Palestine, scattered among the Gentiles. This letter is not written to any Jew, but to Jewish believers.

Theme:

Living Faith. "Faith by itself, if it does not have works, is dead" (James 2:17).

Date:

Probably one of the earliest New Testament books, written about AD 49.

How to Get the Most out of This Study

What makes you feel most alive? Looking at a beautiful sunset? Snuggling a newborn baby? Riding a roller coaster and feeling the rush of adrenaline as you defy gravity? These activities make life enjoyable … even thrilling. But there is so much more to life than day-to-day activities.

God created all creatures with the capacity to live and breathe. But He gave humans an even greater gift—an eternal soul. Not only did God provide us with the chance to live forever, He designed us to live in intimate communion with Him. How amazing that the God who created the heavens and the earth, the stars in the sky and the fish in the sea, wants to know *us* intimately. He wants us to truly live! It's been said that God doesn't add years to our life—He adds life to our years. Jesus said, "I have come that they may have life, and that they may have it more abundantly" (John 10:10).

Are you living life to the fullest, or are you just going through the motions? The secret to truly living rather than merely languishing is found in God's Word. We know that God reveals Himself through His Word. That's why doing a Bible study like this is so vital—because God's Word has the power to do His work in our lives. It is the catalyst that revives your heart, renews your mind, and restores your soul. That helps make life worth living!

The main theme of James can be stated in an acrostic for BIBLE: Basic Instructions Before Leaving Earth. James wanted to make sure that his readers (including you!) understood how to live what they believed. As you travel through this wonderful, practical book, ask yourself, *Am I living what I've learned?*

In this study there are five elements to each day's lesson. They are designed to help you fully "live" as you apply the study to your life:

1. Lift Up … Here we ask you to "Lift Up" prayers to God, asking Him to give you spiritual insight for the day's study.

2. Look At … This portion of the study asks you to "Look At" the Scripture text using inductive questions. These questions help you to discover *What are the facts?* You'll learn the basic who-what-when-where-how aspects of the passage as well as some of the important background material.

3. Learn About … The "Learn About" sidebars correlate to specific questions in order to help you understand *What does this text mean?* These sidebar elements offer cultural insight, linguistic definitions, and biblical commentary.

4. Live Out … These questions and exercises are designed to help you investigate *How should this change my life?* Here you are challenged to personally apply the lessons you have learned as you "Live Out" God's principles in your life.

5. Listen To … We finish with inspiring quotes from authors, speakers, and writers. You'll be able to "Listen To" the wisdom they've gleaned in their lives and relate it to your own.

We know that "the word of God is living and powerful, and sharper than any two-edged sword, piercing even to the division of soul and spirit, and of joints and marrow, and is a discerner of the thoughts and intents of the heart" (Heb. 4:12). We pray that as you walk with God through the book of James that He will teach you to be not only a hearer of the Word but a doer of the Word as well.

Live Faithfully is ideal for discussion in a small-group setting as well as for individual study. The following suggestions will help you and your group get the most out of your study time.

PERSONAL CHECKLIST

- Be determined. Examine your daily schedule, then set aside a consistent time for this study.
- Be prepared. Gather the materials you'll need: a Bible, this workbook, a journal in which to write your thoughts, and a pen.

- Be inspired. Begin each day with prayer, asking the Holy Spirit to be your teacher and to illuminate your mind.
- Be complete. Read the suggested Bible passage and finish the homework each day.
- Be persistent. Answer each question as fully as possible. If you're unable to answer a question, move forward to the next question or read the explanation in the "Learn About …" section, which may offer further insight.
- Be consistent. Don't get discouraged. If you miss a day, use the weekend to catch up.
- Be honest. When answering the "Live Out …" questions, allow the Lord to search your heart and transform your life. Take time to reflect honestly about your feelings, experiences, sins, goals, and responses to God.
- Be blessed. Enjoy your daily study time as God speaks to you through His Word.

SMALL-GROUP CHECKLIST

- Be prayerful. Pray before you begin your time together.
- Be biblical. Keep all answers in line with God's Word; avoid personal opinion.
- Be confidential. Keep all sharing within your small group confidential.
- Be respectful. Listen without interrupting. Keep comments on track and to the point so that all can share.
- Be discreet. In some cases, you need not share more than absolutely necessary. Some things are between you and the Lord.
- Be kind. Reply to the comments of others lovingly and courteously.
- Be mindful. Remember your group members in prayer throughout the week.

SMALL-GROUP LEADER CHECKLIST

- Be prayerful. Pray that the Holy Spirit will "guide you into truth" so that your leadership will guide others.
- Be faithful. Prepare by reading the Bible passage and studying the lesson ahead of time, highlighting truths and applying them personally.
- Be prompt. Begin and end the study on time.
- Be thorough. For optimum benefit, allot one hour for small-group discussion. This

should allow plenty of time to cover all of the questions and exercises for each lesson.

- Be selective. If you have less than an hour, you should carefully choose which questions you will address, and summarize the edited information for your group. In this way, you can focus on the more thought-provoking questions. Be sure to grant enough time to address pertinent "Live Out …" exercises, as this is where you and the other women will clearly see God at work in your lives.

- Be sensitive. Some of the "Live Out …" exercises are very personal and may not be appropriate to discuss in a small group. If you sense that this is the case, feel free to move to another question.

- Be flexible. If the questions in the study seem unclear, reword them for your group. Feel free to add your own questions to bring out the meaning of a verse.

- Be inclusive. Encourage each member to participate in the discussion. You may have to draw some out or tone some down so that all have the opportunity to participate.

- Be honest. Don't be afraid to admit that you don't have all the answers! When in doubt, encourage women to take difficult questions to their church leadership for clarification.

- Be focused. Keep the discussion on tempo and on target. Learn to pace your small group so that you complete a lesson on time. When participants get sidetracked, redirect the discussion to the passage at hand.

- Be patient. Realize that not all people are at the same place spiritually or socially. Wait for the members of your group to answer the questions rather than jumping in and answering them yourself.

A+ Faith
James 1:1–8

The Pew Research Center polled a cross section of Americans in 2010 and learned that nearly six out of ten adults considered religion "very important." Roughly four in ten attended worship services at least once a week. Pew reported that most Americans could correctly answer at least half of the survey's questions about the Bible: of those surveyed, 71 percent knew that Jesus was born in Bethlehem, and 63 percent correctly named Genesis as the first book of the Bible. More than half knew that the Golden Rule—"Do unto others as you would have them do unto you"—is *not* one of the Ten Commandments.[1]

Would you make the grade in the test of faith? Maybe in *Bible Knowledge 101* you could ace the test by answering every question correctly. But an A+ faith is based not only on what we believe but on how we behave. While many Americans profess faith in God, few practice their faith in daily living. A 1990 Roper poll revealed that people who called themselves born-again Christians actually engaged in the following negative behaviors more frequently after conversion than before:

	BEFORE CONVERSION	AFTER CONVERSION
Engaged in illicit sex	2 percent	5 percent
Abused drugs	5 percent	9 percent
Drove while intoxicated	4 percent	12 percent

God wants our talk and our walk to match. How do we improve our faith walk? The book of James was written as an "instruction manual" to help believers attain a *living faith* that practices what is preached. In God's book, that's A+ faith!

Day 1: James 1:1   FAITHFUL TEACHER

Day 2: James 1:2–3   PUT TO THE TEST

Day 3: James 1:4   MAKING THE GRADE

Day 4: James 1:5–6   GUIDANCE COUNSELOR

Day 5: James 1:7–8   FLUNKING OUT

DAY 1
Faithful Teacher

LEARN ABOUT ...

LIFT UP ...

Father, moment by moment, day to day, from my first breath in the morning to my last breath at night, help me to live by faith in You. In Jesus' name. Amen.

LOOK AT ...

Today we meet James, the man of A+ faith who wrote this letter, and the people to whom he wrote.

READ JAMES 1:1.

James, a bondservant of God and of the Lord Jesus Christ, to the twelve tribes which are scattered abroad: Greetings. James 1:1

1. Who was the author of this letter? What do you know about him?

2. According to Galatians 1:19, how was James related to Jesus?

3. Rather than introducing himself as "Christ's half brother" or "Mary's son," how did James describe himself in verse 1? Who were his masters?

4. What does James's description of himself reveal about his character?

1 James

James is widely considered to be the first of Jesus' four younger brothers (see Mark 6:3), not James the apostle. According to church tradition, this James was a leader of the church in Jerusalem for nearly thirty years until his martyrdom. He wrote this book around AD 49 to teach and encourage Jewish Christians.

3 Bondservant

A bondservant is a person bound in servitude to another human being as a laborer—one who has no freedoms and no rights. Paul, Peter, and Jude also considered themselves bondservants. Even Jesus "made Himself of no reputation, taking the form of a bondservant" (Phil. 2:7).

Learn About ...

5 Scattered

Scattered translates the Greek term for sowing seed. It suggests the scattering of the spiritual seed of the Word of Life. James wrote to first-century Jewish Christians dispersed throughout the Roman world, living in mostly Gentile communities. He also wrote to all Christians everywhere.

---

8 His Family

Being members of God's family has its privileges. When you are born again, you become an heir to God's heavenly treasures: "Since we are his children, we are his heirs. In fact, together with Christ we are heirs of God's glory" (Rom. 8:17 NLT).

---

9 Born Again

You can be alive physically but dead spiritually. Until you are born again, you are one of the living dead. "You have been born again.... Your new life will last forever because it comes from the eternal, living word of God" (1 Pet. 1:23 NLT).

5. How did James describe the people to whom he wrote this letter? What was their situation?

6. The twelve tribes of Israel were descended from the twelve sons of Jacob. Why do you suppose James referred to his readers as "the twelve tribes"?

7. a. Read Acts 8:1–4. Why were the Jewish believers scattered?

   b. What was the positive result of the persecution and dispersion?

Live Out ...

8. a. We discovered that Jesus had brothers and sisters in His earthly family. Read Matthew 12:46–50 to discover who else is related to Christ.

   b. How can you be included in Christ's spiritual family? How does that make you feel?

9. Many people wonder whether they have truly been born again into the family of God. Fill in the following chart to discover whether you exhibit the family traits that God's children should display.

Scripture	Family Trait	Self-Evaluation
1 John 2:29		
1 John 3:9–10		
1 John 4:7–8		
1 John 5:1		

10. a. Today we saw that James was a leader and faithful teacher, yet he considered himself a slave to God and Jesus Christ. Check the items below that indicate what things have held you in bondage.

___ The perfect house   ___ Substance abuse

___ Child-centered parenting   ___ Quest for money

___ All-consuming hobby   ___ Other _____

 b. Now journal about how Christ has set you free from that area of bondage.

11. James addressed his letter to his Jewish brethren "scattered abroad." Take the time now to write a letter to a loved one of yours whom God has placed in a faraway location. Encourage him or her to sow the good news of the gospel in the place God has planted him or her.

∘ ∘ • ∘ ∘

Throughout his letter, James faithfully instructed believers how to pass the test of faith with flying colors. This lesson plan does not include reading, writing, or arithmetic; instead it includes lessons James's students must master to prepare for final exams. The book of James persuades us to *act* smart, not just sound smart, so the curriculum contains valuable instruction that requires implementation. Here is James's lesson plan:

- James 1: *Accounting*: Making trials count. "My brethren, count it all joy when you fall into various trials, knowing that the testing of your faith produces patience" (vv. 2–3).
- James 2: *Behavioral Science*: Exhibiting behavior that reflects our

LEARN ABOUT ...

10 Set Free

Being a bondservant of Christ is liberating! "If you were a slave when the Lord called you, you are now free in the Lord.... God paid a high price for you, so don't be enslaved by the world" (I Cor. 7:22–23 NLT).

11 Pen Pals

Far away doesn't have to mean forgotten. Make every effort to keep in touch with friends and loved ones who don't live nearby; you'll comfort their hearts and quench their souls. "Good news from far away is like cold water to the thirsty" (Prov. 25:25 NLT).

beliefs. "Faith by itself isn't enough. Unless it produces good deeds, it is dead and useless" (v. 17 NLT).

- James 3: *Debate 101*: Using our speech to bless others. "Out of the same mouth proceed blessing and cursing. My brethren, these things ought not to be so" (v. 10).

- James 4: *Political Science*: Discovering the source of human conflict. "Where do wars and fights come from among you? Do they not come from your desires for pleasure that war in your members?" (v. 1).

- James 5: *Economics*: Learning how God's economy differs from ours. "Come now, you rich, weep and howl for your miseries that are coming upon you!" (v. 1).

The book of James challenges us to examine the quality of our faith in terms of attitudes and actions. Living faith will produce real changes in your brain as well as your behavior.

LISTEN TO ...

Faith is greater than learning.

—*Martin Luther*

DAY 2

Put to the Test

Norman Vincent Peale once ran into his friend George. The conversation went something like this:

"I'm fed up with problems," George said. "I have nothing but problems. I'd give you five thousand dollars to get rid of all of them."

Norman replied, "Yesterday I was in a place where no one has any problems. Let me take you there."

George agreed.

"Good," Norman answered. "Tomorrow afternoon, I'll take you to the cemetery. The only people without problems are dead."[2]

The Bible tells us to expect trials. The book of James does not say "if" you fall into trials but "when" you fall into them. If you are alive, you will definitely experience trials. They come in all shapes and sizes, and there's one tailor-made to fit your individual circumstances. You see, God uses the trials you face to test your faith. Often, understanding which kind of trial you are experiencing will help you when you are put to the test.

- Cause-and-Effect Trials: These trials are directly related to our actions or lack thereof. In other words, you reap what you sow.
- Spiritual Trials: This kind of trial comes from simply living the Christian life. It includes being persecuted, avoided, or mocked, as well as experiencing spiritual warfare.
- Mysterious Trials: This is the hardest kind of trial because there is no rational or logical reason for it, at least not from a human point of view.

Today we discover that God has a purpose for every trial and that even trials can produce great joy.

LEARN ABOUT ...

3 Adding Up

In this verse, to *count* means to evaluate. When we face life's trials, we must evaluate them in the light of God's will and eternity. Triumph over trials is a question of mind over matter—change your mind about the trials, and they won't matter!

4 Trials

Trials come through temptation or adversity and prove the merit of an individual's faith. Christians experience times of adversity when their faith proves either true or false before God. Since many positive things come about through trials, Christians are urged to rejoice at the occurrence of trials.

LIFT UP ...

Lord, I know that I can't always be happy, but I can always have Your joy no matter what circumstances come my way. Help me to remember Your joy in the midst of trials. In Jesus' name. Amen.

LOOK AT ...

Yesterday we met James, the half brother of Jesus, and learned that he wrote this letter to the Jewish believers scattered throughout the world. Now we dig into the text of the letter and discover how to view the trials we encounter.

READ JAMES 1:2–3.

My brethren, count it all joy when you fall into various trials, knowing that the testing of your faith produces patience. James 1:2–3

1. How did James address his readers here? What does this word choice suggest about his attitude toward them?

2. What emotion did he advise them to display?

3. What phrase makes you think this emotion is a choice?

4. James said "when"—not "if"—you fall into trials. What does the choice of "when" suggest about trials?

5. What is one spiritual reason for trials in a believer's life, according to James?

6. How would you define *patience* in your own words?

7. How do you think having your faith tested produces patience?

LIVE OUT ...

8. Jesus accurately assessed His trials by counting them as joy: "Jesus, the author and finisher of our faith, who for the joy that was set before Him endured the cross" (Heb. 12:2). List some trials you've endured that you once considered deficits. Then write how living faith has transformed those things into assets.

DEFICIT	ASSETS
(*Example: physical weakness*)	(*Example: spiritual strength*)

9. The Old Testament prophet Habakkuk suffered trials that produced the spiritual fruits of patience and joy in his life. Journal Habakkuk's proclamation into a personal prayer concerning a current trial in your life.

> Though the fig tree may not blossom,
> Nor fruit be on the vines; ...
> Though the flock may be cut off from the fold,
> And there be no herd in the stalls—
> Yet I will rejoice in the LORD,
> I will joy in the God of my salvation. (Hab. 3:17–18)

10. a. In the introduction to today's lesson we identified three types of trials: Cause-and-Effect Trials, Spiritual Trials, and Mysterious Trials. Fill in the chart on the next page to describe which type(s) of trial was evident in the following passages.

LEARN ABOUT ...

8 Eternal Joy

Trials are not a sign of God's displeasure. Jesus did not suffer the crucifixion because God the Father was displeased with His Son. Rather, Jesus received and brought eternal joy through the agony of His own soul and through the suffering of the cross.

9 Fruitful Faith

Living faith is productive, bringing forth a harvest of spiritual fruit in a believer's life. In the midst of trials, living faith will develop joy and patience. "But the Holy Spirit produces this kind of fruit in our lives: love, joy, peace, patience" (Gal. 5:22 NLT).

10 Reap and Sow

Don't blame God for the trials you've brought upon yourself. "A man reaps what he sows. The one who sows to please his sinful nature, from that nature will reap destruction; the one who sows to please the Spirit, from the Spirit will reap eternal life" (Gal. 6:7–8 NIV).

SCRIPTURE	TYPE OF TRIAL
Deuteronomy 8:1–3	
2 Samuel 12:7–14	
Luke 22:31–32	
John 9:1–3	

b. Think of your most recent trial. Into which category does it fall, and why?

° ° • ° °

A Midwesterner buys a thirty-thousand-dollar Jeep and invites a buddy to go duck hunting. They load up the Jeep with a dog, guns, and decoys, then head to a nearby frozen lake. In the dead of winter, it's common to park your vehicle on the frozen lake. It's also common (if slightly illegal) to blast a hole in the ice. A construction worker has brought along dynamite to blast a hole in the ice. The Jeep owner lights the fuse and hurls it across the ice.

Remember the vehicle, the guns, and *the dog*? Yes, a black Labrador bred for retrieving (especially things thrown by his owner) sprints across the ice, bent on retrieving the stick-shaped object. The fellows yell at the dog to drop the dynamite. The bewildered dog runs for cover under the nearest refuge—the brand-new Jeep Grand Cherokee. BOOM! Both dog and brand-new Jeep sink to the bottom of the lake. The Jeep owner had no one to blame but himself for this trial.[3]

Understanding what kind of trial you are experiencing can help you know how to defuse the situation. If you're like our mighty hunters, and a trial is blowing up in your life as a result of something you've done, then repentance will restore your joy and help you to remain patient until the trial has passed.

LISTEN TO ...

It is the trial of our faith that is precious. If we go through the trial, there is so much wealth laid up in our heavenly banking account to draw upon when the next test comes.

—*Oswald Chambers*

DAY 3

Making the Grade

One of the primary goals of parenting is to see our children progress. We long for them to graduate from adolescence to adulthood, completing the necessary stages of maturity. Picture your preschool child, twenty years in the future, off at college. One spring break there's a knock at your door. As you open it, there stands your fully grown child saying, "Mama, Dada, I want my baba." Your heart sinks with the realization that your offspring has grown older without growing up. Your child has graduated without making the grade.

I (Lenya) recently saw a bumper sticker that read, "I may grow old, but I refuse to grow up." It reminded me of the storybook figure named Peter Pan. He could be the poster child for Stunted-Growth Syndrome, a tragic malady plaguing our nation. The symptoms include: refusing to grow up; living in Never Land; believing life's a game of make-believe; and kidnapping mothers against their will.

Stunted-Growth Syndrome can be found in Christians who do not progress spiritually. James revealed that trials are good medicine meant to stimulate growth in the Lord. Today we discover that God uses hard times not only to make us stronger but also to make us *complete*, a biblical term for mature. Let's follow Paul's example of seeking maturity: "When I was a child, I spoke as a child, I understood as a child, I thought as a child; but when I became a man, I put away childish things" (1 Cor. 13:11).

LIFT UP ...

Lord, I often pray for "patience—right now!" Yet I realize that becoming patient is a long and sometimes painful process. Help me demonstrate the fruit of patience in my life. In Jesus' name. Amen.

LEARN ABOUT ...

I Let It Be

"Let go, let God" is a popular phrase. James said it better, telling believers to "let patience have its perfect work." When you let go of your plans and patiently let God work out His perfect plan for your life, you are embracing a life of faith.

---

2 Perfection

Since human perfection is impossible for anyone but Jesus, what did James mean by saying we can "be perfect"? The Greek word translated *perfect* means "full-grown or mature." In God's eyes, patient faith makes us spiritually mature Christians who "behave wisely in a perfect way" (Ps. 101:2).

---

4 Completion

Complete means "entire" and carries the idea of wholeness. Have you ever felt like there was something missing inside of you? Learning patience in trials makes you completely whole. If you're looking for the missing piece, it's Jesus! "You are complete in Him" (Col. 2:10).

LOOK AT ...

We've learned that when our faith is tested by trials, we can count it all joy. Now we discover the results of living a life that exhibits patient faith.

READ JAMES 1:4.

But let patience have its perfect work, that you may be perfect and complete, lacking nothing. James 1:4

1. What phrase did James use to convey the idea of allowing trials to run their course?

2. Verse 4 describes three attributes patient faith develops in believers. Fill in the blank with the first attribute. Patient faith will make me p_____.

3. Fill in the following chart to discover where true perfection is found.

SCRIPTURE	PERFECTION FOUND IN
Psalm 18:30	
Colossians 1:28	
Colossians 4:12	
1 John 4:18	

4. Besides becoming perfect, verse 4 reveals that patient faith will make me c_____.

5. a. Read 2 Timothy 3:16–17. List the four things for which Scripture is profitable.

b. How does Scripture affect the man or woman of God?

6. According to James 1:4, patient faith means I live my life
   I_____.

7. Do you think "lacking nothing" means that you can expect every-thing on your wish list? Why, or why not?

Live Out ...

8. a. Patience isn't passive; it is persistence despite struggle, peace in the midst of suffering, and perseverance instead of surrender. With this in mind, name a person or situation that makes you impatient.

   b. Journal a prayer to God by rewriting the following verse and asking Him to grant you patience: "May God, who gives this patience and encouragement, help you live in complete har-mony with each other, as is fitting for followers of Christ Jesus" (Rom. 15:5 NLT).

9. Patient faith will help us become perfect. *Perfect* in this context does not mean without sin; it means spiritually mature. Assess your spiritual maturity by writing a number between 1 and 10 (1 = not mature, 10 = perfectly mature) in the areas the apostle Paul described in Romans 12:9–15:

   ____ "Abhor what is evil. Cling to what is good" (v. 9).
   ____ "Be kindly affectionate, ... giving preference to one another" (v. 10).
   ____ "Not lagging in diligence, fervent in spirit, serving the Lord" (v. 11).

LEARN ABOUT ...

8 Patience

According to *New Unger's Bible Dictionary*, patience is that calm and unruffled temper with which the good man or woman bears the evils of life, whether these evils proceed from persons or things. It manifests itself in a sweet submission to the providential appointments of God. Patience displays fortitude amidst the duties and conflicts of life.

9 Perfect Lord

The suffering caused by trials is meant to make you perfectly mature. Jesus was also perfected through suffering. "For it was fitting for Him, ... in bringing many sons to glory, to make the captain of their salvation [Jesus] perfect through sufferings" (Heb. 2:10).

LEARN ABOUT ...

10 Wholeness

To be whole means to lack nothing—to have everything you need. God sees the big picture and knows the difference between your needs and your greeds. He will "supply all your needs from his glorious riches ... given to us in Christ Jesus" (Phil. 4:19 NLT).

____ "Patient in tribulation, continuing steadfastly in prayer" (v. 12).

____ "Distributing to the needs of the saints, given to hospitality" (v. 13).

____ "Bless those who persecute you; bless and do not curse" (v. 14).

____ "Rejoice with those who rejoice, and weep with those who weep" (v. 15).

10. Being complete means to be made whole. Jesus is the only one who can fill the void in our lives. Journal about a time you felt like your life had a gaping hole, then describe how Jesus made you whole again.

∘ ∘ • ∘ ∘

It was my (Penny's) first Mother's Day. I just knew my husband, Kerry, would give me the perfect gift since I had been working so hard at being the perfect wife and mother. But come Mother's Day, I didn't find a little box with sparkling jewelry inside or a wonderful new outfit to wear—I found a nice, big filing cabinet. I tried to respond maturely, but I had a hard time muttering, "Thank you." My husband, unaware of my feelings, said, "You've been saying you need to get more organized. Isn't this great?"

Now it was true that I needed to get organized. But instead of a practical gift, I wanted to be showered with lavish gifts. And sometimes that's how it is with God. We think we deserve extravagant gifts or great blessings, only to find ourselves disappointed when we receive a trial instead. Yet God, in His wisdom, knows exactly what we need; He understands that oftentimes only trials will mature us. Since that Mother's Day years ago, Kerry has given me some wonderful presents. Ironically, the gifts of clothes have worn out and some of the jewelry has been misplaced, but I use that filing cabinet every day. And the same principle is true in my life with God. While He has blessed me abundantly, it's the lessons from the trials that I tend to remember. Without the trials, I would never have grown up.

LISTEN TO ...

The more experience of [God's] goodness and faithfulness we have, the more he is able to test and develop our faith by teaching us long-suffering and the assurance to wait patiently.

—Hannah Hurnard

DAY 4

Guidance Counselor

When evangelist Billy Sunday was converted, a fellow believer said to him, "William, there are some simple rules I wish you'd practice so no one can ever write 'backslider' after your name." The friend then gave Mr. Sunday three valuable suggestions: "Every day take fifteen minutes to let God talk to you; allow fifteen minutes to talk to Him; and then spend fifteen minutes telling others about the Savior." Impressed, Billy made up his mind that he would use this wise counsel as the pattern for his life. From that time forward, he set aside at least fifteen minutes each morning to meditate upon God's Word. He would spend the same amount of time in fervent prayer, communicating one-on-one with God. Throughout the day he would talk to anyone who would listen about the Lord. Later, when he became a nationally known evangelist, he attributed the success of his ministry to the fact that his wisdom came directly from heaven.

Billy Sunday's wise counselor pointed him to the *wisest* Counselor of all—God. We all need guidance; we need wisdom beyond our limited human resources. And God desires to be our divine Guidance Counselor. The good news is that we don't need an appointment, and He doesn't charge a fee. The wisdom God offers is free of charge and readily available throughout our lives. We can say with the psalmist, "You guide me with your counsel, leading me to a glorious destiny" (Ps. 73:24 NLT).

LIFT UP ...

Father, I need Your guidance every day. Please fill me with Your wisdom. I ask this in faith, knowing that You hold the key to all wisdom. In Jesus' name. Amen.

LOOK AT ...

James pointed out that our goal as believers is to become "perfect and complete, lacking nothing" (James 1:4). Now we find that spiritual maturity and wholeness come only from our divine Guidance Counselor.

READ JAMES 1:5–6.

If any of you lacks wisdom, let him ask of God, who gives to all liberally and without reproach, and it will be given to him. But let him ask in faith, with no doubting, for he who doubts is like a wave of the sea driven and tossed by the wind. James 1:5–6

1. Here James said that a lack of something in particular keeps believers spiritually imperfect or immature. What do believers often lack in the midst of trials?

2. a. To understand biblical wisdom more fully, read 1 Corinthians 2:6–7. What types of worldly wisdom does Paul describe?

   b. Why are they unreliable?

3. According to James 1:5, how can you access the wisdom of God?

4. How did James describe the ways God gives wisdom?

5. What promise did James give to those who ask for wisdom?

6. Explain how we should and should not ask God for wisdom.

7. What image did James use for a person who doubts? Why is it a good one?

LEARN ABOUT ...

1 Wisdom

Wisdom is the ability to judge correctly and to follow the best course of action, based on knowledge and understanding. Biblical wisdom is not only practical understanding of matters relating to this life but also accepting divine revelation.

---

3 A.S.K.

If you need wisdom, just A.S.K.: "*Ask*, and it will be given to you; *seek*, and you will find; *knock*, and it will be opened to you" (Matt. 7:7).

---

6 Faith

According to *Vine's Complete Expository Dictionary*, faith is "(1) a firm conviction, producing a full acknowledgement of God's revelation or truth; (2) a personal surrender to Him; (3) a conduct inspired by such surrender." To have faith is to believe God's Word, surrender to Christ's lordship, and unquestionably obey Him.

LEARN ABOUT ...

8 Fear the Lord

To fear the Lord does not mean being afraid. Rather, it is a feeling of reverence and awe based on love for God. It springs not from dread of punishment but from a desire to please Him. "Those who follow the right path fear the LORD" (Prov. 14:2 NLT).

_____

9 Wise

How can you tell if someone's truly wise? Not by what they know but by what they do with what they know. Jesus said, "Anyone who listens to my teaching and follows it is wise.... Anyone who hears my teaching and doesn't obey it is foolish" (Matt. 7:24, 26 NLT).

_____

10 Doubt

Doubt is distrust or uncertainty usually caused by fear. Doubting God reveals a lack of trust in His love or ability. Like oil and water, faith and doubt don't mix. "'You have so little faith,' Jesus said. 'Why did you doubt me?'" (Matt. 14:31 NLT).

LIVE OUT ...

8. We have learned to ask for the wisdom we lack. Read Job 28:28, then write your own biblical definition of wisdom.

9. Using WISE as an acrostic, list some trials you are experiencing for which you need God's wisdom.

    W (*Example: work is a struggle. I need wisdom to approach my boss.*)
    I
    S
    E

10. a. James described the two attitudes you can display when asking for wisdom—doubt or faith. Doubt will rock your boat, while faith will be an anchor to your soul. With this in mind, think of your recent prayer requests. Place a "d" in the blank of what you have prayed in doubt and an "f" when you have asked by faith.

    ____ My past sins
    ____ My salvation
    ____ My future
    ____ My marriage
    ____ Salvation of family
    ____ My children
    ____ My friendships
    ____ My world
    ____ Other_____

    b. Journal a prayer asking God to give you faith where you are experiencing doubt. Start by saying, "Lord, I believe; help my unbelief!" (Mark 9:24).

· · · · ·

Experience has taught me (Lenya) that faith is not a feeling; it's a choice to believe God despite doubt or fear. It is not a mystical inner state produced by chanting a mantra, or a hyper-charismatic frenzy where I can "name it and claim it." It is a simple obedience to God despite obstacles. Great faith believes God even when circumstances are not favorable or life is a disappointment.

As newlyweds, my husband, Skip, and I both firmly believed that God had called us to start a church in Albuquerque, so by faith we relocated one week after our wedding. Leaving friends, family, and familiar surroundings was harder than we anticipated. We were lonely, homesick, and in culture shock. At first, one of us cried almost every day. We began to doubt God's call on our lives. One day Skip declared, "We're going home." That night God reminded him, "You promised to serve Me for one year in New Mexico." It took all the faith we could muster to keep our hands to the plow for another six months. In that short time, our little Bible study grew from five people to nearly one hundred. Today we pastor the largest church in New Mexico with over fifteen thousand in attendance. If we had surrendered to our doubts, we would never have seen God's hand move so miraculously. We discovered that when Doubt asks, "Can God?" Faith says, "God can."

LISTEN TO ...

Why do we need wisdom when we are going through trials? Why not ask for strength, or grace, or even deliverance? For this reason: ... Wisdom helps us understand how to use these circumstances for our good and God's glory.

—*Warren Wiersbe*

DAY 5

Flunking Out

"Our heart, our reason, history itself, and the word of Christ, all call to us loudly and decisively that a union with Him is an absolute necessity, that without Him we cannot attain our goal, that without Him we are rejected by God, and that only He can save us," wrote Karl Marx in 1835.[4] But by 1844, nine years later, he had abandoned any Christian devotion he may once have felt. In fact, his militant atheism and philosophical ideas of the struggle for a classless utopia, free from the numbing effects of religion, established him as one of the most influential figures of the nineteenth century.

Marx had been baptized into the Lutheran church in 1824 at age six and was confirmed at sixteen. However, at the University of Berlin, he fell under the influence of theologian Bruno Bauer, who taught that the Christian Gospels were no more than a record of human fantasies arising from people's emotional needs and that Jesus had not been a historical person. Marx began to doubt the wisdom of God and placed his confidence in the wisdom of men. In fact, his most famous quote revealed his disdain for Christianity, "Religion is the opiate of the people."

Karl Marx is considered by many to be a brilliant philosopher. On college campuses throughout the land, Marxism is still embraced as the answer to humankind's problems. In the world's eyes, Marx's philosophy received an A+. But according to Scripture, Marx flunked out when it came to divine wisdom: "The fool says in his heart, 'There is no God'" (Ps. 14:1 NIV).

LIFT UP ...

Lord, I'm thankful that though all the philosophies of the world billow around us, Your promises keep me steady. Keep me anchored in Your truth. In Jesus' name. Amen.

LOOK AT ...

We have found that the truly wise person will ask God for wisdom in the midst of trials, in faith, with no doubting. Today we read James's description of one who has flunked the lessons of faith.

READ JAMES 1:7–8.

For let not that man suppose that he will receive anything from the Lord; he is a double-minded man, unstable in all his ways. James 1:7–8

1. Looking back to yesterday's lesson, what person was James referring to here?

2. What can the one who doubts expect to receive from the Lord?

3. Besides doubt, according to Isaiah 59:1–2, why are our prayers unanswered?

4. James described a doubting person as "double-minded." Why is that an appropriate description of doubt?

5. James also called a doubting person "unstable." Why is that appropriate?

LIVE OUT ...

6. a. Read Ephesians 4:14 to learn more about spiritual instability. What are we admonished not to be?

    b. Describe the characteristics of an immature Christian.

LEARN ABOUT ...

2 Nothing

God desires to give His children "everything we need for living a godly life" (2 Pet. 1:3 NLT). Sadly, some receive nothing because they harbor doubt in their hearts. "You must really believe it will happen and have no doubt in your heart" (Mark 11:23 NLT).

---

4 Double-Minded

Double-minded literally means "two-spirited," describing one who vacillates between two opinions. The prophet Elijah challenged Israel to be single-minded: "How much longer will you waver, hobbling between two opinions? If the LORD is God, follow him! But if Baal is God, then follow him!" (1 Kings 18:21 NLT).

---

6 Instability

An unstable person is double-minded, fluctuating, irregular, and characterized by an inability to control his or her emotions. The double-minded crowds who followed Jesus sang "Hosanna" one day and the next day shouted, "Crucify Him!" They were easily swayed by their emotions. Are you?

LEARN ABOUT ...

7 Answers

God answers every prayer, but that doesn't mean you receive everything you ask for. If you haven't received your request, either the answer is no or God is asking you to "pray without ceasing, ... for this is the will of God" (I Thess. 5:17–18).

8 Steadfast

In contrast to the double-minded person, a single-minded person is steadfast, firm in faith, and determined to remain loyal regardless of the crashing waves or blowing winds. "Continue to believe this truth and stand firmly in it. Don't drift away from the assurance you received when you heard the Good News" (Col. 1:23 NLT).

9 Stable

Life can be unstable, with winds of change that blow and threaten to sweep us off our feet. In our own strength, we may not be able to stand, but in God's strength, we're immovable. "When my heart is overwhelmed; lead me to the rock that is higher than I" (Ps. 61:2).

c. What (or who) causes instability in immature believers?

7. a. We've found that sometimes we receive nothing from God because we ask with a heart of doubt. We cannot always know *why* God answers our prayers the way He does, but we can be confident that He will answer them one way or another. With this in mind, journal about some things you've asked of God and how He responded. (Try to think of a time He's said, "Yes," a time He's said, "No," and a time He's said, "Wait.")

REQUEST OF GOD   RESPONSE OF GOD: YES, NO, WAIT

(*Example: heal my illness.*)   (*Example: I must wait until heaven.*)

b. Did you ask for any of these things with a heart of doubt? Why do you think you were filled with doubt in this instance? Did God transform your doubt into faith?

8. We have been warned against being double-minded and vacillating between two opinions. Instead, God wants a steadfast heart that will believe in His goodness. Journal about a situation when you were double-minded in your thinking. What were your varying opinions, and how did you finally decide on a course of action?

9. Double-mindedness brings instability. Put the following phrases in the proper column to help you determine what provides stability and what causes instability in your life (add your own insights to each column): Want things my way / Trust in God / Trust in myself / Grumble / Focus on circumstances / Pray / Do what the Bible says / Do what the world does / Criticize / Help others / Look up / Look around.

STABILITY   **INSTABILITY**

∘ ∘ • ∘ ∘

A man paid a visit to his local psychologist. When the doctor asked him what had prompted the visit, the man said, "I'm suffering from an inferiority complex."

In the ensuing weeks, the psychologist put his new patient through an intensive battery of tests. Next came the long wait while the test results were tabulated and appropriate correlations were made. Finally, the doctor called the man and asked him to return to the clinic. "I have some interesting news for you," the doctor began.

"What's that?" asked the man.

"It's no complex," the psychologist said. "You are inferior."

Outraged, the man said, "I want a second opinion!"

"Fine," replied the doctor. "You're ugly, too."

The world and its opinions will tear you down. Wall Street makes you feel like you don't have enough money, Madison Avenue convinces you that products will make you happy, and Hollywood tells you that you need a face-lift. By the world's standards, many of us feel that we are inferior. We want a second opinion.

A wise woman will not be swayed by the world's opinions; she realizes that the only opinion that matters is God's. God has only one test He asks you to pass—the test of living faith. Will you count it all joy when you fall into trials, grow in patience, seek wisdom from God, and trust Him completely? If you can answer yes, then you are on the road to achieving A+ faith.

LISTEN TO ...

Give me, O Lord, a steadfast heart, which no unworthy affection may drag downwards; give me an unconquered heart, which no tribulation can wear out; give me an upright heart, which no unworthy purpose may tempt aside.

—*Thomas Aquinas*

In God We Trust?
James 1:9–11; 5:1-6

One of the best things about vacations when I (Penny) was a girl was going to the store before the trip. My parents would give my brothers and me a dollar each to buy comic books, hoping we'd stay occupied. My brothers would snatch up *Batman* and *Superman*. Me? I'd head straight for *Archie*.

Remember Archie and the gang? There was Jughead, Archie's ditzy best friend; Reggie, his jealous nemesis; Moose, the dumb jock; and of course, Betty and Veronica, the girls vying for Archie's affection. Veronica was a beautiful brunette, spoiled rotten by her rich daddy. Betty was a bouncy blonde with a great personality.

Who are you more like—Betty or Veronica? While I wanted to be like Betty, growing up I was more like Veronica. We weren't mega-rich, but I was a bit spoiled by my daddy. The problem with Veronicas is that they are often brought down a notch because they only trust in their connections or money. In the end, it's the humble Bettys who come out ahead. In Jesus' words, "Those who exalt themselves will be humbled, and those who humble themselves will be exalted" (Matt. 23:12 NLT).

Early in our marriage, my husband and I were brought down by financial trouble. That's when I learned a valuable lesson: God is more concerned with what is in my heavenly bank account than what is in my pocketbook. I learned that trusting in God makes me truly rich while trusting in gold made me miserably poor.

Day 1: James 1:9–11   RICH MAN, POOR MAN

Day 2: James 5:1–3   STINKIN' RICH

Day 3: James 5:4   MONEY TALKS

Day 4: James 5:5   BUY NOW, PAY LATER

Day 5: James 5:6   TIPPING THE SCALES

DAY I

Rich Man, Poor Man

LIFT UP ...

Lord, I'm so grateful that Your Word is offered freely to everyone—rich and poor, high and low. Help me to listen and to gain insight into the wisdom You offer me today. In Jesus' name. Amen.

LOOK AT ...

We have found that living faith not only allows us to victoriously overcome the trials of life, but also instills joy, patience, and wisdom in the hearts and minds of believers. Now we discover that true living faith will view earthly riches from God's heavenly perspective.

READ JAMES 1:9–11.

Let the lowly brother glory in his exaltation, but the rich in his humiliation, because as a flower of the field he will pass away. For no sooner has the sun risen with a burning heat than it withers the grass; its flower falls, and its beautiful appearance perishes. So the rich man also will fade away in his pursuits. James 1:9–11

1. Whom did James address first here?

2. What attitude is the lowly person to exhibit?

3. What phrase reveals that the lowly person's spiritual condition is the reverse of his financial condition?

LEARN ABOUT ...

I Low Down

"Lowly brother" refers to believers who are cast down, hold a low social station, or are impoverished. God has a special place in His heart for the poor and downcast. He commanded the Israelites, "If one of your brethren becomes poor ... then you shall help him" (Lev. 25:35).

2 Glory

To *glory in* means to rejoice. Even the lowliest Christian can rejoice because of God's blessings. Regardless of our circumstances, like the psalmist we can say, "My heart shall rejoice in Your salvation. I will sing to the LORD, because He has dealt bountifully with me" (Ps. 13:5–6).

3 God's Economy

"'My thoughts are nothing like your thoughts,' says the LORD. 'And my ways are far beyond anything you could imagine'" (Isa. 55:8 NLT). In God's economy the poor are rich, the weak are strong, and the lowly are lifted up and exalted.

LEARN ABOUT ...

4 Humility

To be *humiliated* is to be brought low in rank or emotion. God allows humbling experiences in wealthy believers' lives to teach them that genuine happiness and contentment depend not on earthly wealth, but on the true riches of God's grace: "With humility comes wisdom" (Prov. 11:2 NLT).

9 Exalted

Exalted means highly regarded or esteemed. Jesus was "despised, and we did not esteem Him" (Isa. 53:3). Yet in a heavenly vision, Isaiah "saw the Lord sitting on a throne, high and lifted up" (v. 6:1). Jesus, the despised One, was really Jesus, the Most High.

10 God Decides

You might think your boss decides whether or not you get a promotion. But in reality God is the one who decides. "No one ... can exalt a man. But it is God who judges: He brings one down, he exalts another" (Ps. 75:6–7 NIV).

4. Turning to the next group James addressed, in what is the rich person to glory or rejoice?

5. What comparison did James use to remind us that this life is temporary?

6. Why do you think he reminded rich believers of this?

7. Describe the impact of the sun's burning heat on nature.

8. James compared the fragility of the natural world with the fragility of human beings. What will happen to rich people in their pursuit of pleasure, luxury, and wealth?

LIVE OUT ...

9. We have seen that in God's eyes things are not always what they seem. This was exemplified in the life of Christ. Draw lines to show how Christ's position on earth is the opposite of His true spiritual position.

WORLD'S EYES	GOD'S EYES
A poor man	Glorious abode in heaven
Hungry	Highly exalted by God
Cast down by society	Bread of life
No home on earth	Eternally rich

10. James revealed that the lowly believer is really exalted or lifted up. The Bible teaches that Jesus Christ is to be exalted above all.

    God also has highly exalted Him and given Him

the name which is above every name, that at the name of Jesus every knee should bow, of those in heaven, and of those on earth, and of those under the earth, and that every tongue should confess that Jesus Christ is Lord, to the glory of God the Father. (Phil. 2:9–11)

Journal this passage into a personal declaration, exalting Jesus above everything and confessing Him as *your* Lord.

LEARN ABOUT ...

11 Eternal Riches

You can't take it with you, but you can send treasures to heaven. Paul urged the wealthy "to do good, to be rich in good deeds, and to be generous and willing to share. In this way they will lay up treasure for themselves" (I Tim. 6:18–19 NIV).

11. a. In verse 11, James borrowed vivid imagery from Isaiah the prophet to warn the rich of the danger of trusting in themselves and their wealth. Read Isaiah 40:6–8. Describe what "all flesh"—people and their glory—is compared to.

b. What blows on the grass and flowers?

c. What happens as a result?

d. What "treasure" will last into eternity?

12. a. We learned today that God will often send humbling circumstances so that believers will rely on Him rather than on earthly riches. Fill in the following chart to discover how God humbled His people throughout Scripture.

SCRIPTURE   **HUMBLED BY**
Deuteronomy 8:3
2 Chronicles 32:24–26
Daniel 5:22–28
Luke 18:9–14

b. Now journal about a time when God allowed you to be

humbled or brought low in one of the ways listed above. How did you respond? How did God lift you up?

○ ○ ● ○ ○

The story is told of a shepherd who, given a position of nobility by a Scottish king, often went to a solitary room in the palace. The king became suspicious and asked to look inside this secret room. To his surprise he saw only a chair, a shepherd's crook, and an old plaid scarf. "What does this mean?" asked the king. The nobleman replied, "I was a humble shepherd when your majesty promoted me. I come to this room to look at the crook and the plaid scarf. They remind me of what I used to be, and also that I am nothing but what the grace of the king has made me."

We are all paupers, spiritually speaking, until the King of Kings promotes us to a position of honor beside His dear Son: "God raised us up with Christ and seated us with him in the heavenly realms in Christ Jesus" (Eph. 2:6 NIV). When I (Lenya) forget that and get too big for my britches, I just recall my past as a partying college coed by day and a discotheque bartender by night. Images of me hugging the toilet and waking with a hangover serve as stark reminders of how God can radically change a life by exalting the lowly. If God's hand of favor and His bountiful blessings have caused you to develop an inflated perception of yourself, perhaps you should revisit your own humble beginnings and remember that without Christ we're nothing.

LISTEN TO ...

The call of Christ is always a promotion.

—A. W. Tozer

Stinkin' Rich

In a small town in Florida, a woman known as Garbage Mary could be seen dressed in rags, scavenging through garbage cans for food, which she hoarded in her car or her tiny two-room apartment. A recluse with no friends, she bummed cigarettes and ice from strangers. Those who met her believed that she was a destitute old woman.

Eventually Garbage Mary was arrested and institutionalized. When her apartment was searched, officials were amazed to discover checks, stock securities, oil-drilling rights, and real-estate documents strewn everywhere. Garbage Mary was worth more than a million dollars. They also discovered that she was the daughter of a banking family and had inherited a great deal of money. While her money collected interest, she collected garbage![1]

Where riches are concerned, how much is enough? For Mary, mounds of riches weren't enough. She refused to access her vast resources to benefit herself or others, perhaps out of fear of losing what she already had. The book of James teaches that riches often bring misery to those who possess them. Some rich folks squander their wealth on "riotous living" like the prodigal son in Jesus' parable. Others parade their wealth, using designer labels and status symbols to buy prestige. Any way you look at it, those who waste their wealth are just stinkin' rich.

LIFT UP ...

Lord, I praise You for the heavenly treasures You have blessed me with on earth—the sweetness of Your love, the fruit of the Spirit, and the hope of eternity with You. In Jesus' name. Amen.

LOOK AT ...

A proper perspective on wealth is a recurring theme in James. We now jump ahead to James 5 to continue our study on this important topic. Here we see that God looks unfavorably upon those who selfishly hoard their riches.

LEARN ABOUT ...

1 Riches

Being rich is not a sin. Abraham and Job are examples of godly men blessed with riches. Loving money is sinful: "The love of money is at the root of all kinds of evil. And some people, craving money, have wandered from the true faith" (1 Tim. 6:10 NLT).

---

2 Crying Shame

The foolish rich will experience real misery when they stand before God on judgment day to account for their misuse of wealth: "Riches won't help on the day of judgment, but right living can save you from death" (Prov. 11:4 NLT).

---

3 Hoarding

Riches for people in ancient times consisted of perishable items like grain, oil, and garments. Many wealthy people of James's day stored up goods in case of famine or war, while the poor suffered and starved. Hoarding perishable things is selfish and futile.

READ JAMES 5:1–3.

Come now, you rich, weep and howl for your miseries that are coming upon you! Your riches are corrupted, and your garments are moth-eaten. Your gold and silver are corroded, and their corrosion will be a witness against you and will eat your flesh like fire. You have heaped up treasure in the last days. James 5:1–3

1. James used the words *come now* as an insistent command to pay attention. Whose attention did James want to get?

2. What did James tell the rich to do, and why?

3. Describe what happens to riches and garments that are hoarded.

4. What did James say will happen to gold and silver that is stockpiled?

5. a. Against whom does the corrosion of gold and silver bear witness?

   b. Of what does it bear witness?

6. How will corrosion act as the rich person's executioner?

7. Put into your own words James's indictment against the unrighteous rich person.

LIVE OUT ...

8. Read Romans 2:5–6. According to these verses, what will a hard, unrepentant heart store up in the day of God's judgment?

9. First Timothy 6:9–10 says: "But those who desire to be rich fall into temptation and a snare, and into many foolish and harmful lusts which drown men in destruction and perdition. For the love of money is a root of all kinds of evil, for which some have strayed from the faith in their greediness, and pierced themselves through with many sorrows."

    a. Circle the words above that describe what happens to those who desire to be rich.

    b. Underline the words that describe the love of money and the results of that love.

10. Today we learned that when rich people hoard their earthly wealth, denying its benefits to those in need, they store up the wrath of God on judgment day. Read 1 Timothy 6:17–19. List what these verses command us to do with our earthly wealth and how we will benefit from obedience.

    COMMAND   **BENEFIT OF OBEDIENCE**

11. First Corinthians 4:2 tells us that we must be faithful stewards of what God has given us. In what ways do you spend your money?

    ___ Things I don't really need   ___ Eating at restaurants
    ___ Paying my bills   ___ Entertainment

LEARN ABOUT ...

9 Is It Sin?

Sin has to do with context. Money, like food and sex, is neutral in and of itself. Eating is necessary; gluttony is sin. Sex within God's guidelines is good; prostitution is aberrant. Riches are not evil, but when abused in ways God did not intend, they become harmful.

10 Use or Lose

When it comes to riches, the Bible encourages us to "use it or lose it." Possessions unused are wasted. Grain will rot. Gold will rust. Garments will become moth-eaten. God blesses us with riches and gifts in order that we may bless others.

11 Savings

Saving is not wrong. However, failing to provide for your household is sinful: "If anyone does not provide for his own, and especially for ... his household, he has denied the faith" (1 Tim. 5:8).

    ___ On my vices (e.g., cigarettes)   ___ Supporting a missionary

    ___ Tithing to the Lord   ___ Savings and investments

12. Many people hoard their money because of fear of financial insecurity, or they waste their money on things that do not last simply to impress others. Journal about some of the reasons you have stored up wealth or squandered your resources.

° ° • ° °

Christopher Winans's book *Malcolm Forbes: The Man Who Had Everything* tells of a motorcycle tour the multimillionaire took through Egypt in 1984. Reflecting on the burial tomb of King Tut, Forbes asked an associate: "Do you think I'll be remembered after I die?" Malcolm Forbes is known for his pithy statement, "He who dies with the most toys wins."[2] Author Steve Farrar observed that dying with the most toys was the ambition of Forbes's life: "That's why he collected scores of motorcycles. That's why he would pay over a million dollars for a Fabergé egg. That's why he owned castles, hot air balloons, and countless other toys that he can no longer access."[3]

    Another book has been written that could have been titled *Jesus Christ: The Man Who GAVE Everything.* God knew that all of the silver and gold in the world couldn't open the pearly gates, so He "purchased our freedom with the blood of his Son and forgave our sins" (Eph. 1:7 NLT). If Malcolm Forbes had taken a ride through Israel to the empty garden tomb, he might not have asked, "Will I be remembered after I die?"—but like the thief on the cross, he would have requested, "Jesus, remember me when you come into your Kingdom" (Luke 23:42 NLT). He who dies with the most toys doesn't win—he just dies. But whoever dies believing in Jesus gains all of eternity.

LISTEN TO ...

I would not give one moment of heaven for all the joy and riches of the world, even if it lasted for thousands and thousands of years.

—Martin Luther

DAY 3

Money Talks

My husband called and said, "Penny, put on a nice outfit. We're going out to celebrate!" Kerry had started his own architectural company, and business had been slow. Then he got a call from a developer who wanted him to design a new subdivision. That meant that we'd be financially secure for the first time in years. We were overjoyed.

In good faith, Kerry spent months visiting the site and supervising the building of several high-end southwestern homes nestled in the foothills of the Sandia Mountains. The developer had said, "As soon as the first house sells, I'll pay you." Naively, we believed him and kept waiting to receive a check. But the first house sold, and then the second, and we didn't get paid. Finally, Kerry confronted the man, who taunted, "You can sue me; I'm not gonna pay you." That's when we realized we'd been had by a smooth-talking con man.

This businessman thought he would get ahead by defrauding honest laborers like Kerry. But time has shown that God's Word is true; the businessman's heaped-up riches have corroded. He has filed bankruptcy several times, and so many people refused to work with him that he left town. His heart has also grown hard. He divorced his wife and severed relationships with personal friends.

Anyone who has been defrauded by a dishonest employer will be encouraged to learn that the wages you're owed call out to God—money talks.

LIFT UP ...

Father God, it gives me great comfort to know that when the oppressed and needy cry out, You always hear them. I praise You that in Your sovereign time You deliver us from the hands of our enemies. In Jesus' name. Amen.

LEARN ABOUT ...

1 Fraud

According to *Merriam-Webster's Dictionary*, fraud is the "intentional perversion of the truth to induce another to part with something of value; to deceive or misrepresent." Jacob defrauded Esau: "Jacob ... has cheated me twice. First he took my rights as the firstborn, and now he has stolen my blessing" (Gen. 27:36 NLT).

2 Laborers

In a rural farming economy, most laborers depended on daily wages to survive. To withhold pay from a workman was a serious sin in God's eyes: "Woe to him ... who uses his neighbor's services without wages and gives him nothing for his work" (Jer. 22:13).

5 Sabaoth

Sabaoth is derived from the Hebrew word *tsaba*, meaning "hosts or armies." "The Lord of Sabaoth" describes God as Commander of the armies of heaven. God, the mighty warrior, will hear the cries of the downtrodden and oppressed, and He will judge righteously.

LOOK AT ...

We have learned that hoarding wealth is a sin, but when we use our possessions for God's glory, those things become treasures—and we invest in eternity. This passage looks at the ways the unrighteous rich deal with their employees.

***

READ JAMES 5:4.

Indeed the wages of the laborers who mowed your fields, which you kept back by fraud, cry out; and the cries of the reapers have reached the ears of the Lord of Sabaoth. James 5:4

1. What happened to the wages of the laborers?

2. Describe what the laborers had done to earn their wages.

3. How did the money talk?

4. Whose cries were also heard?

5. Who heard these cries?

6. a. Read Deuteronomy 24:14–15. What did God command *shall not* be done to the hired servant?

    b. What did God command *shall* be done? Why?

LIVE OUT ...

7. a. Today we have seen that God condemns financial fraud. Read Jeremiah 22:13–14. Upon whom did Jeremiah pronounce this "woe"?

    b. In what ways had this person committed fraud?

    c. How did the person spend his ill-gotten gain?

8. Today's text focuses on laborers who didn't receive their due. Has there ever been a time in your life when you were owed money but were denied payment? Journal about your experience. How does it make you feel to learn that your lost wages actually "cry out" to God?

9. We have been warned against defrauding others of their well-earned pay. Journal the truths of this proverb into a personal prayer to God:

    > Remove falsehood and lies far from me; give me neither poverty nor riches—feed me with the food allotted to me; lest I be full and deny You, and say, "Who is the LORD?" Or lest I be poor and steal, and profane the name of my God. (Prov. 30:8–9)

° ° • ° °

Most of us would never think of defrauding someone we know. But there are subtle ways of defrauding that you may never have considered: holding back an allowance, underpaying a babysitter, or cheating the IRS. Ann Landers received this letter about a very creative act of fraud:

LEARN ABOUT ...

7 Cheaters

Those who cheat others may seem to come out ahead, but in the long run, cheaters never prosper. "You yourselves do wrong and cheat, ... to your brethren! Do you not know that the unrighteous will not inherit the kingdom of God?" (I Cor. 6:8–9).

8 Indebted

"The laborer is worthy of his wages" (I Tim. 5:18). God wants all people to receive their due. Yet there is one debt that we will always owe: "Owe nothing to anyone—except for your obligation to love one another" (Rom. 13:8 NLT).

9 Honesty

Honesty is always the best policy. According to *Merriam-Webster's Dictionary*, honesty is the "refusal to lie, steal, or deceive in any way. It suggests an active or anxious regard for the standards of one's profession or position." An honest person exhibits fairness and a trustworthy character.

Dear Ann Landers:

Aunt "Emma" was married to a tightwad who was also a little strange. He made a good salary, but they lived frugally because he insisted on putting 20 percent of his paycheck under the mattress. (The man didn't trust banks.) The money, he said, was going to come in handy in their old age.

When Uncle "Ollie" was sixty, he was stricken with cancer. Toward the end, he made Aunt Em promise, in the presence of his brothers, that she would put the money he had stashed away in his coffin so he could buy his way into heaven if he had to. They all knew he was a little odd, but this was clearly a crazy request. Aunt Em did promise, however, and assured Uncle Ollie's brothers that she was a woman of her word and would do as he asked. The following morning she took the money (about twenty-six thousand dollars) to the bank and deposited it. She then wrote a check and put it in the casket four days later. This is a true story, and our family has laughed about it ever since.

"Don't let the world around you squeeze you into its own mould," the apostle Paul wrote in Romans 12:2 (PH). Honor God by being honest in all your financial dealings, and God will honor you.

LISTEN TO ...

Ill-gotten gains never prosper.

—*Anonymous*

DAY 4
Buy Now, Pay Later

In 1923, seven of the world's most successful financiers met at Chicago's Edgewater Beach Hotel. These guys were rich—rich—rich!

1. Charles Schwab, the president of the largest steel company
2. Samuel Insull, the president of the largest electric utility company
3. Howard Hopson, the president of the largest gas company
4. Arthur Cutten, the great wheat speculator
5. Richard Whitney, the president of the New York Stock Exchange
6. Albert Fall, the Secretary of Interior in President Harding's Cabinet
7. Jesse Livermore, the greatest "bear" on Wall Street

Financially, these high rollers could have anything money could buy. Wouldn't you like to change positions with them? Before deciding, look to what the future held for these men:

1. Charles Schwab went bankrupt, living his last years on borrowed money.
2. Samuel Insull died penniless in a foreign land, a fugitive from justice.
3. Howard Hopson lost his sanity.
4. Arthur Cutten became insolvent and died abroad.
5. Richard Whitney spent time in Sing Sing prison.
6. Albert Fall was pardoned from prison so he could die at home—broke.
7. Jesse Livermore committed suicide.

These men lived for the "now" without any regard for "later." If they'd had a proper perspective on money, perhaps they wouldn't have lost their fortunes. Solomon counseled, "Don't wear yourself out trying to get rich.... In the blink of an eye wealth disappears, for it will sprout wings and fly away like an eagle" (Prov. 23:4–5 NLT). James also warns that with a "buy now" mentality, you are sure to "pay later."

LEARN ABOUT ...

1 At Home

Too at home here on earth? Maybe it's time to renovate your heart and mind. "Store your treasures in heaven.... Wherever your treasure is, there the desires of your heart will also be" (Matt. 6:20–21 NLT). Home is where the heart is.

3 Hedonists

The Greek word translated "pleasure" here is related to our word *hedonism*, which describes the lustful gratification of the natural/sinful desires. "In the last days ... men will be ... lovers of money ... lovers of pleasure rather than lovers of God" (2 Tim. 3:1–4).

LIFT UP ...

Thank You, Lord, that my contentment does not depend on what I have or what I do, but on delighting myself in You. In Jesus' name. Amen.

LOOK AT ...

Wealth unjustly gained will bear testimony against those who steal it. The book of James now introduces us to the sin of self-indulgent spending.

READ JAMES 5:5.

You have lived on the earth in pleasure and luxury; you have fattened your hearts as in a day of slaughter. James 5:5

1. Where do the unrighteous rich live? Why do you think James focused on this?

2. a. Read Hebrews 11:13–16. What did these saints understand about life on the earth, and what were they looking for (vv. 13–14)?

   b. Explain why returning to their birthplace wouldn't make them feel at home (v. 15).

   c. Describe their true home (v. 16).

3. According to James 5:5, how do the unrighteous rich live?

4. Describe the hedonist's end.

LIVE OUT ...

5. In Luke 12:16–21, Jesus told the parable of the rich fool. Underline the self-indulgent statements of the rich fool. Circle God's responses to him.

A rich man had a fertile farm that produced fine crops. He said to himself, "What should I do? I don't have room for all my crops." Then he said, "I know! I'll tear down my barns and build bigger ones. Then I'll have room enough to store all my wheat and other goods. And I'll sit back and say to myself, 'My friend, you have enough stored away for years to come. Now take it easy! Eat, drink, and be merry!'"

But God said to him, 'You fool! You will die this very night. Then who will get it all?"

Yes, a person is a fool to store up earthly wealth but not have a rich relationship with God. (Luke 12:16–21 NLT)

6. Read Philippians 3:17–21. Contrast those who live for earthly pursuits with those who understand that heaven is their true home.

7. a. Using FAT as an acrostic, describe how people today have fattened themselves with pleasure and luxury.

F

A

T

LEARN ABOUT ...

5 Self-Indulgent

Scripture never condones self-indulgent living. This lifestyle is inconsistent with the very purposes for which God made us. God views a life of ease and luxury, especially at the expense of others, as foolish and deadly. "She who lives in pleasure is dead while she lives" (I Tim. 5:6).

6 Heavenly Home

All things earthly are perishing, but heavenly things will last throughout eternity. "When this earthly tent we live in is taken down (that is, when we die and leave this earthly body) we will have a house in heaven, an eternal body made for us by God himself" (2 Cor. 5:I NLT).

7 F.A.T

Earthly F.A.T. is Foolish Acquisition of Treasures. However, spiritually F.A.T. represents a person who is Faithful, Available, and Teachable. "To you who fear My name ... you shall go out and grow fat like stall-fed calves" (Mal. 4:2).

LEARN ABOUT ...

8 Possessions

God loves to give good things, but your possessions should never possess you. "Command those who are rich ... not to ... trust in uncertain riches but in the living God, who gives us richly all things to enjoy" (I Tim. 6:17).

b. Journal about the ways you have overindulged in pleasure and luxury. Then write a prayer telling God how you will start a heavenly diet.

8. The unrighteous rich will be corrupted by their possessions. The riches that your heavenly Father gives are meant to be a blessing. Fill in the following chart to discover some of the rich blessings God offers.

SCRIPTURE	RICH BLESSINGS
1 Chronicles 29:11–12	
Psalm 112:1–3	
Proverbs 24:3–4	

· · • · ·

An old man had built a prosperous business through hard work. Childless, he worried about who would be his heir. His three nephews were the most likely candidates. He gathered the young men and said, "I'm giving you each an equal sum of money. Buy something to fill this office from floor to ceiling. Whoever comes up with the best solution to this problem will be my heir."

The nephews hurried to fulfill their task. The first nephew brought bales of hay that filled the room two thirds of the way. The second brought in large bags of goose-down, which filled three fourths of the room. Then the third nephew walked in empty-handed. "What did you bring?" the benefactor asked. The nephew replied, "I spent half of my money to feed a hungry child and gave almost all the rest to the church. With what I had left, I bought these matches and this candle." He lit the taper, and light filled every corner of the room! The old man realized that here was the best purchase of all. He freely gave his wise nephew all his possessions.

God bestows financial blessings not so we can live lives of idle luxury, but so we can bless others and help light their way. Jesus said, "Let your light so shine before men, that they may see your good works and glorify your Father in heaven" (Matt. 5:16).

LISTEN TO ...

If money be not your servant, it will be your master.

—Francis Bacon

DAY 5

Tipping the Scales

The judge glared down from his bench at the prospective juror. "And why do you not want to serve on this jury?" he asked.

The man replied, "Well, judge, I'm biased. One look at that man convinced me that he is guilty."

The judge scowled and replied, "That man is not the defendant; he's the district attorney."

Stacking a jury with those prejudiced against the defendant is just one way to tip the scales of justice. Other imbalanced tactics may include enlisting false witnesses, denying the defendant's right to legal representation, conducting a trial behind closed doors, or bribing the judge. The crafters of the Declaration of Independence dreamed of justice for all when they wrote, "We hold these truths to be self-evident, that all men are created equal...." Sadly, the rich often seem more "equal" than others within the jurisprudence system.

Ancient Israel, like the United States, was established with laws meant to ensure each citizen a fair trial. But the book of James reveals that society in James's day was plagued with corruption just as ours is today. The wealthy were making the ancient legal system lopsided through bribery. They hoped their deep pockets would tip the scales of justice in their favor.

LIFT UP ...

Jesus, I am grateful for Your sacrifice on the cross for my sins. Thank You for saving me from the bondage of my flesh and eternal condemnation. I praise You for my new life in the Holy Spirit. In Jesus' name. Amen.

Look At ...

We have discovered that being self-indulgent with God-given wealth is sin. Continuing in chapter 5, James addressed another sin of the wicked rich.

Read James 5:6.

You have condemned, you have murdered the just; he does not resist you.
James 5:6

1. What are the crimes of the overindulged rich?

2. How did James convey that the "sentence" the rich pass on the poor is unfair?

3. How have the poor responded to the unjust rich?

4. The prophet Amos gave some insight into the corrupt judicial system in Israel in the Old Testament. Read Amos 5:12–15 to learn more.

   a. In what three ways did the judges sin against the poor (v. 12)?

   b. How did the people respond and why (v. 13)?

   c. What was God's ideal for the judicial system? How would the nation benefit (v. 15)?

5. Though Israel's courts were corrupt, God established a system of judicial fairness. Fill in the following table to discover what God expected of judges.

Learn About ...

1 Condemned

To *condemn* is a judicial term meaning to declare guilty, convict, or doom. God alone is our Judge, and He demands righteousness. "What does the LORD require of you but to do justly, to love mercy, and to walk humbly with your God?" (Mic. 6:8).

2 Injustice

Some Bible commentators say that the rich used the judicial system to condemn the poor. Often they literally murdered to maintain their luxurious lifestyle (as when Jezebel had Naboth murdered to obtain his vineyards). The poor had no resources and thus no way to resist.

4 Fair Play

When God established Israel, He set up a system of fair and impartial courts to protect His people. The judges were commanded to be fair and honest. They were not to be greedy, show partiality, or take bribes. The Jews in James's day knew this.

LEARN ABOUT ...

6 Hypocrisy

According to *Merriam-Webster's Dictionary*, *hypocrisy* (from the Greek word for an actor) is "feigning to be what one is not; the false appearance of virtue or religion." "What is the hope of the hypocrite, though he may gain much, if God takes away his life?" (Job 27:8).

---

7 Murder

Throughout history, murder has been considered the worst of crimes. God considers the taking of human life a capital offense. Murder is an outrage because human beings are created in the image of God.

SCRIPTURE	FAIR JUDGE
Exodus 18:21–22	
Leviticus 19:15	
Deuteronomy 19:15–19	

LIVE OUT ...

6. We have learned that ancient Israel was plagued by a corrupt judicial system, as was the Roman society in James's day. Jesus condemned hypocritical rulers who exploited others while pretending to be righteous. Fill in the chart to unmask the hypocrisy.

SCRIPTURE	SEEMS RIGHT	ACTS WRONG
Matthew 23:14		
Matthew 23:23		
Matthew 23:25–27		

7. James rebuked the rich for pronouncing a death sentence on the poor—in effect murdering them. In the Sermon on the Mount, Jesus said anger is as lethal as murder: "You have heard that our ancestors were told, 'You must not murder. If you commit murder, you are subject to judgment.' But I say, if you are even angry with someone, you are subject to judgment!" (Matt. 5:21–22 NLT). Journal about a time when you were angry enough to wish another person harm. Confess this anger as sin, and ask God to forgive you.

8. a. James said the just don't resist the actions of the unjust. Jesus also spoke to this in Matthew 5:39–42. Read the passage, then rewrite in your own words the principles Christ taught.

b. Have you ever put these principles to work in your life? If so, what happened? If not, why not?

· · • · ·

The judges in James's day were willing to tip the scales in favor of the rich for a price. But justice is never true if it can be sold to the highest bidder. The cries of the poor fell on deaf ears—the jangling of gold coins drowned out the truth. The poor were helpless to resist the inequity of the system.

Jesus knew what it felt like to be the victim of a rigged trial. Caiaphas, the chief priests, and the elders (the supreme court of New Testament Israel) sought out false witnesses to accuse Jesus. They even resorted to bribery in an attempt to subvert justice: "Judas Iscariot … went to the chief priests and said, 'What are you willing to give me if I deliver Him to you?' And they counted out to him thirty pieces of silver" (Matt. 26:14–15). The prophet Isaiah described Jesus like this: "He was led as a lamb to the slaughter. And as a sheep is silent before the shearers, he did not open his mouth" (Isa. 53:7 NLT). Perhaps James was thinking of his brother Jesus when he wrote this passage about the just not resisting the unjust.

But don't be deceived; God will one day even the scales of justice. As believers, we can confidently say with the psalmist, "The LORD loves justice, and he will never abandon the godly. He will keep them safe forever" (Ps. 37:28 NLT).

LISTEN TO …

Injustice anywhere is a threat to justice everywhere.

—*Martin Luther King Jr.*

Triumph over Temptation

James 1:12–18

James began this discourse on temptation by saying, "Blessed is the man who endures temptation" (1:12). The word *blessed* can be translated "O how happy." I don't know about you, but I do not feel blessed when temptations come my way. In fact, I assume I've done something terribly wrong when temptation knocks on my door. But temptation is not a sin; it's what you do in response to temptation that can cause sin. Martin Luther once quoted a "wise man" who said, "You cannot prevent birds fleeing over your head, but you can hinder them building in your hair."[1] Even Jesus was tempted when He sojourned here on earth, but He triumphed over temptation. The writer of Hebrews said that Jesus, our great High Priest, "was in all points tempted as we are, yet without sin" (Heb. 4:15).

Over twenty years ago, before I (Lenya) was a Christian, I thought getting high was a way to escape reality. After salvation, I was delivered from the desire to smoke marijuana. But a few years ago at a reunion, I smelled a familiar pungent aroma coming from the basement of the home I was visiting. I was shocked at the random thought that ran through my mind: *A joint sounds relaxing; I could get away with it here.* My palms began to sweat when I realized I was being tempted. That's when the Lord spoke to my heart: "Lenya, you can triumph over temptation, ... just flee!" And that's exactly what I did.

Day 1: James 1:12	BLESSED TEMPTATION
Day 2: James 1:13–14	TEMPTATION UNMASKED
Day 3: James 1:15	DEADLY TEMPTATION
Day 4: James 1:16–17	TEMPTED TO DOUBT
Day 5: James 1:18	TEMPTATION TRANSFORMED

LEARN ABOUT ...

1 Blessed

A *beatitude* is a declaration of blessedness, meaning spiritual well-being and prosperity, the deep joy of the soul. The blessed have a share in salvation and have entered the kingdom of God. Some scholars render each beatitude as: "O the bliss [or blessedness] of."

DAY 1

Blessed Temptation

LIFT UP ...

When temptations come my way, Lord, help me discover the blessing of resisting them and obeying Your Word. Help me to seek You with all my heart. In Jesus' name. Amen.

LOOK AT ...

Through James we have learned that those with living faith will count it all joy when facing the trials life brings their way. We have also learned that a right perspective on earthly wealth is evidence of a true living faith. Now we discover how to turn temptation into a blessing.

READ JAMES 1:12.

Blessed is the man who endures temptation; for when he has been approved, he will receive the crown of life which the Lord has promised to those who love Him. James 1:12

1. What beatitude did James pronounce?

2. Fill in the following chart to discover other beatitudes found in Scripture.

SCRIPTURE	BEATITUDE
Psalm 1:1	
Psalm 128:1–2	

Matthew 5:3–10

John 20:29

3. Explain what a person must do to receive this blessing, according to James 1:12.

4. What phrase reveals that the one who endures temptation has done well in God's eyes?

5. What will this person receive?

6. To whom will the Lord give this gift?

7. How can you be sure you will receive this gift?

LIVE OUT ...

8. There are times when we look at temptations as a curse. James told his readers to view temptations as blessings when they are faithfully endured. Recall a situation in which God transformed your curse (temptation) into a blessing. How were you able to resist the temptation? How did God bless you?

9. Scripture promises various crowns to believers. Check which crowns you have obtained from the Lord.

___ Wisdom is a crown of glory (Prov. 4:7–9).

___ An excellent wife is a husband's crown (Prov. 12:4).

___ Gray hair is a crown of glory (Prov. 16:31).

✓ Grandchildren are a crowning glory (Prov. 17:6).

LEARN ABOUT ...

3 Temptation

Temptation means to put to the test, examine, or try. Therefore a temptation either puts something good to the test or entices us to do something evil. Depending upon our response to it, temptation can be helpful or harmful to our spiritual growth.

5 Crown

A crown shows a person's status or honor. Royalty and high priests in Old Testament times wore crowns signifying their authority. Athletes were crowned with wreaths of leaves. As Christians, we are promised several types of crowns symbolic of our inheritance in heaven.

8 Blessing

Our blessed Savior became a curse to transform our curse into a blessing: "Christ has redeemed us from the curse of the law, having become a curse for us ... that the blessing of Abraham might come upon the Gentiles in Christ Jesus" (Gal. 3:13–14).

LEARN ABOUT ...

9 Hold Fast

Jesus warned that Christians could forfeit their crowns if they aren't careful to persevere in the faith. Focusing on Christ's return helps us cling to what we already possess. "Behold, I am coming quickly! Hold fast what you have, that no one may take your crown" (Rev. 3:11).

---

11 Endurance

More than physical endurance, we need spiritual endurance in the race of life. "Let us lay aside every weight, and the sin which so easily ensnares us, and let us run with endurance the race that is set before us" (Heb. 12:1).

___ Temperance brings an imperishable crown (1 Cor. 9:25).

___ Others brought to faith are a crown of rejoicing (1 Thess. 2:19).

✓ A crown of righteousness to those who love His appearing (2 Tim. 4:8).

✓ The crown of life to those who endure temptation (James 1:12).

10. James did not say "if " you are tempted but "when" you are tempted. Temptation is common to all humanity. Fill in the following chart to discover how others have been tempted.

SCRIPTURE	TEMPTATION
Joshua 7:20–21	
2 Samuel 11:1–3	
Matthew 4:1–4	
Acts 8:18–20	

11. a. Describe a situation in which you have been greatly tempted.

    b. Journal a prayer to God by rewriting the following verse and asking Him for endurance in the midst of temptation: "Do not throw away this confident trust in the Lord. Remember the great reward it brings you! Patient endurance is what you need now, so that you will continue to do God's will. Then you will receive all that he has promised" (Heb. 10:35–36 NLT).

° ° • ° °

Saint Augustine was a famed fourth-century bishop who was one of the great leaders of the early Christian church. His writings have had a strong impact on religious thought throughout the ages. His mother, Saint

Monica, was a devout Christian while his father was a pagan. As a young man Augustine pursued worldly success and pleasure.

At the age of thirty-two, after a life steeped in sexual immorality, Augustine repented and devoted his life to the gospel. Soon after his conversion, he was walking down a street in Milan, Italy, when he encountered a prostitute whom he had known intimately. She called to him, but he would not answer. He kept right on walking. "Augustine," she called again. "It is I!" Without slowing down and by the grace of God, he exclaimed, "Yes, but it is no longer I." Even though he was a recent convert, he understood that God would bless him if he resisted temptation. His reply, "It is no longer I," proved that he had a supernatural power available to combat the forces of sin and evil that had dominated his life in the past. He was a changed man. Through patient endurance, Augustine was able to "flee the evil desires of youth, and pursue righteousness, faith, love and peace" (2 Tim. 2:22 NIV). So take heart. God will give you power to face temptations, and He has promised to bless you through them, working all things for good in your life.

Listen To ...

Holiness is not freedom from temptation, but power to overcome temptation.

—*G. Campbell Morgan*

DAY 2

Temptation Unmasked

Young Jamie wanted a new baseball bat, so he was desperately saving his money. But it wasn't easy. One night his mother overheard his bedtime prayer: "God, help me save my money for a bat. And please don't let the ice-cream man come down the street!"

What areas tempt you? Shopping malls? TV shows? All-you-can-eat buffets? Affection? Temptations can be described as good desires run amok. Sarah and Abraham's temptation began with a good desire to have a child. This was in God's will for them, but they went about it the wrong way. Sarah encouraged Abraham to use her servant Hagar as a surrogate mother. Hagar conceived Ishmael, but God declared that Ishmael was *not* the son of promise—Sarah's own son, Isaac, would be God's chosen heir. In this case (and most others), giving in to temptation carried long-lasting consequences. Ishmael was a ruthless bully to Isaac, and Ishmael's descendants antagonize Israel to this day.

In drawing a distinction between trials and temptations, James unmasks the tempter. Trials usually come from the outside; temptations frequently happen on the inside. God may send trials, but temptations are authored by Satan and encouraged by our own sinful nature. If we aren't careful, the testings on the outside may become temptations on the inside. When our outside circumstances are difficult, we may find ourselves inwardly complaining against God, questioning His love, and resisting His will. That's when Satan provides us with an "opportunity" to escape the difficulty—this opportunity is temptation.

Lift Up ...

Thank You, God, that You can help me stand against temptation. When I am tempted, Lord, show me the way of escape. In Jesus' name. Amen.

LOOK AT ...

James encouraged patient endurance of temptations. This passage unmasks the source of temptation.

READ JAMES 1:13–14.

Let no one say when he is tempted, "I am tempted by God"; for God cannot be tempted by evil, nor does He Himself tempt anyone. But each one is tempted when he is drawn away by his own desires and enticed. James 1:13–14

1. Who should we *never* blame when we are tempted? Why not? (James gave more than one reason.)

2. Why do you think James made this point so forcefully?

3. Look up Genesis 3:11–13. Summarize whom Adam and Eve each blamed for their sin, and why.

4. What phrase reveals that no one is exempt from temptation?

5. If God does not tempt, then how is a person tempted?

6. Give an example of how a person might be tempted by desires from within.

7. Give an example of how a person might be enticed from outside himself or herself.

LEARN ABOUT ...

1 Blameless

It stands to reason that if God can't be tempted by evil, then He cannot and will not tempt others. God hates sin; therefore He would never promote what is repugnant to His nature. "God is light and there is no darkness in him at all" (1 John 1:5 NLT).

---

3 Blame Shifting

Since the fall in the garden, we have played the blame game when yielding to temptation: Eve blamed the serpent, and Adam blamed Eve. During James's time, Jewish philosophers theorized that God was to blame for having "created" us with the propensity to sin.

---

7 Predator

Drawn away means to bait a trap. *Enticed* refers to baiting a hook. As a predator, Satan knows how to catch his prey. "Watch out for your great enemy, the devil. He prowls around like a roaring lion, looking for someone to devour" (1 Pet. 5:8 NLT).

LEARN ABOUT ...

8 Solace

God is not to be blamed for tempting you; He is to be blessed for praying for you in temptation. Jesus told Peter, "Simon, Simon! Indeed, Satan has asked for you, that he may sift you as wheat. But I have prayed for you, that your faith should not fail" (Luke 22:31–32).

9 Safety

While God does not tempt us, He does set parameters for the temptations that come our way. Satan wasn't allowed to tempt Job above what he could endure: "Satan ... said, 'Does Job fear God for nothing? Have You [God] not made a hedge around him?'" (Job 1:9–10).

10 Satan

Other names for Satan include "the Devil," meaning slanderer or false accuser; "the tempter"; "Beelzebub"; "the wicked one"; "the ruler of this world"; "the god of this age"; "the prince of the power of the air"; and "the accuser of our brethren."

LIVE OUT ...

8. a. James warned us against blaming God for the temptation to sin. When you're enticed by sin, whom do *you* blame?

    ___ The Devil

    ___ My upbringing

    ✓ Myself

    ___ My husband

    ___ My boss

    ___ My hormones

    ___ My kids

    ___ God

    ___ Others

    b. If you've been blaming others for the sin in your life, then it's time to take personal responsibility. Write a prayer admitting that you are a sinner who still needs a Savior.

9. Our evil desires and outward enticements tempt us. Read 1 Corinthians 10:13 to discover more about the dynamics of temptation.

    a. Are you the only one who is tempted? How do you know?

    b. Are the temptations you face insurmountable? Explain.

    c. What makes temptation bearable?

10. Temptations are often the result of satanic warfare. Fill in the following chart to discover Satan's predatory tactics.

Scripture	**Satan's Tactics**
Matthew 4:3	
John 8:44	
Revelation 12:9	
Revelation 12:10	

∘ ∘ • ∘ ∘

What do advertisers and our adversary have in common? They push the right buttons so we'll succumb to the weakness of the flesh. Ad executive Jerry Della Femina said, "Advertising deals in open sores.... Fear. Greed. Anger. Hostility.... We play on all the emotions and on all the problems, from not getting ahead ... to the desire to be one of the crowd. Everyone has a button. If enough people have the same button, you have a successful ad and a successful product."[2] But advertising can be deceptive. The right toothpaste won't give you sex appeal, and driving a European car doesn't mean you're successful.

We are all susceptible to temptation in three areas: bodily appetites, beautiful things, and boastful pride. John called these "the lust of the flesh, the lust of the eyes, and the pride of life" (1 John 2:16). Like a successful advertising executive, Satan takes advantage of our lusts. And like a concert pianist, Satan knows how to get us to sing his tune. On a piano, when the sustain peddle is pressed while a specific note is struck, the coordinating strings will recognize the note and vibrate in harmony. That's what Satan does; he sings out a sinful tune and hopes our coordinating fleshly desires will sing along. To stop the vibration on a piano, you take your foot off the pedal. To resist temptation, you unmask the real tempter, then "get up and pray, so that you will not give in to temptation" (Luke 22:46 NLT).

Listen To ...

The devil tempts that he may ruin; God tests that he may crown.

—*Saint Ambrose*

DAY 3
Deadly Temptation

Have you heard about a tricky method used by monkey hunters? Trappers take a small cage out into the jungle with a tasty bunch of bananas locked inside. Then a monkey comes along and spots the bananas. The unsuspecting primate reaches his greedy paw through the narrow rungs of the cage and grabs a banana. But he can't get the paw back out. And no matter how hard he tries—twisting his hand back and forth—he can't pull his hand through the rungs while hanging on to the banana. The trappers merely have to grab the unrelenting monkey. Now if you were standing there in the jungle, watching all of this happen, and wanted to save the monkey, you might yell in exasperation, "Drop the banana!"

Satan employs a similar clever strategy on unsuspecting Christians. He takes advantage of the appetites of our flesh, hoping we will grasp the enticing temptations he puts in our path. If we refuse to release the alluring bait, we will be unable to escape Satan's trap. Our evil desires cry out, "Don't let go! Hang on to this pleasure for as long as it will last!" If you are clinging to sinful practices that are destroying your testimony and preventing you from growing in grace, "Drop the temptation!" Get out of Satan's trap before it's too late.

LIFT UP ...

Father, You have power over sin and death. Give us strength to let go of temptation and look to You. In Jesus' name. Amen.

LOOK AT ...

James unmasked our true Enemy who tempts us. Now the book continues to explain the power of our own sinful desires.

READ JAMES 1:15.

Then, when desire has conceived, it gives birth to sin; and sin, when it is full-grown, brings forth death. James 1:15

1. Remembering yesterday's lesson, explain what happens when we give in to our desires.

2. How can yielding to sinful desire be compared to pregnancy?

3. What phrase lets you know that sin develops over time?

4. What does it mean to say that sin brings forth death?

5. a. Sin is a process that begins with the conception of evil desires and ends in death. Read Acts 5:1–11. What did Ananias and Sapphira conceive in their hearts (vv. 1–4)?

   b. What happened to Ananias as a result (vv. 5–6)?

   c. Explain how Sapphira allowed the conspiracy to grow (vv. 7–10).

LIVE OUT ...

6. a. We have learned that good desires can be fulfilled in wrong ways, making us susceptible to the attacks of Satan. In the following chart, list some good desires you have that could be fulfilled the wrong way.

LEARN ABOUT ...

1 Desire

Desire here means "lust"—a longing for what is forbidden or an intense craving or need. Desires can be deadly. Before you yield to desires, consider where they may lead you. "The righteousness of the upright delivers them, but the unfaithful are trapped by evil desires" (Prov. 11:6 NIV).

2 Conceived

To *conceive* means to take into one's being. Physical conception occurs by taking in male seed; intellectual conception comes by taking in thoughts; emotional conception begins with taking in a desire for good or evil. "They trust in empty words and speak lies; they conceive evil and bring forth iniquity" (Isa. 59:4).

4 Stillborn

James uses the imagery of childbirth to depict the birth of sin. Desire is the "mother" who conceives the child, "sin." Giving birth to a child is a painful experience that is transformed into joy; giving birth to sin is a seemingly pleasurable experience transformed into grief and death.

LEARN ABOUT ...

6 Step-by-Step

Sin is a four-step process resulting in death: (1) desire: we experience a strong compulsion to have or do something we should not; (2) deceit: we justify our desire; (3) design: we consciously plan to satisfy our desire; (4) disobey: we disregard God's Word to gratify our sinful urge.

---

7 Full-Grown

Sinful behavior can make us adult-sized sinners while godly behavior will make us full-grown saints. "We should no longer be children, tossed to and fro, ... but, speaking the truth in love, may grow up in all things into Him who is the head—Christ" (Eph. 4:14–15).

---

8 New Life

As surely as sin gives birth to death, repentance gives birth to new life. Resurrection is just a prayer away. "Anyone who belongs to Christ has become a new person. The old life is gone; a new life has begun!" (2 Cor. 5:17 NLT).

GOOD DESIRES	WRONG FULFILLMENT
(Example: to be accepted by others)	*(Example: succumbing to peer pressure)*

b. Journal about how one of the good desires, fulfilled the wrong way, gave birth to trouble in your life.

7. James revealed that sin has a maturation process. Complete the exercise to show how different desires and temptations can become full-grown sins. This takes creative thinking, but try it.

BIRTH OF SIN	CHILDHOOD	ADOLESCENCE	ADULTHOOD
Illegal drugs	*Occasional partying*	*Weekly habit*	*Complete addiction*
Pornography			
Anger			
Materialism			
Other			

8. We know that the birth of sinful desires will ultimately lead to death. If you are reaping the consequences of your sinful desires, take heart! God promises new life to those who repent. Journal a prayer by rewriting the following Scripture and asking God to give you new life in Christ:

> I have been crucified with Christ; it is no longer I who live, but Christ lives in me; and the life which I now live in the flesh I live by faith in the Son of God, who loved me and gave Himself for me. (Gal. 2:20)

° ° • ° °

News stories of the rich and famous often read like tombstones in a graveyard. They carve in our memories people who have followed the tragic cycle of sin that leads to death—people such as Jimi Hendrix, Janis Joplin, and Jim Morrison, the forefathers of rock and roll who literally partied themselves to death. More recently, we have read about Whitney Houston who, even with all the trappings of fame and fortune, died an unfortunate death.

But it's not just the rich and famous whose lifestyles can lead to an early grave. I (Penny) grew up with a promising young man I'll call Chad. He was tall, blond, and handsome and was always the life of the party. It started out innocently enough: he'd sneak liquor from his parents' cabinet. Later, he and his buddies began to host keggers on a weekly basis, relying on fake IDs to get them the beer. After high school, Chad became a fixture at the local bar scene.

As we grew up, most of our gang got married, had families, and put our partying days behind us. But not Chad. He ended up a severe alcoholic. The last time I saw him, he reeked of tobacco and bourbon even though it was early in the day. A short while later, I heard that in a state of drunken despondence, Chad had shot and killed himself. Ignoring the warning James gave about sin really can have deadly consequences.

LISTEN TO ...

Sin may open bright as the morning, but it will end dark as night.

—*Thomas DeWitt Talmage*

DAY 4

Tempted to Doubt

September 11, 2001, was a day that made Americans doubt. After hijackers turned commercial airplanes into missiles, Americans doubted the nation's security. They doubted that President Bush was up to the task. They doubted whether they could ever trust an immigrant again. And some of them began to doubt God.

Skeptics asked, "Where was Jesus on September 11?" He was on Flight 93, inspiring the passengers to recite the Lord's Prayer before taking action to thwart their captors' plans. He was helping over fifty thousand people (94 percent) escape before the World Trade Center collapsed. He was in the smoke-filled Pentagon, accompanying those who walked through the valley of the shadow of death. He was with Father Mychal Judge, who offered last rites to the mortally wounded.

The question is not where was God on September 11, but where was Satan? *He* was there, too: working in the terrorist training camps and in the hearts of the hijackers and inspiring Osama bin Laden to zealously promote his demonic agenda. The Bible tells us that "the devil … was a murderer from the beginning. He has always hated the truth" (John 8:44 NLT).

When we are tempted to doubt God, the book of James reminds us that evil begins with the "Evil One"—while God is the One who can bring good out of evil.

LIFT UP …

Lord, thank You for Your faithfulness even when I doubt. I praise You that when darkness seems so strong, Your never-changing love and goodness are always stronger. In Jesus' name. Amen.

LOOK AT ...

We've seen that our evil desires can lead to tragic consequences. Today the book of James brings us back to the goodness of God.

READ JAMES 1:16–17.

Do not be deceived, my beloved brethren. Every good gift and every perfect gift is from above, and comes down from the Father of lights, with whom there is no variation or shadow of turning. James 1:16–17

1. What did James implore his readers to do?

2. What was James's attitude toward his readers? How did he show it?

3. What things are from above?

4. Why do you think James reminded his readers that God is the source of these gifts?

5. How do you think this knowledge helps prevent us from accusing God when we face temptation?

6. God is described as the Father of lights. This description refers to Genesis 1:14–19 and Psalm 136:7–9. What do you learn about God from these scriptures?

7. Why do you think James made the point that God is unchanging?

LEARN ABOUT ...

1 Deception

Deceive means "to cheat or beguile; that which gives a false impression, whether by appearance, statement or influence." James implored believers not to be deceived into thinking that God is responsible for temptations.

3 Every Gift

Every means every. Therefore, every gift that God gives, without exception, is beneficial to His children. "If you sinful people know how to give good gifts to your children, how much more will your heavenly Father give good gifts to those who ask him" (Matt. 7:11 NLT).

7 Unchanging

In a world of change—from the seasons to the latest fashions—it's comforting to know that God is a constant. "I am the LORD, and I do not change" (Mal. 3:6 NLT). God cannot change for the worse because He's flawless. He can't get any better because He's the best.

LEARN ABOUT ...

8 Be a Berean

Before you believe what others say about God, make sure the Bible agrees with what they've said. "The people of Berea ... searched the Scriptures day after day to see if Paul and Silas were teaching the truth" (Acts 17:11 NLT).

---

9 Faithful

Faithfulness implies dependability, loyalty, and stability. It is difficult to depend on someone who is erratic or switches allegiance. It is hard to find stability in a relationship with someone who is always changing. You can depend on God to be loyal and steadfast.

LIVE OUT ...

8. a. James strongly commanded, "Do not be deceived." Unfortunately, there are many misconceptions about God. Check the boxes below to indicate how you have been deceived about God in the past.

    ❏ There are some things God can't do.

    ❏ There are some things God doesn't see.

    ❏ There are some times God doesn't care.

    ❏ There are some people God won't forgive.

    ❏ There are some places God won't go.

    b. Journal about which of the above deceptive ideas ensnared you the most and caused you to doubt God's goodness. How did God correct your unrealistic view of Him? What scripture reinforced the truth about God?

9. The following hymn was inspired by this passage in James and Lamentations 3:22–23. Read or sing it out loud as you spend time worshipping our unchanging God.

    Great is Thy faithfulness, Oh God my Father,

    There is no shadow of turning with Thee;

    Thou changest not, Thy compassions they fail not;

    As Thou hast been Thou forever wilt be.

    Great is Thy faithfulness!

    Great is Thy faithfulness!

    Morning by morning new mercies I see.

    All I have needed Thy hand hath provided;

    Great is Thy faithfulness, Lord, unto me!

    —*Thomas O. Chisholm*

10. a. God is the giver of every good and perfect gift. Make a list of some of the good things (gifts) He has given to you (home, health, happiness, etc.).

b. Journal your own psalm of praise to God, thanking Him for His goodness.

∘ ∘ • ∘ ∘

It's hard to believe that *everything* in our lives is a good and perfect gift from the Father of lights. In addition to acknowledging the obvious blessings we have, all of us can look back at something tragic from our past and respond by doubting God or blaming others. It's easy to do. Yet James's teaching implies that what happens here below has its origin in heaven above. Paul shed light into the dilemma of the seemingly bad being actually good when he wrote, "We know that all things work together for good to those who love God, to those who are the called according to His purpose" (Rom. 8:28). Somehow, in some miraculous way, God promises to transform "bad things" into "beautiful things" in His children's lives. But between the bad-into-beautiful is time—time when we can doubt God's motives or His ultimate intentions.

For me (Lenya), I could simultaneously doubt God and blame my father for my problems: "Why did God allow me to be born to parents who would split?" Before I was a Christian, the divorce broke me, turning me into a partyer to hide the pain. But once I was born again, the divorce made me a reconciler, sensitive to the pain of others. Amazingly, God used my past to define my future. My greatest joy is counseling and praying for fractured families to be reconciled to God and each other. As I have seen relationships restored, I thank God for His good and perfect gifts!

LISTEN TO ...

God's gifts put man's best dreams to shame.

—*Elizabeth Barrett Browning*

DAY 5
Temptation Transformed

During the Victorian era, an English paper factory boasted that it made the finest stationery in the world. One day an American businessman toured the factory and inquired, "What is the secret ingredient for making such fine stationery?" The supervisor showed him a huge pile of dirty old rags and told him that the rag content was the key to producing the highest quality paper. The skeptical man thought he was being misled in order to keep the secret ingredient a secret. Sometime later he received a package of fine writing paper embossed with his initials. An enclosed note simply read: "Dirty rags transformed."

God's view of us is similar to the factory supervisor's view of the dirty rags. He sees beyond who we are and looks instead at who we can become. He looked at Peter, the rough fisherman who denied Jesus, and saw a man who could become the rock on which His church was built. He saw the late Chuck Colson, a man tempted by power and position, and saw a man who would build Prison Fellowship International into an organization that preaches the gospel to thousands of incarcerated prisoners throughout the world. He looks at *you* and looks past the things that tempt you to see the person you can become. He says: "Give your life to Me. I will transform you." And when you turn your heart over to Him, your life will become a rags-to-riches story.

LIFT UP ...

Dear God, when I give in to temptation and I'm tempted to give up, help me remember that Your Word has the power to transform and give new life. In Jesus' name. Amen.

LOOK AT ...

James's words have reminded us not to doubt that God is a faithful giver of good gifts. We discover today that God will continue His transforming work in our lives.

READ JAMES 1:18.

Of His own will He brought us forth by the word of truth, that we might be a kind of firstfruits of His creatures. James 1:18

1. James repeated the analogy of birth. Explain who is being "born" and how.

2. How do you know that this birth is in God's plan?

3. Explain what the Word of Truth is.

4. God's Word is very important to believers; it is the basis of faith. Look up the following scriptures to discover what the Word of God does.

SCRIPTURE	WHAT THE WORD DOES
Isaiah 40:8	
Romans 10:17	
1 Thessalonians 2:13	
2 Timothy 3:16	

5. James called his readers "firstfruits." Look up Romans 1:16. Why do you suppose he referred to Jewish believers as "firstfruits"?

LIVE OUT ...

6. a. James reminded believers that they have been born again through the Word of Truth. Read 1 Peter 1:22–23. Describe the characteristics those who have been born again display.

LEARN ABOUT ...

1 Two Births

God designed two types of birth: (1) the flesh, born through human parents, and (2) the spirit, born again through God's Word implanting new life. Jesus said, "Humans can reproduce only human life, but the Holy Spirit gives new life from heaven" (John 3:6 NLT).

2 God's Will

God's will is His specific design, intent, or purpose; His acting with a specific objective. Here, God's will is His desire for humanity to experience new birth. "[God is] not willing that any should perish but that all should come to repentance" (2 Pet. 3:9).

5 Firstfruits

In Old Testament times, the Israelites offered their "firstfruits," the first and best of their crops, to God. In the New Testament, "firstfruits" refers to (1) the first converts in a place, (2) the Christians of that generation, or (3) Christ, who first rose from the dead.

6 Life

In biology one criterion for being categorized as alive is to be capable of procreation. Life springs from life. God's Word—the Bible—is living and breathes new life into those who believe its message: "The word of God is alive and powerful" (Heb. 4:12 NLT).

Learn About ...

7 Free Will

God's will is that we follow His perfect plan found in Scripture. Yet, in His love, God has given us free will to make choices, even if our choices oppose His will. But how much better to pray, "I want your will to be done, not mine" (Luke 22:42 NLT).

---

8 Gospel

Gospel literally means "good news." The gospel is the story of the saving work of God in His Son, Jesus Christ, and a call to faith and new life in Him. Jesus is more than a messenger of the gospel; He is the living embodiment of the gospel.

b. What type of seed does God implant for our new birth?

c. What do you learn about the Word of God from this passage?

7. Today we learned that God's will is for us to be born again. Fill in the chart to discover other aspects of God's will for us.

Scripture	God's Will
John 1:12–13	
1 Thessalonians 4:3–5	
1 Thessalonians 5:18	
1 Peter 2:15	

8. The Jewish believers were the "firstfruits," or first crop, of people to embrace the gospel message and become born again. From them, God's spiritual seed was spread throughout the world. With this in mind, work through the following exercise.

Step One: Journal about your "firstfruits"—the first people from whom you heard the gospel message.

Step Two: Write about when and how the message took root in your own heart so that you believed the Word of Truth.

Step Three: List some people in your acquaintance who have not heard about the new birth Christ offers.

Step Four: Journal a prayer asking God to give you the boldness to be "firstfruits" to them as you plant the seed of God's Word in their lives.

o o • o o

A rabbi desired his wisdom to live on after he died, and he wondered whom he could trust to carry on his work. He decided to test the honesty of his pupils. Calling them all together, he posed a question: "What would you do if you were walking along and found a purse full of money laying in the road?"

The first disciple answered, "I'd return it to its owner." The rabbi thought to himself, *His answer comes so quickly, I must wonder if he really means it.*

"I'd keep the money if nobody saw me find it," said another. *He has a frank tongue, but a wicked heart,* the rabbi told himself.

"Well, rabbi," said a third disciple, "I believe I'd be tempted to keep it. So I would pray to God that He would give me the strength to resist such temptation and do the right thing." *Aha,* thought the rabbi, *here is the man I would trust!*

As with the rabbi, God is looking for people He can trust. He wants to know if we'll be able to carry on the work of spreading new life through the gospel message. He allows temptations to test us to see what's in our hearts—have we truly been born again? He wants to know how we'll handle difficult situations—will we glorify Him by resisting or grieve Him by succumbing? When your temptation is transformed into triumph, you prove you are trustworthy to carry His life-giving message to others.

LISTEN TO ...

He who made us also remade us.

—*Saint Augustine*

Mirror, Mirror in the Word
James 1:19-27

The most famous mirror was a mirror that could speak. We all know Grimm's fairy tale of Snow White, whose wicked stepmother would gaze into her magical mirror and ask, "Mirror, mirror on the wall, who is the fairest one of all?" The mirror, which could not lie, answered, "Thou, O Queen, art the fairest one of all," and the queen was content, because she knew the mirror spoke the truth.

As time passed, Snow White grew more beautiful. By the time she was seven, she was even lovelier than the queen herself. Once again the queen asked, "Mirror, mirror on the wall, who is the fairest one of all?" The mirror answered, "Famed is thy beauty, Majesty. But hold, a lovely maid I see…. Alas, she is more fair than thee." The queen was horrified, and from that moment envy and pride grew in her heart like rank weeds.[1]

All mirrors have one thing in common: they don't lie. Whether we have bad hair or a beautiful smile, mirrors faithfully reflect the truth. James teaches us that God's Word is a supernatural mirror that can look beneath the surface to expose the heart. Instead of asking, "Am I the fairest in the land?" we should be discovering, "Am I faithful in word and deed?" God's mirror reveals the inconsistencies between religious activity that is useful or useless. This week, gaze into God's looking glass and ask yourself: Do I hear God's Word? And am I doing what I hear and see?

Day 1: James 1:19–20   DO YOU HEAR?
Day 2: James 1:21–22   DO YOU DO?
Day 3: James 1:23–25   DO YOU SEE?
Day 4: James 1:26   DO YOU SPEAK?
Day 5: James 1:27   DO YOU GO?

DAY 1
Do You Hear?

LIFT UP ...

Father, I want to be righteous in Your sight. Teach me how to pluck out any "weeds" in my heart and plant Your Word deep so I can act in a way that pleases You. In Jesus' name. Amen.

LOOK AT ...

In his instruction manual on living faith, James taught believers how to pass the tests of trials, riches, and temptations. His words in the next passage ask us to pass the test of responding faithfully to God's Word.

READ JAMES 1:19–20.

So then, my beloved brethren, let every man be swift to hear, slow to speak, slow to wrath; for the wrath of man does not produce the righteousness of God. James 1:19–20

1. Why do you think James kept calling his readers things like "my beloved brethren"?

2. What phrase did James use to show that no one was exempt from his instruction?

3. What must every person "be swift" to do?

LEARN ABOUT ...

1 Beloved

Beloved translates the Greek word *agape*, which is used of God's unconditional love for Christ, His Son. James loved the early church like God loves His Son. "Beloved, if God so loved us, we also ought to love one another" (1 John 4:11).

3 Do You Hear?

"Be swift to hear" is preceded by the phrase "so then," referring back to verse 18 and the "word of truth." Jesus' followers must listen to God's infallible Word and evaluate every idea, philosophy, or piece of advice against it.

4. What was the first thing James said to be "slow" to do?

5. Rewrite in your own words the meaning of the phrase "slow to wrath."

6. Fill in the following chart to discover how to become slow to wrath.

SCRIPTURE	SLOW TO WRATH
Psalm 37:8	
Proverbs 15:1	
Proverbs 29:8	
Romans 12:19	
Ephesians 4:26	
James 1:20	

7. Why should we be slow to wrath?

8. Explain in your own words what God's righteousness is.

LIVE OUT ...

9. a. James considered the church "beloved" family members and friends. As an older brother, he offered some loving advice. Fill in the chart to discover further advice, given by the apostle Paul, to those beloved by God.

SCRIPTURE	INSTRUCTION TO THE BELOVED
1 Corinthians 10:14	
2 Corinthians 7:1	
Philippians 2:12	
Colossians 3:12	

b. Based on those scriptures in the chart, journal about which piece of advice you needed to hear the most right now in your life, and why.

10. James exhorted believers to be "swift to hear" the Word of Truth. Check off the things that dull your ability to hear God's Word clearly.

___ Advice from friends   ___ Self-help books

___ Hollywood hype   ___ Talk show tips

___ Political pundits   ___ Latest gossip

___ Your own ideas   ___ Other_____

11. a. We know that people's wrath does not produce righteousness. Use the word *ANGRY* as an acrostic to describe some things that provoke you to anger.

A (*Example: arrogant people who think they know it all.*)

N

G

R

Y

b. Now journal a prayer asking God to help you become slow to wrath.

○ ○ ● ○ ○

A story is told of Franklin Roosevelt, who often endured long receiving lines at the White House. He complained that people paid no attention to what was said as they went through these lines. One day he tried an experiment. To each person who passed by, he murmured, "I murdered my grandmother this morning." The guests responded with, "Marvelous!" "Keep up the good work." "God bless you, sir." Finally, Roosevelt greeted the ambassador from Bolivia, who actually heard the president's words. Nonplussed, the ambassador leaned over and whispered, "I'm sure she had it coming."

Sometimes we, too, are "hard of hearing." There are times when our eyes glaze over and people's words just float through our ears and past the brain. Haven't we all responded with a vague "Uh huh" to a story we're not really listening to? Or maybe at dinner we say a cursory "That's nice, dear" in response to our husband's stories about work?

When it comes to hearing God, many times we are also spiritually hard of hearing. Like the people in the receiving line, we want to be in a position to hobnob with God, but we don't *really* listen to what He says. Often we are so busy thinking of what we want to say to God that we don't pay attention to what He's saying to us. The next time you spend time with God, spend more time listening than talking.

LISTEN TO ...

Half an hour's listening is essential except when you are very busy. Then a full hour is needed.

—*Saint Francis de Sales*

DAY 2
Do You Do?

Only time will tell whether a person is an authentic fruit-bearing Christian or a showy imposter. By outward appearances it is impossible to determine whether those who attend church are saints or ain'ts. In Matthew 13 Jesus told a parable of the tares and the wheat to illustrate the problem of mistaken identity—those who seem to be Christians in word but never in deed. Tares are a kind of darnel weed that grow in grain fields. Tares appear identical to wheat and barley, with a similar beard and stature. Ancient Jews considered tares degenerate wheat because the seeds are poisonous to man and animals, producing sleepiness, nausea, convulsions, and even death. The plants can be separated only at the time of harvest—to divide them earlier would destroy the good wheat.

God wants spiritual fruit, not religious nuts. He can tell the difference between the frauds and the fruitful: "Do not be deceived, God is not mocked; for whatever a man sows, that he will also reap" (Gal. 6:7).

James teaches that a person of living faith is one who produces fruit by incorporating four key elements into his or her Christian walk: (1) repenting of all filthiness; (2) receiving the Word of Truth; (3) reproducing righteousness through doing what God says; and (4) realistically examining one's life in light of God's Word.

LIFT UP ...

Lord, I don't want to deceive myself. Help me to hear Your Word clearly and then do what You say. In Jesus' name. Amen.

LOOK AT ...

We have learned to be swift to hear and slow to speak because we've received the Word of Truth. "Therefore" we must *do* something with what we've received.

Learn About ...

2 Lay Aside

To lay aside means to put away, cease, or depart from. James told his readers to prepare the soil of their hearts by pulling out the weeds. Before God will produce righteousness in us, we must weed out the sin that stands between us and the fruits of righteousness.

3 Implanted

James compared God's Word to seed and the human heart to soil. Metaphorically, God's Word is implanted in our hearts at salvation. In the parable of the sower, Jesus described four types of soil: (1) hard heart; (2) shallow heart; (3) crowded heart; (4) fruitful heart (Matt. 13).

5 Do You Do?

Some people mistakenly believe that attending church or hearing a good sermon makes them grow as Christians. However, it is not the hearing but the doing that brings about spiritual fruit. We must do the Word. Don't just mark your Bible; let the Bible mark your life.

Read James 1:21–22.

Therefore lay aside all filthiness and overflow of wickedness, and receive with meekness the implanted word, which is able to save your souls. But be doers of the word, and not hearers only, deceiving yourselves. James 1:21–22

1. James began this verse with a "therefore." Whenever you see a "therefore," it's good to find out what it's there for. Look back to verse 20 and write the scriptural principles James connected with verses 21–22.

2. Describe what James wanted his readers to lay aside.

3. Once we've weeded out sin, what should we receive, and how?

4. What is the spiritual benefit of meekly receiving God's Word?

5. What are we to be and not to be?

6. What is the danger of being only hearers?

Live Out ...

7. Laying aside sinful behavior is like weeding a garden. Fill in the following chart to discover what weeds must be pulled from the garden of your heart.

Scripture	Lay Aside
Ephesians 4:22–24	
Colossians 3:8–10	
Hebrews 12:1	
1 Peter 2:1–2	

8. God desires to implant His Word deep in our hearts, bringing forth fruit. In the parable of the sower (Matt. 13:3–9, 18–23), Jesus described the kinds of soil (hearts) God's Word encounters. Journal about some of the people you know who have hearts similar to those described below. Write a prayer asking God to make their hearts fruitful.

Hard Heart: Does not understand or receive the Word of God, so it does not bring forth fruit.

Shallow Heart: Receives the Word with great emotion but has no depth, so it withers over time and bears no fruit.

Crowded Heart: Lacks repentance and permits sinful attitudes and behaviors to crowd out the Word, so it bears no fruit.

Fruitful Heart: Receives the Word, allows it to take root, and produces a bountiful harvest.

9. James warned against self-deception. Paul gave the Corinthians a list of those who would not inherit the kingdom of God because they had been deceived. Journal 1 Corinthians 6:9–10 into a personal prayer asking God to reveal to you the ways *you've* been deceived about sin. Ask Him to help you spot the lies so that you can inherit the kingdom.

> Do you not know that the wicked will not inherit the kingdom of God? Do not be deceived: Neither the sexually immoral nor idolaters nor adulterers, … nor homosexual offenders nor thieves nor the greedy nor drunkards nor slanderers nor swindlers will inherit the kingdom of God. (1 Cor. 6:9–10 NIV)

LEARN ABOUT ...

8 Meekness

We are to receive the implanted Word with meekness. Meekness is an attitude of humility toward God and gentleness toward others, springing from a recognition that God is in control. God promises blessings for those who exhibit this characteristic. "The meek shall inherit the earth" (Ps. 37:11).

9 Deceit

In lesson 3 we learned that Satan deceives us, tempting us to sin. Self-deception is every bit as dangerous as Satan's deception. It's important not to fool ourselves and, as a result, act foolishly. "If we say that we have no sin, we deceive ourselves" (1 John 1:8).

∘ ∘ • ∘ ∘

Along with discovering electricity, Benjamin Franklin discovered a way to make his harvest more fruitful. He learned that gypsum plaster sown in the fields would make things grow better. He told his neighbors, but they didn't believe him and turned a deaf ear to his advice. He said no more about it, but he went into the field early the next spring and sowed some grain. Near the path where his neighbors walked, he traced some letters with his finger, sowed seed, and fertilized it with plaster. After a couple of weeks, the seed sprang up. As his neighbors passed that way, they were surprised to discover a message in bright green letters growing from the soil: "This has been plastered." Benjamin Franklin never needed to argue with his neighbors again about the benefit of plaster for the fields—the fruit of his labor said it all.

God has sown something amazing in the soil of our hearts—the implanted Word. For the Word to grow, not only do we need to weed out "all filthiness," but we must also make our hearts more fertile by doing what the Word instructs us to do. God's Word is much more than water to a parched soul; it is Miracle-Gro that will produce a bountiful harvest in the lives of Christians who have living faith.

LISTEN TO ...

There are two things to do about the Gospel—believe it and behave it.

—*Susanna Wesley*

Do You See?

A cameraman working on the Merv Griffin Show kept circling the waif-like model Twiggy during the pre-show lighting check. Merv became distracted and then irritated with the constant movement of the man and his camera. Finally, Merv asked why the man kept rotating around Twiggy. The cameraman answered, "I always check our guests for their bad side, but Twiggy looks great from every angle."

Photographers say there are very few naturally beautiful people in the world. Careful lighting, posing, and airbrushing help people appear more attractive. Many are shocked to discover they have a crooked smile, one small eye, an off-centered nose, or some other flaw. Often when we look into a mirror, some type of activity like putting on makeup, plucking eyebrows, or combing hair distracts us. This is deceiving. When we're in motion, physical defects are not as noticeable. But when we're caught standing still, as in a photograph, our less-than-perfect features become obvious.

James revealed that in the spiritual realm, motion is also a great deceiver. When we read God's Word hastily, as we would read the daily news, we fail to see our spiritual flaws and stop long enough to do something about them. Today as you hold the mirror of God's Word up to your life, don't rush away before you have the chance to ask yourself, "Do I really see myself?"

LIFT UP ...

Lord, thank You for offering a mirror that truly reflects what I look like, inside and out. Help me to see myself the way You see me. In Jesus' name. Amen.

LEARN ABOUT ...

2 Mirror

Ancient mirrors were polished brass or bronze. Only the rich could afford mirrors of gold or silver. These metal mirrors, more primitive than the glass mirrors developed in the fourteenth century, gave distorted reflections. "For now we see in a mirror, dimly" (I Cor. 13:12).

3 Glance

The word *observes* implies that people often merely glance at their reflection. The problem with glancing is that we're likely to forget what we've seen. So, too, when we only give God's Word a cursory glance, we're less likely to remember what we've read.

4 Perfect Law

God's Word is perfect because it is inerrant, flawless, and complete. The law emphasizes God's commands requiring obedience. Liberty focuses on redemption from sin and bondage. "The instructions of the LORD are perfect, reviving the soul" (Ps. 19:7 NLT).

LOOK AT ...

We have read James's exhortation to "be doers of the word, and not hearers only" (1:22). James also challenged his readers to remember what we look like when we gaze into the mirror of God's Word.

READ JAMES 1:23–25.

For if anyone is a hearer of the word and not a doer, he is like a man observing his natural face in a mirror; for he observes himself, goes away, and immediately forgets what kind of man he was. But he who looks into the perfect law of liberty and continues in it, and is not a forgetful hearer but a doer of the work, this one will be blessed in what he does. James 1:23–25

1. In your own words, what does it mean to be a hearer but not a doer of the Word?

2. To whom is such a person compared?

3. What shows that this person's observation has little impact?

4. James encouraged us to look into "the perfect law of liberty." How is this a good description of the Bible?

5. How do you know that this action is more than just a glance?

6. Describe the person who continues in "the perfect law of liberty."

7. What does God promise this kind of person?

LIVE OUT ...

8. Looking into God's Word helps us to really see our spiritual appearance. Answer the questions by circling your response.

    a. How often do you look into a mirror to check your physical appearance?

    Never   Once/month   Once/week   Once/day   Twice/day or more

    b. Do you like what you see?

    Never   Sometimes   Frequently   Usually   Always

    c. How often do you look into the mirror of God's Word?

    Never   Once/month   Once/week   Once/day   Twice/day or more

    d. Do you like what you see?

    Never   Sometimes   Frequently   Usually   Always

9. Today we learned that we must continually look into God's Word, putting into practice what we read. Journal a prayer to God, committing to live out what you have learned from God's Word by rewriting the following verse:

    > This Book of the Law shall not depart from your mouth, but you shall meditate in it day and night, that you may observe to do according to all that is written in it. For then you will make your way prosperous, and then you will have good success. (Josh. 1:8)

10. James called the Bible "the perfect law of liberty." Read Psalm 19:7–9, then fill in the following chart to record what this psalm teaches you about God's Word.

LEARN ABOUT ...

8 Do You See?

The purpose of a mirror is to see yourself as you are and do something about what you see. The mirror of God's Word reflects the true nature of our hearts. "The Word of God ... exposes our innermost thoughts and desires" (Heb. 4:12 NLT).

9 Look Intently

The looking that James encouraged comes from a word meaning "to bend beside; lean over; peer within; look intently; or stoop down." In contrast to casually observing an image in a mirror, gazing carefully and with serious intent at God's Word requires time, attention, and sincere devotion.

10 God's Word

The Bible is such an indescribable book that one name alone can't convey all it contains: "Scripture"; "our daily bread"; "the perfect law of liberty"; "the sword of the spirit"; "pure milk"; and "water" are just a few names given for God's Word.

WHAT IT'S CALLED	WHAT IT IS	WHAT IT DOES
Law of the Lord	*Perfect*	*Converts the soul*

When you get what you want in your struggle for self
And the world makes you king for a day,
Just go to God's mirror and look at yourself,
And see what The Man has to say.

For it isn't your father or mother or wife
Who judgment upon you will pass;
The fellow whose verdict counts most in your life
Is the One whose Word is the glass.

Some people may think you're a straight-shootin' chum
And call you a wonderful guy,
But the "Man of the Glass" says you're only a bum
If His Word you've neglected to try.

God's the One you must please, never mind all the rest,
For it's Him that you'll meet in the end.
And you've passed your most dangerous, difficult test
If the "Man of the Glass" is your friend.

You may fool the whole world down the pathway of years
And get pats on the back as you pass,
But your final reward will be heartaches and tears
If you forsake the "Man of the Glass."[2]

—*Adapted from "The Guy in the Glass" by Peter Dale Wimbrow Sr.*

LISTEN TO ...

The Bible is the book that holds hearts up to the light as if held against the sun.

—*William A. Quayle*

DAY 4

Do You Speak?

A man sat down to dinner with his family and solemnly said, "Let us pray." Everyone bowed their heads, and the father intoned, "Thank You, Lord, for this food and for the hands that prepared it." During the meal, however, he began to complain: "This bread is stale!" "I don't like broccoli!" "This coffee's too weak!" And on it went throughout the meal.

As dessert was served, his young daughter asked, "Dad, do you think God heard you when you said grace today?" He answered confidently, "Of course." Then she asked, "Do you think God heard what you said about the bread, the broccoli, and the coffee?" Less confidently he answered, "Yes, I believe so." The little girl then asked, "Well, which of your words do you think God believed?"

To all appearances, this fault-finding father was very religious: he made sure he prayed with his family. But his words told a different story. The same is true with us. What we say speaks volumes about our character. Our words expose whether we are compassionate or critical; loving or hateful; generous or greedy.

We've all heard the saying that actions speak louder than words. But the Bible teaches that our words loudly proclaim the condition of our hearts. It has been estimated that we spend one-fifth of our lives talking, speaking on average sixteen thousand words per day.[3] Today the book of James reminds us to ask ourselves, "*What* do I speak?" because what we say reveals whether we are righteous or merely religious.

LIFT UP ...

Father, help me to bridle my tongue and, by my words, reveal to the world that I have a relationship with You. Keep me mindful that religion without relationship is worthless. In Jesus' name. Amen.

LOOK AT ...

This week we have learned the importance of receiving God's Word, looking intently into it, and responding in obedience. Now we discover that true religion, based upon God's Word, will result in righteous speech.

READ JAMES 1:26.

If anyone among you thinks he is religious, and does not bridle his tongue but deceives his own heart, this one's religion is useless. James 1:26

1. What phrase lets you know that James was addressing everyone who professes faith?

2. What specific type of person was James addressing here?

3. Describe the action this person fails to take.

4. What effect does this failure have on the heart?

5. Jesus revealed that the tongue and the heart are intimately linked. Explain the connection, according to Matthew 12:34.

6. Looking back at James 1:26, what does an unbridled tongue reveal about a person's religion?

7. Read Mark 7:6–7. How do the words Jesus quotes from Isaiah about hypocrisy expand on James's point here?

LIVE OUT ...

8. Rather than engaging in outward religious rituals for the sake of appearances, the Bible instructs us to pursue inner godliness for the sake of disappearances—"He must increase, but I must decrease" (John 3:30). With this in mind, journal the following passage into a personal prayer, asking God to help you grow in godliness:

> Giving all diligence, add to your faith virtue, to virtue knowledge, to knowledge self–control, to self–control per-severance, to perseverance godliness, to godliness brotherly kindness, and to brotherly kindness love. (2 Peter 1:5–7)

9. James encouraged believers to bridle their tongues. Check the areas in which you struggle to determine if you need a muzzle for your mouth.

     ____ I chatter mindlessly.

     ____ I gossip brutally.

     ____ I boast about accomplishments.

     ____ I remind people I'm religious.

     ____ I talk if it's quiet.

     ____ I interrupt conversations.

     ____ I use profanity.

     ____ Other

10. What we say reflects what is in our heart and our relationship with God. Fill in the chart to discover how to engage in godly speech.

SCRIPTURE	GODLY SPEECH
Psalm 35:28	
Psalm 119:171–172	

LEARN ABOUT ...

8 Godliness

Godliness speaks of piety or reverence toward God. More than religious profession, it is the power of a vital union with God that results in godly speech and conduct. "But you ... pursue righteousness, godliness, faith, love, patience, gentleness" (I Tim. 6:11).

9 Holy Speech

The words that we believers speak are a reflection of the One we serve. If we speak carelessly or thoughtlessly, we misrepresent God. Before speaking we should pray, "Let the words of my mouth and the meditation of my heart be acceptable in Your sight, O LORD" (Ps. 19:14).

10 Edification

As believers, we should exalt God and uplift one another with our speech. To *edify* literally means to build up. Christians are edified not only by godly speech but also by understanding spiritual truth through the work of evangelists, pastors, and teachers.

Ephesians 4:15
Ephesians 4:29

° ° • ° °

"You're grounded, Penny," my mom exclaimed when I used a swear word at home. "You've got an awful potty mouth!" When I was a teenager, all the cool kids cussed. And it was important to me to be cool. Though I had been raised in the church and knew better, I became proficient at profanity. Sadly, what came out of my mouth was a picture of what I had allowed into my heart. I had turned my back on my faith, thinking it was much more important to be a popular party girl than a prim and proper church girl. My friends swore, the movies I watched were drenched in bad language, and the music I listened to should have been rated R.

After I rededicated my life to Christ, one of the first sins God brought to my attention was my bad language. I repented and made a conscious effort to delete all expletives from my vocabulary. I didn't want my children to learn swear words from me. But old habits die hard. Once when I was teaching my oldest daughter to drive, she made a scary move. Without thinking I yelled, "%@X!#, Erin, watch where you're going!" She looked at me and said, "Mom, you've got a potty mouth." I realized that my words made me look like a total hypocrite in front of my daughter. I asked her to forgive me, and I asked God to cleanse my heart and tongue.

Listen To ...

Never let an indecent word slip from your mouth. Even if you don't mean it in an evil way, others may be offended. An evil word dropping into a weak person grows and spreads like a drop of oil on linen.

—*Saint Frances de Sales*

Do You Go?

Having grown up an atheist, in college I (Lenya) decided that if there truly was a God, I would do a little investigating. I started this pursuit of God by taking a class on eastern religions. It gave an overview of Hinduism, Buddhism, Taoism, and Islam. From this smorgasbord of religious options, I admired Hinduism the most because of the Hindu belief that all paths lead to God. It was so nice of this religion to accommodate hundreds of millions of gods; perhaps I could sample the "flavor of the month" god.

Simultaneously I began to take random surveys of my friends' religious belief systems. When I asked, "Do you believe in God?" they would respond, "I'm a Catholic," or "I go to the Lutheran church." While attending the same party, drinking from the same keg, and smoking the same joint, my pseudo-religious friends would condemn me to hell for disbelief in "a God," as they sat smugly secure in their church membership, without practicing their faith. They had been inoculated by a religious system that prevented them from catching the real thing—a relationship with God rather than with a denomination.

James encountered some people who were similar to my friends. They said they were religious, but they had never repented. They had all the right rituals, but they weren't living righteously. So James decided to give some clear instruction on what makes Christians relevant.

LIFT UP ...

Father, I want to go where You say, to love whom You love, to keep myself unsullied by the world. Please empower me to exhibit pure and undefiled religion. In Jesus' name. Amen.

LOOK AT ...

James taught that true inward conversion manifests outwardly in righteous speech. Now we examine some other marks of true religion.

LEARN ABOUT ...

1 Religion

The word *religion* comes from *religare*, which means reading over or paying careful attention to divine things. It refers to a system of worship with specific patterns of behavior. Religious rituals are not bad so long as they reflect true reverence and obedience to God.

---

3 Helpless

To God, neglecting helpless widows and orphans is as bad as witchcraft, lying, or adultery. "'I will be a swift witness against sorcerers, against adulterers, against perjurers, against those who exploit ... widows and orphans ... because they do not fear Me,' says the LORD" (Mal. 3:5).

---

6 Stain Free

Unspotted means unstained. The spiritual stains of sin can only be washed clean by Christ's blood. Once cleansed we can stay clean through obedience and confession. "If we confess our sins to him, he is faithful and just to forgive us our sins and to cleanse us from all wickedness" (1 John 1:9 NLT).

READ JAMES 1:27.

Pure and undefiled religion before God and the Father is this: to visit orphans and widows in their trouble, and to keep oneself unspotted from the world. James 1:27

1. What kind of religion did James want believers to practice?

2. What phrase did James use to indicate that God notices your religion?

3. How will those with pure religion treat the helpless?

4. According to Psalm 68:5, what will our holy God be for widows and orphans?

5. Read Matthew 25:35–40. Explain whom Jesus encouraged us to help, and whom we're *really* helping when we do this.

6. According to James 1:27, if we have pure religion, how will we look after ourselves?

7. What are some ways the world can stain a person's life?

LIVE OUT ...

8. James encouraged us to be pure concerning our religion. Fill in the table to discover in what areas of your life God expects purity.

SCRIPTURE	BE PURE IN ...
Proverbs 21:8	
Matthew 5:8	

1 Timothy 3:9

2 Peter 3:1

9. Today we learned that God's desire is for His people to help the helpless. Think about a widow, orphan, or other vulnerable person you know personally. Journal about when you will visit this person and how you will help her or him.

10. James strongly urged his readers to remain unspotted from the world. Fill in the table to discover some characteristics of the world.

SCRIPTURE	WORLD
John 7:7	
Galatians 4:3	
Colossians 2:8	
1 John 5:19	

° ° • °°

Over a thousand people lost spouses and over three thousand children lost a parent on September 11, 2001.[4] As I (Lenya) watched the September 11 attacks, my thoughts became a prayer, *What can I do, Lord?* Thinking about the thousands killed proved too difficult to wrap my brain around. Instead I needed to pray for one widow. I remembered the POW bracelet I once wore and thought, *Perhaps a similar bracelet could be made to remember the victims and offer their families mercy.*

With the Lord's leading, I founded an organization called Mercy B.A.N.D. (Bearing Another's Name Daily), manufacturing bracelets to serve as a reminder to pray for the survivors and as a living memorial to those who died so tragically. Within a week a jeweler, a silver provider, and a manufacturer were on board. Compassionate Christians donated

LEARN ABOUT ...

8 Pure

Pure means clean; *undefiled* means free from contamination. Spiritually, religion becomes defiled when mixed with sinful motives. "The commandments and doctrines of men ... have an appearance of wisdom in self-imposed religion ... but are of no value" (Col. 2:22–23).

9 Do You Go?

To visit means more than casually dropping by. It means to look out for, care for, and offer relief. In the early church, the neediest people were orphans and widows who, without the benefit of life insurance or welfare programs, were often in desperate straits.

10 World

The *world* refers not to planet Earth but to sinful humanity alienated from God. The world's systems of ungodly philosophies and values oppose God's holy precepts. Paul said, "We have received, not the spirit of the world, but the Spirit who is from God" (I Cor. 2:12).

computers, telephones, graphic design, and printing. Within four months, over forty thousand people had donned the bracelets. After a *New York Daily News* story, calls began coming from New York City. A mother who lost a son wanted bracelets engraved with his name. Four widows in a support group passed the phone around, spelling their husbands' names for me. Hundreds of victims' family members have received the bracelets.

It's my hope that these simple silver bands made a difference to the widows and orphans. I wanted the families to know that although there are a few people with evil in their hearts, there are infinitely more people who have mercy in their hearts—and now on their wrists.

LISTEN TO ...

Please give me those daily graces necessary to be fruitful in virtue and in good works.

—*Marie of the Incarnation*

Class Warfare
James 2:1–13

Class warfare has many different faces: the haves versus the have-nots; Democrats versus Republicans; and educated versus uneducated. In India, Hindus organized society into groups called *castes*, which determined one's social class within the community. The caste system included the Brahmans (priests and scholars), Kshatriyas (rulers and warriors), Vaishyas (merchants and professionals), Shudras (artisans, laborers, and servants), and Dalits (menials known as the untouchables). The caste system has been strictly enforced: no one could intermarry or find employment above his or her station in life.

Medieval Europeans had their own caste system known as *feudalism*, based on the social system of large manor estates. The social classes within this system were the lords (the rulers of the land), the vassals (aristocrats and warriors), and the peasants (farmers and servants). Socially, the peasants were at the bottom of the heap.

Ancient Israel was guilty of class warfare, ranking the rich above the poor and the Jews above the Gentiles. Obviously, it's human nature to put people into categories and rank them by their looks, clothing, social status, intelligence, ethnicity, or bank accounts. James urged believers to abolish class warfare because in God's eyes we are all equal. God does not show favoritism toward anyone, and neither should we: "For the LORD your God is God of gods and Lord of lords, the great God, mighty and awesome, who shows no partiality" (Deut. 10:17).

Day 1: James 2:1	**A CLASS OF HIS OWN**
Day 2: James 2:2–4	**CLASSY CLOTHES**
Day 3: James 2:5–7	**LOW CLASS**
Day 4: James 2:8–11	**CLASS ACT**
Day 5: James 2:12–13	**CLASS RULES**

DAY 1
A Class of His Own

LIFT UP ...

Lord Jesus, I praise You that we are all precious in Your sight. I pray You will open my eyes to see others around me with Your love, dignity, and compassion. In Jesus' name. Amen.

LOOK AT ...

Last week we learned that believers with living faith will obey the Word of God. Today we will see that those with living faith realize that believers should treat one another equally.

READ JAMES 2:1.

My brethren, do not hold the faith of our Lord Jesus Christ, the Lord of glory, with partiality. James 2:1

1. What title did James give to Jesus?

2. Read 2 Corinthians 4:6. In whose face did the glory of God shine?

3. Read 1 Corinthians 6:19–20. Where does the Lord of glory reside today?

4. What did James warn his brethren not to do?

LEARN ABOUT ...

1 Lord of Glory

Glory is part of God's character. The word emphasizes His greatness and authority. While God's glory is not a substance, at times God reveals His perfection and presence visibly. It's often seen as fire or dazzling light, but sometimes it's seen as an act of power.

3 Our Glory

After Old Testament times, God's glory is shown mainly in Christ and His church. Christ shares His glory with us, transforming us into the glorious image of God. "[We] can see and reflect the glory of the Lord" (2 Cor. 3:18 NLT).

4 Partiality

Partiality can be translated "favoritism" or "with respect of person." Originally, the word referred to raising someone's face or elevating the person. It came to refer to exalting someone strictly on a superficial, external basis, such as appearance, race, wealth, rank, or social status.

LEARN ABOUT ...

8 Black Sheep

Tamar committed incest by seducing her father-in-law, Judah, in order to bear a child. Rahab was a prostitute in Jericho who hid the Israelite spies. Ruth was a Gentile from the despised Moabites, a race the Jews were strictly forbidden to marry. Bathsheba, Uriah's wife, committed adultery with King David.

---

9 Reflection

We reflect Jesus' glory by developing godly character; doing good deeds; operating in His miraculous gifts; and separating ourselves from sin. "When Christ, who is your life, is revealed to the whole world, you will share in all his glory" (Col. 3:4 NLT).

5. Read Job 34:19. What does this verse say about why God is not partial?

6. Look up the following Scripture references. Record some of the people to whom Jesus ministered while on earth.

SCRIPTURE	JESUS'S MINISTRY
Matthew 8:5–7	
Luke 18:35	
Luke 19:1–2	
Luke 23:32	
John 8:3	

7. Based on the definition of partiality and what you discovered from the chart, do you think Jesus was partial or impartial toward people? Why?

8. Jesus' genealogy included notable and godly believers such as Abraham, David, and Solomon. But God also chose to include in the Savior's bloodline some people with socially unacceptable pasts, such as Tamar, Rahab, and Ruth (see Matt. 1:1–16). Why do you think God did this? Why did Matthew make a point of naming those people?

LIVE OUT ...

9. Jesus is the Lord of glory. His glory is revealed in His character, His miraculous deeds, and His transforming work within His people. Using GLORY as an acrostic, journal about some of the ways you have beheld the Lord of glory.

G (*Example: God's miraculous deliverance of my life from sin.*)

L

O

R

Y

Learn About ...

10 Favoritism

Playing favorites with friends or family may cause others to stumble through jealousy and strife. When Jacob favored Joseph over his brothers, they were jealous and lashed out. When James and John requested places of honor in heaven, it caused strife among the other disciples.

10. James exhorted believers to be impartial toward others. By what criteria do you show partiality or judge people?

____ Past experiences   ____ Color of skin

____ Initial impressions   ____ Social standing

____ Level of education   ____ God's view of them

____ Way they dress   ____ Other_____

11. Jesus said the way you treat others will determine how others will treat you. Place the phrases from the following verse that contain *you* or *others* in the appropriate column.

> Do not judge others, and you will not be judged.
> For you will be treated as you treat others. The standard you use in judging is the standard by which you will be judged.
> And why worry about a speck in [another's] eye when you have a log in your own? (Matt. 7:1–3 NLT)

You   **Others**

∘ ∘ • ∘ ∘

With just a tad of self-righteousness, my (Lenya's) father would say, "I don't smoke, I don't chew, and I don't go with girls who do." It was his funny way of saying there were plenty of people worse than him in this world. Have you ever overheard other believers talk about things that made you feel spiritually inferior? "I don't go to the movies!" "I'm a homeschooler—I'd never send my kids to public school." "If he'd cut his hair and take those earrings off, he'd look more like a Christian."

Jesus told a parable about people who compare themselves with others:

> One was a Pharisee, and the other was a despised tax collector. The
> Pharisee stood by himself and prayed this prayer: "I thank you, God, that
> I am not a sinner like everyone else. For I don't cheat, I don't sin, and I
> don't commit adultery. I'm certainly not like that tax collector! I fast twice
> a week, and I give you a tenth of my income."
>
> But the tax collector stood at a distance and dared not even lift his eyes
> to heaven as he prayed. Instead, he beat his chest in sorrow, saying, "O
> God, be merciful to me, for I am a sinner." I tell you, this sinner, not the
> Pharisee, returned home justified before God. (Luke 18:10–14 NLT)

Comparing ourselves with others is futile: there's always someone better or someone worse. Instead, we should judge ourselves by the Lord of glory. Everyone else pales in comparison.

LISTEN TO ...

The greatest, in the judgment of God, are the least in their own opinion; the more worthy they are, the more humility will be seen in them.

—Thomas à Kempis

DAY 2

Classy Clothes

In a simple experiment, two friends of equal education, background, and economic status—one Caucasian, the other African American—visited a Midwestern city to see if they would be treated alike. When they went into a shoe store, the white man was welcomed with a handshake; the black man waited for more than four minutes and never got waited on. At the car dealership, the white man got a better deal. At the apartment for rent, he was encouraged to look it over, but his African American friend was told that the unit had already been taken. When interviewed, the people in this experiment who had shown prejudice said they weren't biased at all. But their actions belied their words.

Prejudice is a preconceived judgment or opinion. It is an irrational attitude of hostility directed against an individual or groups of people. Humans are susceptible to prejudice and partiality, but God has never had a prejudiced thought. Jill Briscoe offered some practical suggestions to overcome prejudice and partiality: (1) Become friends with someone you don't like because of their religious or political views, race, or economic standing; (2) join a club whose members come from different socioeconomic levels; and (3) invite people you feel prejudice against into your home for a meal.[1]

LIFT UP ...

Lord, I praise You that You consider a person's heart and not her appearance. Help me not to judge others by their dress, color of skin, or possessions. Rather, help me to look past people's external shells and look for Your presence in their lives. In Jesus' name. Amen.

LOOK AT ...

James told us that personal prejudice and the gospel of Jesus Christ cannot coexist. Today the passage introduces us to two imaginary visitors—one in classy clothes and one in dirty duds—to illustrate the evils of partiality.

LEARN ABOUT ...

I Classy Clothes

In ancient Israel, well-to-do people wore numerous rings on their fingers to parade their wealth. These people were referred to as "gold-fingered." Fine clothing was also a status symbol. The word translated *fine* literally means "bright or brilliant." These people tried to dazzle others with glitter and glamour.

2 Dirty Duds

The poor could afford only cheap clothing—probably castoffs. Water was such a precious commodity that they had less opportunity to wash. The sin was not that the first man wore finery or that the second man wore dirty duds. The sin was that the people treated them differently based on appearances.

5 Disrepect

Failing to offer a visitor a footstool was extremely disrespectful. Telling a visitor to sit down beside one's footstool was a double show of contempt, because it essentially said, "Sit by my stool like a dog."

READ JAMES 2:2–4.

For if there should come into your assembly a man with gold rings, in fine apparel, and there should also come in a poor man in filthy clothes, and you pay attention to the one wearing the fine clothes and say to him, "You sit here in a good place," and say to the poor man, "You stand there," or, "Sit here at my footstool" have you not shown partiality among yourselves, and become judges with evil thoughts? James 2:2–4

1. Who is the first visitor, and what is he wearing?

2. Who is the second visitor, and what is he wearing?

3. What phrase lets you know that this scenario takes place in the church?

4. Describe how the two men are treated differently.

5. What question did James ask the brethren?

6. How do the actions in the passage reveal evil thoughts?

LIVE OUT ...

7. James gave a scenario of two different types of people—now it's your turn. Picture yourself standing in the checkout line at the grocery store. A woman wearing diamonds and designer clothes is waiting in front of you. What judgments do you make about her because of her apparel?

____ "I bet she's a snob."

____ "Her children probably go to a private school."

____ "Her money can't buy her happiness."

____ "I wonder if she is rich in the Lord?"

____ Other_____.

Now imagine yourself sitting in your car at a stoplight. A man in filthy clothes is sitting on the corner with a "Will Work for Food—Jesus Loves You" sign. What judgments do you make about him?

____ "He needs to get a job."

____ "If I give him money, he'll go buy liquor."

____ "He doesn't know Jesus—he's just using His name."

____ "I wonder if he would let the Lord change his life?"

____ Other_____.

8. Can you recall a time when you tried to impress others by wearing classy clothes? How did it make you feel? Did others respond like you expected?

9. a. James told about the poor who were treated with disrespect in the early church. Name some people or groups today that modern society marginalizes or treats with disdain.

   b. How can you treat one of those people respectfully this week?

· · • · ·

Children are naturally greedy and selfish. Their favorite words are *I*, *me*, and *mine*. My (Lenya's) son was no different from other preschoolers, so

LEARN ABOUT ...

7 Class Warfare

Class warfare works both ways. Oftentimes it's the rich judging the poor. But the poor can be guilty of judging the rich, thinking they don't deserve their money or have obtained it easily. Lydia, the seller of purple, worked hard for her money and used it to further the gospel.

8 Filthy Rags

Humans obsess about what they wear on their bodies, but the Bible teaches that we should be more concerned about how our hearts are adorned. "We are all infected and impure with sin. When we display our righteous deeds, they are nothing but filthy rags" (Isa. 64:6 NLT).

9 Respect

Respect means to look back or to give particular attention and consideration. We don't just ignore the poor; oftentimes we don't even see them or their plight. Train yourself to notice, then considerately meet their needs. More than giving them a handout, offer them a hand up.

my husband, Skip, found a way to train him to be generous and not show prejudice. One night while reading the Bible together, they read: "Do not be hard-hearted or tightfisted toward [the poor]. Instead, be generous and lend them whatever they need" (Deut. 15:7–8 NLT). Skip tightly clenched his hands into fists and said, "Don't be tightfisted." Then he opened his fists, holding out his hands and said, "Be open-handed." With childlike exuberance, Nathan imitated his father, walking around the house clenching and releasing his fists, chanting, "Don't be tightfisted, be open-handed!"

One day this lesson was put to the test. Nathan and I drove by a homeless person holding a sign that said, "Will Work for Food." Nathan said, "Mama, let's be open-handed and give him some money." I didn't want to quench Nathan's generosity, but I didn't want our money to be squandered. Then I got an inspired idea. "Let's go to the grocery store and buy him some food." After that, we prepared a dozen lunch bags filled with nonperishable food and a note about God to carry wherever we traveled. Keep your eyes open this week to your hidden prejudices, and ask God for new ways to share His love without favoritism.

LISTEN TO ...

Very few people take the trouble to use their brains as long as their prejudices are in working condition.

—*Roy L. Smith*

DAY 3

Low Class

Everybody knows some of the basic rules of etiquette: "Don't talk with your mouth full."
"Respond to an RSVP within five days of receiving an invitation." "Offer your seat to
a pregnant woman or your elders." Etiquette is a code of behavior that helps people get
along with one another. Many people think it applies to high-class members of society who
have a rigid set of rules concerning appropriate party attire and proper table manners. But
true etiquette doesn't exist to make you look good; its goal is to make others feel good.
Like my grandma used to say, "A person with good manners will always make others feel
comfortable."

Emily Post, who made a career out of good manners, wrote, "Best Society is not a fellowship of the wealthy, nor does it seek to exclude those who are not of exalted birth; but it
is an association of gentle-folk, of which good form in speech, charm of manner, knowledge
of the social amenities, and instinctive consideration for the feelings of others, are the cre-
dentials by which society the world over recognizes its chosen members."[2] In other words,
you can possess the impeccable manners of high society, but if you make other people feel
bad about themselves, you behave like a member of the lower class, not the upper crust.

Our instructor James wanted to make sure believers have proper etiquette when it
comes to their dealings with others, especially the poor.

LIFT UP ...

Lord, I praise You that no matter what my social status is, You have blessed me abundantly
with faith to believe the gospel, be saved, and persevere to eternal life. In Jesus' name.
Amen.

LEARN ABOUT ...

2 Rich Faith

When God speaks of riches, He doesn't necessarily mean money. He wants us to be rich in faith, mercy, and good works, and then He will take care of the rest. "Seek first the kingdom of God and His righteousness, and all these things shall be added to you" (Matt. 6:33).

4 Kingdom

The kingdom of heaven, the kingdom of God, and eternal life are one and the same. People who have placed their faith in Jesus Christ have the kingdom of God reigning in their hearts now, and later they will enter the kingdom of heaven and experience eternal life.

7 Blasphemy

Blasphemy is cursing, slandering, or showing contempt or lack of reverence for God. In the Old Testament, blaspheming God was a serious crime punishable by death. "Anyone who blasphemes the name of the LORD must be stoned to death by the whole community of Israel" (Lev. 24:16 NLT).

LOOK AT ...

Yesterday we learned that being rich or poor is not a sin, but playing favorites is. Today we discover that God's grace produces people rich in faith and that those who treat the poor badly exhibit low-class behavior.

READ JAMES 2:5–7.

Listen, my beloved brethren: Has God not chosen the poor of this world to be rich in faith and heirs of the kingdom which He promised to those who love Him? But you have dishonored the poor man. Do not the rich oppress you and drag you into the courts? Do they not blaspheme that noble name by which you are called? James 2:5–7

1. What phrase did James use to gain his readers' attention?

2. Describe whom God has chosen and why.

3. Read Psalm 41:1–3. List the blessings for those who consider the poor and weak.

4. What promise does God make in James 2:5 to those who love Him?

5. How did James say the poor man was treated? Reflect on yesterday's lesson, then describe how this could happen within the church.

6. What question did James use to remind his readers how the rich treated them?

7. James said that when the rich oppress poor believers, they are really blaspheming the name of Christ. Why do you suppose God regards injustice as blasphemy?

8. Often the financially poor are rich in faith. But there is another type of poverty the Bible teaches about: "Blessed are the poor in spirit, for theirs is the kingdom of heaven" (Matt. 5:3). Think about how you were "poor in spirit"—spiritually bankrupt— before you experienced the kingdom of heaven. Journal about how, in God's grace, you've become spiritually rich in faith, mercy, or good deeds.

9. God has promised that those who believe will be heirs to His kingdom. Fill in the chart to discover some of the riches we will inherit.

SCRIPTURE	INHERITANCE
Psalm 37:11	
Proverbs 3:35	
Matthew 19:29	
Revelation 21:7	

10. We have seen that in the early church the rich often oppressed the poor. Read the definition of oppression in the sidebar, then journal about some ways people are oppressed today.

° ° • ° °

Shrink the earth's population to a village of one hundred people, and it looks something like this:

- Fifty-seven Asians, twenty-one Europeans, fourteen people from the Western Hemisphere, and eight Africans
- Fifty-two female, forty-eight male
- Seventy non-Christian, thirty Christian

LEARN ABOUT …

8 Poor in Spirit

In order for you to be rich in faith, Jesus became poor in spirit. "You know the generous grace of our Lord Jesus Christ. Though he was rich, yet for your sakes he became poor, so that by his poverty he could make you rich" (2 Cor. 8:9 NLT).

9 Heirs

In heaven we will all be rich in the things that really matter. Every child of God equally inherits eternal life, a heavenly home, crowns for the faithful, and a place at the Lord's table. "Since we are his children, we are his heirs" (Rom. 8:17 NLT).

10 Oppress

To oppress someone is to crush or burden them by an unjust exercise of power or authority; to weigh down mentally; a sense of heaviness or obstruction in the body or mind. Besides instructing not to oppress the poor, the Bible exhorts, "Do not oppress widows, orphans, [or] foreigners" (Zech. 7:10 NLT).

Six people would possess 59 percent of the entire world's wealth, and all six would be from the United States. Eighty people would live in substandard housing, seventy would be unable to read, fifty would suffer from malnutrition, one would be near death, one would be near birth, one (yes, only one) would have a college education, and only one would own a computer.

When you consider our world from such a compressed perspective, the following is something to ponder:

- If you have food in the refrigerator, clothes on your back, a roof overhead, and a place to sleep, you are richer than 75 percent of this world.
- If you have never experienced war, imprisonment, torture, or the pangs of starvation, you are ahead of 500 million other people.
- If you have money in the bank, in your wallet, and spare change in a dish someplace, you are among the top 8 percent of the world's wealthy.

For those of us who have much, James's teaching reminds us to honor the poor, not insult them or play favorites. This is the way to a living faith that is truly rich.

LISTEN TO ...

Half the world is starving; the other half is on a diet. We are not privileged because we deserve to be. Privilege accepted should mean responsibility accepted.

—*Madeleine L'Engle*

DAY 4

Class Act

Catherine Booth, wife of William Booth and "mother" of the Salvation Army, was truly a class act. "Wherever Catherine Booth went," said G. Campbell Morgan, pastor of Westminster Chapel, "humanity went to hear her. Princes and peeresses merged with paupers and prostitutes."

One night Morgan took part in an evangelistic meeting with Mrs. Booth, and a great crowd of lower-class people attended. Her message of compassion to the downtrodden brought many to Christ. After the meeting, Morgan and Mrs. Booth went to a fine home for dinner. The elegant lady of the manor, dressed in the latest fashions, said, "My dear Mrs. Booth, that meeting was dreadful!"

In her down-to-earth way, Mrs. Booth asked, "What do you mean, dearie?"

"Well, when you were speaking, I was looking at those people…. Their faces were so terrible…. I don't think I shall sleep tonight!"

"Why, dearie, don't you know them?" Mrs. Booth asked.

The hostess replied in a huff, "Certainly not!"

"That is interesting," Mrs. Booth said. "I did not bring them with me from London; they are *your* neighbors!"[3]

It's easy to love the lovely, but it's godly to love the unlovely. Mrs. Booth demonstrated true class by extending her hand to those less fortunate than herself, treating them with the same dignity she would offer to those who were well-to-do. James reminded believers to obey Christ's royal command to love their neighbors as themselves.

LIFT UP …

Thank You, Lord, for liberating me from the bondage of sin and for clothing me with Your perfect righteousness. Thank You that I'm a brand new person in Christ Jesus, free to obey, serve, and live a faithful, righteous life. In Jesus' name. Amen.

LEARN ABOUT ...

1 Royal Law

James quoted Leviticus 19:18 in this passage, reminiscent of the Golden Rule: do unto others as you would have them do unto you. "Whatever you want men to do to you, do also to them, for this is the Law and the Prophets" (Matt. 7:12). By doing this we fulfill the royal law.

4 Law Breakers

To *sin* means to miss the mark of God's holy purity. *Transgress* means to go over or beyond; to willfully violate God's laws. Transgression implies rebellion. If God drew a line in the sand, then sinners would inadvertently stumble over the line while transgressors would willfully step over it.

5 Law Maker

The Law—the Ten Commandments—comes from God, reflecting His nature of holiness, righteousness, and goodness. As the great King, God gave laws that were binding on His people. Furthermore, His laws are universal and are an expression of His love for His people.

LOOK AT ...

Our lesson yesterday taught us that rich or poor, those who love Jesus and have placed their faith in Him will inherit God's kingdom. Now we will learn that if we obey the royal law of love, in God's eyes we'll be a class act.

READ JAMES 2:8–11.

If you really fulfill the royal law according to the Scripture, "You shall love your neighbor as yourself," you do well; but if you show partiality, you commit sin, and are convicted by the law as transgressors. For whoever shall keep the whole law, and yet stumble in one point, he is guilty of all. For He who said, "Do not commit adultery," also said, "Do not murder." Now if you do not commit adultery, but you do murder, you have become a transgressor of the law. James 2:8–11

1. What did James encourage his readers (and us) to fulfill?

2. Explain the royal law.

3. What behavior did James consider sinful?

4. How does showing partiality break the royal law?

5. If a person breaks even one of God's laws, what is that person guilty of? Why do you suppose that's the case?

6. What two commandments did James mention?

LIVE OUT ...

7. By comparing the sin of partiality to the sins of adultery and murder, what was James saying about partiality?

8. We've been told to love our neighbor, but "who is my neighbor?" Read Luke 10:29–37 to see how Jesus answered that question.

   a. Describe what happened to the traveler (v. 30).

   b. How did the priest and Levite treat the traveler (vv. 31–32)?

   c. Explain how the Samaritan responded (vv. 33–35).

   d. Describe what a good neighbor is (v. 37).

9. Journal about a specific way you can "do unto others as you would have them do unto you" this week. Then do it!

10. The Ten Commandments (see Exodus 20) were given to govern our relationships with God and with others. Place each commandment in the appropriate column: have no other gods besides God; do not make idols; do not take God's name in vain; keep the Sabbath; honor your father and mother; do not murder; do not commit adultery; do not steal; do not bear false witness; do not covet.

   GOD   **OTHERS**

LEARN ABOUT ...

8 Good Neighbor

Samaritans were a mixed race (Jewish and Gentile), contaminated by foreign blood and false worship, and had built a rival temple on Mount Gerizim. Jews hated Samaritans. Yet the "Good Samaritan," a despised foreigner, was a better neighbor than a pious priest.

9 Golden Rule

Sin of commission means doing something you know is wrong. Sin of omission is not doing what you know is right. The Golden Rule is of no value until you practice it. "To him who knows to do good and does not do it, to him it is sin" (James 4:17).

10 Commandments

The ten laws given by God are guidelines for daily living. They are part of a covenant between God and His people. Although given more than three thousand years ago, they're still relevant today. Jesus upheld them and summed them up into two commandments: (1) loving God and (2) loving others.

○ ○ ● ○ ○

Following World War II, soldiers were released from a prison camp in Siberia. Although the officers tried to repatriate as many men as possible, it looked like many would have to remain in the bitter cold region when winter threatened to close up the port. As the last boat prepared to sail, it was apparent that only a few would be welcomed aboard. Among those waiting to be transported were two buddies who had developed a deep friendship throughout the war. Only one man was selected; the other seemed doomed to remain behind.

Those who were leaving were limited to one piece of luggage. The lucky soldier who was chosen to board the ship emptied his duffle bag of his prized possessions and personal belongings, then told his best friend to get into the canvas sack. Carefully lifting the bag on his shoulders, he boarded the ship with his friend as his single possession. This man truly loved his neighbor as himself.

Loving your neighbors requires sacrifices of time, energy, and resources. Jesus showed His love by sacrificing everything for us. He fulfilled the royal law by giving His life for everyone: "Greater love has no one than this, than to lay down one's life for his friends" (John 15:13). He was completely impartial. He died for the whole world—from Ted Bundy to Mother Teresa—including you and me, and He challenges you to follow in His footsteps. Show how much you love Him by loving your neighbor, no matter who it is.

LISTEN TO ...

Though we do not have our Lord with us in bodily presence, we have our neighbor, who, for the ends of love and loving service, is as good as our Lord himself.

—*Saint Teresa of Avila*

DAY 5

Class Rules

Many years ago, a well-to-do Christian who abhorred slavery paid a high price for a slave at auction. When the two met for the first time, the wealthy man said, "I have bought you, but I did it only to free you from the terrible bondage you have known." Then he handed the other man some papers that guaranteed his freedom.

The slave looked at him in sheer amazement. "Am I truly free? May I go where I wish?"

"Yes," said the Christian, "that's why I bought you, so you could be loosed from those chains forever." Overwhelmed by these words, the slave fell at the feet of his liberator and said with heartfelt devotion, "Then my greatest joy and freedom will be to stay with you and serve you gladly for the rest of my life."

The Bible is the story of God's quest to liberate humanity. His Son, Jesus, paid a very high price—His life. Through His sacrifice, those who call on His name are set free from the bondage of sin. The only reasonable response for those of us who have been liberated by His mercy is to serve Christ gladly in all that we say and do for the rest of our lives. Like the former slave we will be able to say, "Serving Christ has been my greatest joy and freedom." James taught that showing love and mercy are part of the class rules in the school of faith.

LIFT UP ...

Lord, I long to do what is pleasing and good in Your sight. Help me to love and extend mercy to everyone who needs it, just as You extend mercy to me. In Jesus' name. Amen.

LOOK AT ...

We have found that living faith obeys the royal law of God by extending love to our neighbors. Today we discover that we must follow the class rules and uphold God's merciful law of liberty.

LEARN ABOUT ...

2 Judged?

Believers are judged differently than unbelievers. The judgment seat of Christ does not judge a believer's sins; those have been atoned for by Christ's death. Rather, the works of every child of God will be evaluated, resulting in reward or loss of reward. See 2 Corinthians 5:10.

3 Law of Liberty

The Ten Commandments were the law of Moses; the gospel of Christ represents the law of liberty because it sets transgressors free from the bondage, judgment, and penalty of sin. "If the Son sets you free, you are truly free" (John 8:36 NLT).

7 Mercy

Mercy moves God to help the miserable just as grace moves Him to forgive the guilty. Mercy implies compassion that withholds punishment even when it is deserved. "Our God is merciful and forgiving, even though we have rebelled against him" (Dan. 9:9 NLT).

READ JAMES 2:12–13.

So speak and so do as those who will be judged by the law of liberty. For judgment is without mercy to the one who has shown no mercy. Mercy triumphs over judgment. James 2:12–13

1. Based on yesterday's lesson, what is the "law" that should affect our speech and actions?

2. According to James, how should we speak and act?

3. What do you think it means to be judged by the law of liberty?

4. The law of liberty was designed to set us free from sin. Read Galatians 5:13–14. What should we *do* and *not* do with the liberty we've been given?

5. Who will receive judgment without mercy?

6. When do you think this type of judgment will be delivered?

7. Describe the power of mercy.

LIVE OUT ...

8. We've been urged to speak and do as those obeying the royal law. Fill in the chart to discover some things believers are to speak or do.

SCRIPTURE	SPEAK/DO
John 13:15	
1 Corinthians 11:25	

Ephesians 4:25

Titus 2:1

9. Many people think that God's law is restrictive. James said it is a law of liberty setting us free from the bondage of sin. Check off the things that have held you captive.

____ Food   ____ Drugs

____ Relationships   ____ Bitterness

____ Legalism   ____ Materialism

____ Tobacco   ____ Swearing

____ Lust

10. James said mercy triumphs over judgment. With this in mind, complete the following steps:

Step One: Write the name of someone you know in bondage to sin who needs God's mercy.

Step Two: Describe the circumstances this person is in and the consequences that may occur because of his or her actions. (*Example: my friend has been gambling at the casino and could squander the rent.*)

Step Three: Journal a prayer of mercy for your friend by rewriting the following verse: "So let us come boldly to the throne of our gracious God. There we will receive his mercy, and we will find grace to help us when we need it" (Heb. 4:16 NLT).

LEARN ABOUT …

8 Your Gospel

"You are writing a Gospel / A chapter each day / By deeds that you do / By words that you say. / Men read what you write, / Whether faithless or true. / Say! What is the Gospel / according to you?" ("The Gospel According to You," author unknown)

9 Bondage

People think they can handle a little sin. An alcoholic might say, "Just one drink, then I'll quit." But this slippery slope leads to destruction. When we obey sin, it masters us. "You can be a slave to sin, which leads to death, or you can choose to obey God, which leads to righteous living" (Rom. 6:16 NLT).

10 Triumph

Triumph refers to the celebratory parade hailing a Roman general's victory over an enemy. Jesus was triumphant over the power of sin, ensuring that mercy could prevail. "Having disarmed principalities and powers, [Jesus] made a public spectacle of them, triumphing over them" (Col. 2:15).

○ ○ ● ○ ○

What if things were reversed? Think about what would happen if God's judgment triumphed over His mercy. Break one—just *one*—of the Ten Commandments, and you're toast. No second chances; immediate death sentence. That moment of loving your child more than God? Death! That little white lie you told your husband? Death! That instant of longing for your neighbor's new car? Death!

Now think about society. If judgment triumphed over mercy, then the moment you broke the speed limit, your license would be rescinded. The first class you missed would be your last—you'd be expelled from school. No calling in sick to work—judgment doesn't allow for sick days. At home, every time your child acted naughty—immediate punishment. Your husband broke his promise and came home late—no smiles of understanding, only the cold shoulder. You mention a handsome movie star and end up in divorce court. No mercy, only judgment.

Living under judgment would make the world a desperate and despairing place. Perhaps the birds would not sing, nor would the grass turn green. People wouldn't smile or laugh—why should they? There'd be no need for prayer because we couldn't be forgiven.

Aren't you grateful that God is a God of mercy? His very name is mercy; His character is mercy; He delights in mercy; His mercy is new every morning; His mercy is never ending. And, hallelujah, His mercy triumphs over judgment!

LISTEN TO ...

There's a wideness in God's mercy.

—*Frederick William Faber*

Flatline Faith
James 2:14–26

The eerie scream of sirens shatters the lazy afternoon. Paramedics rush into the ER calling out, "Code Blue! We've got a flatline!" Quickly doctors assess the patient, then pull out the defibrillation paddles, sending bursts of electricity into the body to shock the heart into activity. While the patient is being hooked up to an EKG to measure the heart rate, a doctor pulls out her stethoscope and listens intently to the patient's breathing to make sure the lungs are working properly. The crisis is averted—the patient will survive.

Human beings need two vital organs to survive: a heart and lungs. Without both functioning properly, life will cease. You can't stay alive if you stop breathing. You can't stay alive if your heart stops beating. These two functions are inseparable: the heart pumps the blood, and the lungs oxygenate the blood. If either system fails, you're dead.

Just as physical bodies need the heart and lungs to work together, the spirit needs two vital components to function together: faith and works. Faith and works are to our souls what the heart and lungs are to our bodies. We must have both to be spiritually alive. Faith allows us to be born again—it gives us spiritual breath. Works help us grow to maturity, pumping spiritual vitality into our lives. This week the book of James reminds us that people without the two functioning elements of faith and works are in a spiritual crisis, resulting in flatline faith—faith that is dead.

Day 1: James 2:14	**DOUBTING FAITH**
Day 2: James 2:15–17	**DEAD FAITH**
Day 3: James 2:18–20	**DEMONIC FAITH?**
Day 4: James 2:21–23	**DIVINE FAITH**
Day 5: James 2:24–26	**DYNAMIC FAITH**

DAY 1
Doubting Faith

LIFT UP ...

Father, I want my faith to be genuine, beyond any doubt. Help me examine myself closely and determine whether I merely say I believe, or whether I show what I believe in both word and deed. In Jesus' name. Amen.

LOOK AT ...

Lesson 5 taught us that people with living faith will not show partiality based on worldly wealth. In this lesson, we see that there is good reason to doubt the sincerity of those who profess faith in Christ if they fail to put their words into action. People with living faith will not just say they believe; they will show it.

READ JAMES 2:14.

What does it profit, my brethren, if someone says he has faith but does not have works? Can faith save him? James 2:14

1. How do you know James was addressing professing Christians?

2. What was the first question that James raised?

3. Put this question into your own words.

LEARN ABOUT ...

2 Profit

Profit means "a return above an expenditure; a gain or advantage." In God's eyes, when we expend godliness, we gain contentment: "Now godliness with contentment is great gain" (1 Tim. 6:6). Following God provides many advantages that money can't buy.

3 F.A.I.T.H.

Faith is firm belief in God that involves commitment to His will and a personal surrender to Christ. *Faith* could be an acrostic: Forsaking All I Trust Him. "Faith is the substance of things hoped for, the evidence of things not seen" (Heb. 11:1).

LEARN ABOUT ...

5 Works

Our works can be either good or bad. Works are bad when they are works of darkness, works of the flesh, idolatry, hypocrisy, or works of the law. "Have no fellowship with the unfruitful works of darkness, but rather expose them" (Eph. 5:11).

9 Profitable

God isn't concerned whether we make a financial profit; He is concerned that we prosper spiritually. By investing in good works, we will reap eternal treasures. Jesus said, "What profit is it to a man if he gains the whole world, and loses his own soul?" (Matt. 16:26).

4. According to Romans 10:9, in order for us to be saved, what must accompany our words?

5. Returning to James 2:14, what sorts of works do you think James had in mind?

6. How would you state James's second question in your own words?

7. What answer do you think James expected believers to give?

8. a. Read Ephesians 2:8–10. According to Paul, how have we been saved (v. 8)?

   b. Explain what has *not* purchased our salvation and why (vv. 8–9).

   c. Why did God create us in Christ Jesus (v. 10)?

LIVE OUT ...

9. We've seen that God desires for us to profit spiritually. However, to benefit God's kingdom, we must invest something. Using the acrostic PROFIT, journal about how *you* will invest in kingdom work.

   Pray for _____.

   Remind _____ that Jesus loves them.

   Offer my time to _____.

   Forgive _____.

   Invest in _____ ministry.

   Tell _____ about Christ.

10. a. Not all who *say* they have faith truly do have saving faith. Read Matthew 7:21. What will people *say* to Jesus?

    b. What did Jesus reveal about some of these people's eternal fate?

    c. Explain who will enter the kingdom of heaven.

11. a. James revealed that those with living faith will not only say they believe but also will do good works. Fill in the table to discover some good works we are instructed to do.

SCRIPTURE	GOOD WORKS
1 Timothy 5:10	
1 Timothy 6:18	
Titus 2:6–9	
Hebrews 6:10	

    b. Journal about which of the above good works you exhibit in your life, then write a prayer asking God to help you incorporate the good works you do not yet exhibit into your life.

LEARN ABOUT ...

10 Saying

Saying something doesn't make it true. You can say you're twenty-nine, but that doesn't make it so. You can say you have faith, but your actions might betray you. "We are lying if we say we have fellowship with God but go on living in spiritual darkness" (I John 1:6 NLT).

11 Doing

Christians will do what the Bible instructs, revealing a genuine faith. Jesus rebuked the scribes and Pharisees for saying the right words without doing the right deeds: "They say, and do not do" (Matt. 23:3). Doing good works will not save us, but it does prove we are saved.

∘ ⋅ • ∘ ∘

A Christian worked transporting tourists across a lake in his rowboat. Sometimes he illustrated the gospel in a most unusual way. He painted the word *faith* on one oar of his rowboat and the word *works* on the other. Stopping in the middle of the lake, he would row with just the oar marked *faith*, causing the boat to go in circles to the left. Reversing the process, he'd row with just *works* and circle in the opposite direction. The bewildered passengers would ask what he was doing. Explaining the truth of salvation, he would add, "You see, neither faith nor works can go it alone. They are twins that cannot be separated."

This story is reminiscent of Lazarus's two sisters: Mary, the faithful devotee, and Martha, the hardworking servant. When Jesus came to their home for dinner, Mary was found worshipping at the Lord's feet while Martha was spinning her wheels in a flurry of activity. Disgruntled, Martha said, "Lord, doesn't it seem unfair to you that my sister just sits here while I do all the work?" Jesus defended Mary's choice saying, "My dear Martha, you are so worried and upset over all these details! There is only one thing worth being concerned about. Mary has discovered it, and it will not be taken away from her" (Luke 10:40–42 NLT).

As Christians, there are seasons when we become more involved in the work and less concerned about the worship, and that's when we go in fruitless circles. Pray for a balance of believing and doing in your faith walk.

LISTEN TO ...

Only the Word of God makes us wholesome and blessed. The divine Word brings faith. Faith brings love. Love results in good deeds.

—*Martin Bucer*

DAY 2

Dead Faith

Mother Teresa said, "The poor come to all of us in many forms. Let us be sure that we never turn our backs on them, wherever we may find them. For when we turn our backs on the poor, we turn them on Jesus Christ." Is this true? Did Mother Teresa really mean that neglecting the poor is neglecting Christ?

Jesus explained this phenomenon during the Olivet Discourse. He warned that upon His return He will separate the sheep from the goats. The sheep represent those followers who express living faith through generous works. The goats are those who display dead faith by not practicing what they preach. This litmus test of dead or living faith is based on a person's treatment of the poor and needy.

Jesus takes it personally when the poor are neglected. He chastised the goats, "Depart from Me, … for I was hungry and you gave Me no food; I was thirsty and you gave Me no drink; I was a stranger and you did not take Me in, naked and you did not clothe Me, sick and in prison and you did not visit Me" (Matt. 25:41–43). The dismayed goats couldn't understand how they had neglected Jesus. He said, "Inasmuch as you did not do it to one of the least of these, you did not do it to Me" (v. 45).

James's litmus test for true faith was the same as our Lord's. Will we assist the poor or avoid them? Your answer reveals whether you are more like a sheep or a goat.

Lift Up …

Lord, You have promised life to those of us who choose to walk in it. If my faith is dead in any area, please breathe new life in me through the power of Your Holy Spirit. In Jesus' name. Amen.

LEARN ABOUT ...

1 Destitute

Destitute means "forsaken or abandoned; suffering extreme poverty." The world thinks the rich get ahead while the poor are left behind, but Jesus said, "The last will be first, and the first last" (Matt. 20:16), and "I will never leave you nor forsake you" (Heb. 13:5).

3 Family of God

We are to help anyone in need. But if the needy are members of God's own family, we should treat them especially well. "Whenever we have the opportunity, we should do good to everyone— especially to those in the family of faith" (Gal. 6:10 NLT).

LOOK AT ...

James asked us to contemplate whether merely *saying* we have faith proves we truly believe. Now we learn that true living faith expresses itself not only in good words but in generous works as well.

READ JAMES 2:15–17.

If a brother or sister is naked and destitute of daily food, and one of you says to them, "Depart in peace, be warmed and filled," but you do not give them the things which are needed for the body, what does it profit? Thus also faith by itself, if it does not have works, is dead. James 2:15–17

1. James used another hypothetical situation to reflect the lifelessness of faith without works. Describe the condition of the needy people in this situation.

2. What platitude did the church offer the needy brother or sister in James's example?

3. Describe what the church failed to do.

4. What question did James repeat from verse 14?

5. a. John also addressed people who say the right words but fail in acts of mercy. Read 1 John 3:17–18. Describe the kind of people John was addressing here.

   b. Explain the true nature of these people's relationship with God.

   c. Contrast the way John expected true believers to behave.

Not:

But:

6. What conclusion did James reach about faith?

7. What does faith need to be alive?

Live Out ...

8. a. In the Old Testament book of Jeremiah, the Lord rebuked His people for neglecting the poor. Read Jeremiah 5:28–29. How are these people described?

   b. What two things did they fail to do?

   c. What indictment did God make against them? What were the consequences?

9. The people in today's lesson offered pious platitudes instead of necessary nourishment. Check off some modern platitudes you've heard offered to those in need.

   ___ "God bless you."
   ___ "Have you called the homeless shelter?"
   ___ "I'll pray for you."
   ___ "I feel your pain."
   ___ "Will Medicaid cover that?"
   ___ "What about food stamps?"
   ___ "I gave at the office."
   ___ "God helps those who help themselves."
   ___ Other _____.

Learn About ...

6 Lonely Faith

The New Century Version translates James 2:17, "Faith by itself—that does nothing—is dead." It is faith alone that saves us, but faith that saves us can never be alone. Just as Jesus sent the disciples out two by two, faith and works must keep each other company.

---

8 National Sin

If individuals neglect the poor, so will the nation. "This was the sin of your sister Sodom: ... her daughters were arrogant, overfed and unconcerned; they did not help the poor and needy.... Therefore I did away with them as you have seen" (Ezek. 16:49–50 NIV).

---

9 Empty Words

Words of caring without acts of sharing are a sham. Jesus saw through people who say one thing but do another: "You hypocrites! Isaiah was right when he prophesied about you, for he wrote, 'These people honor me with their lips, but their hearts are far from me'" (Mark 7:6–7 NLT).

10 Dead Faith

People with dead faith know the proper prayers and can quote memory verses, but they fail to live what they've learned. Any proclamation of faith that does not result in the performance of good deeds is in danger of dying. Does your faith need to be resuscitated?

10. Actions really do speak louder than words. Journal about a time when you showed your faith by your actions rather than your words.

・ ・ ● ・ ・

During the Great Depression, a group of Christians gathered to pray for a family that had lost everything when the stock market crashed. While one of the men was praying fervently on their behalf, the young son of a local farmer knocked loudly at the door.

"What do you want?" the people inquired.

The boy said, "Pa says he can't join you at this prayer meetin', but he asked me to bring his prayers in the wagon!"

They went outside to see what the young boy meant. When they reached the wagon, they saw that Pa's "prayers" consisted of potatoes, flour, beef, oatmeal, turnips, apples, jars of jelly, fruit, and a bundle of clothing. Convicted for failing to take action, the group decided to become the answer to their own prayers. That same day, they each loaded up a wagonload of "prayers" to help their needy neighbors.

Like James, Jesus taught that we can become the answer to our own prayers. At the conclusion of Matthew 9, He told the disciples, "The harvest truly is plentiful, but the laborers are few. Therefore pray the Lord of the harvest to send out laborers into His harvest" (vv. 37–38). Matthew 10 begins with Jesus sending the disciples themselves out to become the answer to their own prayers: "These twelve Jesus sent out and commanded them, saying, ... 'As you go, preach, saying, "The kingdom of heaven is at hand"'" (vv. 5, 7).

LISTEN TO ...

You do right when you offer faith to God; you do right when you offer works. But if you separate the two, then you do wrong. For faith without works is dead; and lack of charity in action murders faith.

—Saint Bernard of Clairvaux

Demonic Faith?

All I really need to know about demons I learned from deviled ham! The gospels of Matthew, Mark, and Luke all provide an in-depth course in Demonology 101 in their record of how Jesus exorcised demons from a possessed man, sending the demons into a herd of swine. The demons knew more about Jesus Christ's position of authority, His power, and the judgment to come than the twelve disciples did. Let's look at the unclean spirits' response to Jesus more closely.

That the demon-possessed man "ran and worshiped him" (Mark 5:6) showed the demons' profound respect for Jesus. Bible teacher John MacArthur said, "Demons hate and loathe everything about God, yet they are powerless to do anything but bow down before Him when in His presence."[1]

They called Jesus the "Son of the Most High God" (Luke 8:28), revealing that the demons understood His incarnation—the Son, fully man, and Most High God, fully deity.

Their statement "If you cast us out" (Matt. 8:31) proves that the evil spirits knew that Jesus had compassion for this man and that He had the power to destroy them.

The question "Have You come here to torment us before the time?" (Matt. 8:29) shows the demons knew there would be a divinely appointed time for judgment and eternal damnation. Their eschatological theology was impeccable.

James knew about Jesus' power too and about what real faith in Christ was. As he continued his discussion of faith and works, he used the demons' faith to make a point.

LIFT UP ...

Father, I believe in You. I believe that Jesus died for my sins. I don't want to have just an intellectual faith, Lord. Help me to put feet to my faith. In Jesus' name. Amen.

Look At ...

We have found that faith without works is dead faith. Today we learn that mere intellectual faith, the type even the demons have, is not living faith either.

Read James 2:18–20.

But someone will say, "You have faith, and I have works." Show me your faith without your works, and I will show you my faith by my works. You believe that there is one God. You do well. Even the demons believe— and tremble! But do you want to know, O foolish man, that faith without works is dead? James 2:18–20

1. What might a person say to separate faith from works?

2. In response, what did James ask to see?

3. How was James willing to prove that belief and behavior are inseparable?

4. What did James acknowledge that the reader believes?

5. In what sense do the demons believe in Christ?

6. In what sense do they not believe in Christ? How do they respond to Him?

7. Summarize James's main point. Why do you think James repeated this message?

Learn About ...

3 Show Me

James was from the "Show Me" state. He knew that seeing is believing. How can you tell an apple tree from a peach tree? By the fruit! Jesus said, "You can identify them by their fruit, that is, by the way they act" (Matt. 7:16 NLT).

---

4 Orthodox

Jewish orthodoxy believes the *Shema:* "Hear, O Israel: The LORD our God, the LORD is one! You shall love the LORD your God with all your heart" (Deut. 6:4–5). Christian orthodoxy says, "There is one God and one Mediator between God and men, the Man Christ Jesus" (1 Tim. 2:5).

---

6 Unorthodox

Demons are monotheistic; their orthodoxy believes in one true God, but they don't love Him. This intellectual belief cannot save them. They accept Deuteronomy 6:4 without obeying 6:5, and that kind of faith is worthless. As a result, they tremble at their certain judgment to come.

LIVE OUT ...

LEARN ABOUT ...

8 Show and Tell

"Do you love me?" a young wife asks her husband. "Of course I do. I married you, didn't I?" he replies. "If you really love me, then why don't you show me?" she responds. True love will both show and tell sincere devotion. Jesus said, "If you love me, obey my commandments" (John 14:15 NLT).

9 Foolish

Only a fool would fail to act upon what he or she knows. If you know an earthquake is coming, you fortify your house. If you know a flood is flowing, you head for higher ground. Don't be foolish. If you know that Jesus saves, make sure He's your Savior.

10 Demons

Demons are fallen angels who joined against God. This fall occurred before God's creation of the world, leaving Satan and his angels free to contaminate the human race with wickedness (Rev. 12:9). The New Testament (Jude v. 6) speaks of the ultimate imprisonment of demons.

8. James challenged people to show him their faith without works, while he would show them his faith by his works. Journal about a time when someone told you how much they loved you but failed to show you that they really cared. How did it make you feel?

9. a. James commended his readers for believing in the one true God. But what we believe should impact how we behave. Make a list of the things you believe about God.

   b. Now journal about what you will do in response to what you believe.

10. The demons, as well as their leader, Satan, believe in God and are afraid. Fill in the chart to learn what they know.

SCRIPTURE	WHAT EVIL POWERS KNOW
Matthew 4:5–6	
Matthew 25:41	
Luke 4:33–35	

° ° • ° °

The demons are one example of spiritual beings who believe but are doomed anyway. Even Satan believes. Let's imagine a conversation between God and Satan.

Satan smoothly approaches the pearly gates and beseeches, "Let me into heaven. I *believe* in You."

God replies, "Let me give you the test of faith and we'll see. First, do you believe that I created the heavens and the earth?"

Satan smugly says, "Of course I believe that. I was there!"

Next God says, "Do you believe that Jesus is God made man?"

"Of course I do. I was stalking—I mean watching Him in Bethlehem."

"But do you believe that My Son died for humanity's sins?"

Satan quickly answers, "I believe that. I saw the crucifixion," then mutters to himself, "I thought I had Him there."

"Do you believe," God asks, "that Jesus rose from the dead and now sits beside Me in glory?"

"Unfortunately, I wasn't able to stop the stone from being rolled away. I saw Him walking and talking after His resurrection—yes, I believe."

"Well, then," said God, "what good works have you done to further my kingdom?" Lucifer thinks for a long time but can't come up with one single good work. Firmly God says, "Though you believe in My Son, you oppose Him. You have done only evil works. You would never call Him Lord. Depart, you worker of iniquity; you have no place here."

But to those who believe and obey, our loving Father says, "Well done, good and faithful servant" (Matt. 25:21).

LISTEN TO ...

The devil is perfectly willing for a person to profess Christianity, so long as he doesn't practice it.

—Anonymous

DAY 4

Divine Faith

Faith has made people do some pretty peculiar things. John the Baptist wore camel's hair, ate locusts, and lived out in the wilderness. The prophet Ezekiel ate an entire book, locked himself in the house and bound himself in ropes, lay on his right side for forty days, then alternated to his left side for forty more days. Hosea married a prostitute, knowing she would be unfaithful and would accept her lovers' food and clothing. Why did they do these things? Because, by faith, they heard God speak, and they obeyed.

What would you do if you "heard" a strange inner voice telling you, "Say good-bye to everyone you know, pack up, and move to a place you have never seen"? Perhaps your well-intentioned mother would call Dr. Phil, or some misguided zealot would try to cast out the demon of deception. Or maybe, as a last resort, you'd swallow a small white lithium pill to make the voices stop.

Abraham had no Bible, no TV or radio evangelist, no pastor, no church, and no prayer partner when he heard God say, "Leave your native country, your relatives, and your father's family, and go to the land that I will show you" (Gen. 12:1 NLT). But amazingly Abraham responded to God's unfamiliar voice with absolute obedience. God considered this a response of faith, "and it was accounted to him for righteousness" (James 2:23). Today we see that the book of James presents Abraham as an example of a man who possessed divine faith.

LIFT UP ...

God, thank You for the example of the faithful people in the Bible. I want to have a faith like theirs—a faith that is willing to work, to wait, and to watch for You. In Jesus' name. Amen.

LOOK AT ...

James showed that a belief in God is useless if it is only intellectual in nature. Now we learn that a faith that acts is what God seeks.

READ JAMES 2:21–23.

Was not Abraham our father justified by works when he offered Isaac his son on the altar? Do you see that faith was working together with his works, and by works faith was made perfect? And the Scripture was fulfilled which says, "Abraham believed God, and it was accounted to him for righteousness." And he was called the friend of God. James 2:21–23

1. Why do you think James called Abraham "our father"?

2. How was Abraham justified?

3. What was working together in Abraham's life?

4. Explain the result of these working together.

5. What was fulfilled through Abraham's actions?

6. Because Abraham believed God, what was put into his spiritual account? Try to say this in your own words.

7. Describe the honor Abraham received.

LEARN ABOUT ...

2 Just Faith

Justified means (1) acquittal: to declare and treat a person as righteous and (2) vindication: evidence of righteousness. To be justified means we are excused from judgment and give evidence of our faith through obedience to God. "The doers of the law will be justified" (Rom. 2:13).

4 Perfect Faith

The Greek word translated *perfect* means "complete, fully grown, or mature." Absolute perfection is an attribute of God alone. In the highest sense, He alone is complete, wanting nothing. His perfection is eternal and without defect and is the standard of all other perfection.

6 Right Faith

Righteousness is conforming to God's will, obeying God's commands, or fulfilling God's requirements. Abraham accepted God's Word through faith and submitted himself to its control. Therefore God accepted him as one who fulfilled the whole of His righteous requirements.

LEARN ABOUT ...

8 Foreshadowing

Abraham's good works were a mere foreshadowing of God's best work. Abraham willingly offered his only son on an altar on Mount Moriah, pointing to the time when God would willingly sacrifice His only begotten Son on a cross on a hill called Calvary.

---

9 Imperfect

Abraham was faithful, not sinless. Twice he lied about his wife, saying Sarah was his sister. However, the majority of Abraham's life he faithfully obeyed God. Christians aren't perfect either, just forgiven. "If we confess our sins, He is faithful and just to forgive us our sins" (I John 1:9).

---

10 God's Friend

You might think God chooses friends based on their stellar qualities. But Jesus came to be "a friend of tax collectors and sinners" (Matt. 11:19)! When Jesus becomes your friend, He's "a friend who sticks closer than a brother" (Prov. 18:24).

LIVE OUT ...

8. Read Hebrews 11:8–10 and 17–19 to learn more about Abraham and his acts of faith.

   a. In what way did Abraham first display his faith in God (vv. 8–9)?

   b. How did Abraham's faith affect his future (v. 10)?

   c. What test of faith did he endure (vv. 17–18)?

   d. What knowledge of God prompted this faithful response (v. 19)?

9. Fill in the table to learn more about Abraham, the father of faith.

SCRIPTURE	ABRAHAM
Genesis 20:2–7	
Nehemiah 9:7–8	
Isaiah 41:8	
John 8:56	
Romans 4:2–3	

10. Today we learned that Abraham believed God and so was considered a friend of God. Jesus also called Christians His friends. Journal a prayer thanking God for calling you His friend. Use the following verse: "You are my friends if you do what I command. I no longer call you slaves, because a master doesn't confide in his slaves. Now you are my friends, since I have told you everything the Father told me" (John 15:14–15 NLT).

· · • · ·

What is faith anyway? Is it an overwhelming feeling or a serene inner state of consciousness? Since faith is at the core of practical Christian living, it's very important to understand what it is and what it is not.

In the classic book *The Fight*, John White wrote,

> Faith is man's response to God's initiative.... To realize that faith is your response to something God does or says, will take pressure off you and enable you to adopt a more constructive attitude to it. Do not look inside yourself and ask, 'How much faith do I have?' Look to God and ask, 'What is he saying to me? What would he have me do?' When Jesus praised the great faith of different men and women in the Gospels, he was not praising a mystical inner state. He was usually commenting on a concrete action by which someone responded to him. It might have been the action of the Roman centurion who sent his servants to Christ asking only that Christ speak the word of power or the pathetic struggle of a feeble woman to touch his robe.... [Faith] was the person's response, usually in overt action, to God's call.[2]

Abraham is called the "father of faith" because of his obedient response to God's voice. By leaving his home, journeying to the Promised Land, circumcising his flesh, and offering up Isaac, Abraham made step-by-step decisions to obey God. Do *you* follow in Father Abraham's footsteps?

LISTEN TO ...

Faith is not only a means of obeying, but a principal act of obedience. It is ... not only as an altar on which to sacrifice; but it is a sacrifice itself.

—Edward Young

DAY 5

Dynamic Faith

James might logically have followed his teaching on Abraham, the "father of faith," with other examples of godly, faithful men—maybe David, the man after God's own heart, or Elijah, the miracle-working prophet. Instead, James told his readers about Rahab. In James's day, Rahab had three strikes against her: she was a Gentile pagan, a prostitute, and a woman! But James chose an unlikely Old Testament character to make his point that faith is available to all who will hear and obey God's call on their lives.

Jesus chose unlikely people too. He called lowly fishermen, despised tax collectors, and radical zealots to follow Him. He also called women. One woman was like Rahab—a desperate woman with a past. Remember the story? A Pharisee invited Jesus to his house for dinner and didn't even offer the common courtesy of washing Jesus' feet. Then a woman, who was a known sinner, came to the house and stood at Jesus' feet, weeping. "She began to wash His feet with her tears, and wiped them with the hair of her head; and she kissed His feet and anointed them with the fragrant oil" (Luke 7:38). The Pharisee rebuked Jesus for allowing this prostitute near Him. But Jesus commended her, saying, "Her sins, which are many, are forgiven, for she loved much" (v. 47). From these unlikely women, we learn that dynamic faith is love put in action.

LIFT UP ...

I know, Lord, that I am a sinner. Thank You for allowing Your Son, Jesus Christ, to justify me before You. Thank You for viewing me just as if I'd never sinned. In Jesus' name. Amen.

LOOK AT ...

James continued his discussion on faith and works by showing that we exhibit a dynamic faith when we believe in and obey God despite all obstacles.

Read James 2:24–26.

You see then that a man is justified by works, and not by faith only. Likewise, was not Rahab the harlot also justified by works when she received the messengers and sent them out another way? For as the body without the spirit is dead, so faith without works is dead also. James 2:24–26

1. Based on Abraham's example, what are we supposed to see?

2. What key phrase reveals that faith is but one aspect of justification?

3. What Old Testament figure did James next mention?

4. Why did he mention her here?

5. Describe the good works she performed.

6. Skim Matthew 1:5–16, then describe the honor Rahab received for her allegiance to God.

7. Summarize James's comparison here by filling in the blanks.

Just as the body needs the spirit to be _____,
faith must have works to prove it is _____.

Live Out ...

8. This week we have learned that living faith is a process—the grace of God leads to faith in God, which results in good works for God. The "Hall of Faith" found in Hebrews 11 is a monument to those who exhibited this kind of faith.

Learn About ...

2 Justified

When we are justified by God, He pardons our sin and makes us acceptable to Him. This happens by the grace of God: "By grace you have been saved" (Eph. 2:8); *through faith* in Jesus: "... through faith" (v. 8); *for good works* to others: "... created in Christ Jesus for good works" (v. 10).

3 Rahab

Rahab was a pagan Gentile who lived in Jericho, the first city conquered by the Israelites (Josh. 2:1). Rahab is described as a harlot, but she also manufactured and dyed linen. According to rabbinic tradition, Rahab was one of the four most beautiful women in the world.

5 Treason?

Rahab risked her life for the Jews, her people's enemies. Harboring spies was a treasonable offense that would bring the death penalty not only to her but to her family as well. By choosing to ally herself with God's friends, Rahab found new life.

8 Role Models

Those in the hall of faith are role models of faith for believers. But these people were not sinless. Jacob stole his brother's inheritance, Moses murdered a man, and David was an adulterer. Their lives teach that God is not looking for perfect people, only faithful ones.

Learn About ...

9 Hearing

Rahab heard about God's mighty power, and it brought her to a dynamic living faith. She became one of God's own despite her despised race, occupation, and gender. "There is no longer Jew or Gentile, slave or free, male or female.... You are one in Christ Jesus" (Gal. 3:28 NLT).

---

10 Family Faith

Faith is not passed on genetically; birth into a family of faith does not ensure salvation. However, being born into a family that believes has advantages. Families can pass on a faith heritage by teaching Scripture, living godly lives, and praying for those who are not yet saved.

a. Skim Hebrews 11. Write down the members of the Hall of Faith who stand out to you, then describe the good works that accompanied their faith.

HALL OF FAITH	ACT(S) OF FAITH

b. Which of these people would *you* most want to be like? Why?

9. Rahab is the only Gentile mentioned by name in the Hall of Faith. Read part of her story in Joshua 2:8–14.

a. Explain what she realized and how she came to this realization (v. 9).

b. Describe what the inhabitants of Jericho had heard about the Lord and their response (vv. 10–11).

c. What declaration of faith did Rahab make to the spies (v. 11)?

d. Explain what she asked of the spies and what they promised in return for her help (vv. 12–14).

10. Rahab received mercy for herself as well as the members of her household because of her faith. Journal the following verse into a personal prayer asking God to show mercy to the members of your household: "Believe on the Lord Jesus Christ, and you will be saved, you and your household" (Acts 16:31).

° ° • ° °

A king once organized a great race ending in the courtyard of his palace. Every young man in the kingdom participated, hoping to win the bag of gold offered to the winner. The runners lined up, and the starting bell rang out. They set off quickly but were dismayed to find a great pile of rocks and stones in the middle of the course. The runners frantically scrambled over and around the obstacle to complete the race.

Every runner but one crossed the finish line in record time. But the king did not declare a winner. Finally, a solitary runner came through the gate. Lifting a bleeding hand, he said, "O King, forgive my tardiness! I found a pile of rocks and stones in the road, and I wounded myself removing the obstacles from the path." Then he lifted his other hand, saying, "But I found this bag of gold beneath the pile." The king proclaimed, "My son, *you* have won the race, for he runs best who makes the way safe for others to follow."

Like the runner, Rahab's course was not easy. She faced the obstacles of being a woman and a pagan Gentile. She risked everything she had—including her life—to pave the way for others to enter God's kingdom. Yet her victory was assured. Because of her faith working together with faithfulness, she holds a place in Messiah's genealogy, stands proudly in the Hall of Faith, and wears a victor's crown in heaven.

LISTEN TO ...

We can prove our faith by our committal to it, and in no other way.... And it might shock some of us profoundly if we were brought suddenly face to face with our beliefs and forced to test them in the fires of practical living.

—*A. W. Tozer*

Loose Lips Sink Ships
James 3:1–12

On December 7, 1941, Japanese aircraft attacked Pearl Harbor in Hawaii. This sneak attack disabled much of the US Pacific naval fleet and destroyed many aircraft, propelling enraged Americans to arms. World War II took place on both land and sea, but it was clear that, for the war being waged in the Pacific, aircraft carriers were the most important weapon.

The fear of enemy spies finding out key locations of US naval vessels prompted the government to wage a publicity campaign. They sent advice to GIs about what to say and not say when writing letters home, when carrying on conversations, or if captured by the enemy. Posters carried the message to the home front: *Loose Lips Might Sink Ships.*

The epistle of James also warns those in the Lord's army that the lips can do devastating damage: our lips can make our ships sink or float! Last week James emphasized what we do—our works—not what we say. Just in case his readers got the wrong idea, James gave clear instructions to counterbalance the works-only idea: *saying* and *doing* go hand in hand.

Modern Christians have the same problem with works, thinking, *If I don't drink, smoke, or swear, I'm okay.* Yet they engage in gossip, slander, and backbiting. They may build up the body of Christ with their actions while their loose lips spring leaks in the body of Christ.

Day 1: James 3:1–2   **NAVIGATING TROUBLED WATERS**
Day 2: James 3:3–4   **STEERING THE SHIP**
Day 3: James 3:5–6   **BELOW DECK**
Day 4: James 3:7–8   **FIRE TORPEDOES!**
Day 5: James 3:9–12   **GOURMET GALLEY**

DAY 1
Navigating Troubled Waters

LIFT UP ...

Heavenly Father, I know that whatever is in my heart eventually will come out of my mouth. Please help my words and my actions honor You. In Jesus' name. Amen.

LOOK AT ...

It is interesting to note that every chapter in the book of James includes an admonition about our speech. As James began his teaching on loose lips, he reminded believers that those who teach God's Word are held to a higher standard as they help navigate their students through troubled waters.

READ JAMES 3:1–2.

My brethren, let not many of you become teachers, knowing that we shall receive a stricter judgment. For we all stumble in many things. If anyone does not stumble in word, he is a perfect man, able also to bridle the whole body.
James 3:1–2

1. What phrase lets you know that teaching is not for everyone?

2. Did James include himself as a teacher? How do you know?

3. Why do you think God holds teachers to a higher standard?

LEARN ABOUT ...

1 Navigator

Teacher means "master or instructor," carrying the idea of ruling over another. A teacher, like a navigator, charts the course for others to follow. Since there's a danger in leading others astray, not everyone in the church should teach. Too many navigators could take a ship off course.

3 Inspector

Some desire to be spiritual leaders for power or prestige, forgetting that how and what they teach will affect their eternal reward. Jesus said, "When someone has been given much, much will be required in return; and when someone has been entrusted with much, even more will be required" (Luke 12:48 NLT).

LEARN ABOUT ...

6 Perfecter

Stumble means "to fall, trip, sin, or offend." Stumble in word, and you'll stumble in deed. Controlling your tongue helps you become perfect—mature or complete. Christ is our perfecter, so "let us fix our eyes on Jesus, the author and perfecter of our faith" (Heb. 12:2 NIV).

8 Gifted Teacher

The "gift of teaching" is the ability to understand and communicate Christian truths clearly. The result is the maturing of believers into more effective Christian disciples. "Preach the word of God.... Patiently correct, rebuke, and encourage your people with good teaching" (2 Tim. 4:2 NLT).

9 Millstone

A millstone was part of a mortar used to grind wheat or olives. About two feet thick, a millstone weighed hundreds of pounds. Just like cement shoes, a millstone would make you sink like a rock! "A woman on the roof dropped a millstone that ... crushed his skull" (Judg. 9:53 NLT).

4. a. To learn more about the gift of teaching, read Ephesians 4:11–12. Who decides what gift an individual receives?

    b. How do you know that not everyone has the same gift?

    c. Why are these gifts given?

5. Teachers offer spiritual instruction. Yet, teachers themselves must be taught. Fill in the table to learn who teaches the teacher.

SCRIPTURE	THE TEACHER
Job 36:22	
John 13:13	
John 14:26	

6. Explain what all human beings do.

7. What are the characteristics of someone who does not have loose lips?

LIVE OUT ...

8. a. In the school of life, some are pupils, and some are teachers. God calls and gifts some people to be teachers of spiritual truth. Name some of the people appointed by God to be your spiritual teachers.

    b. Journal about some of the spiritual truths you have learned from them.

9. If a teacher stumbles, he or she often causes the pupils to stumble as well. The gospel of Matthew teaches about the consequence of

causing others to trip up spiritually. Read Matthew 18:6–7, and describe the offense and resulting punishment.

10. The apostle Peter said that if you add some key elements to your Christian faith, "you will be neither barren nor unfruitful in the knowledge of our Lord Jesus Christ.... If you do these things *you will never stumble!*" (2 Pet. 1:8, 10). Read 2 Peter 1:5–10. Place a + by the elements you have added, and a – by those things you lack.

___ Faith in the Lord

___ "Add to your faith virtue"

___ "To virtue [add] knowledge"

___ "To knowledge [add] self–control"

___ "To self-control [add] perseverance"

___ "To perseverance [add] godliness"

___ "To godliness [add] brotherly kindness"

___ "To brotherly kindness [add] love"

11. Those who do not stumble are considered perfect, mature in the faith. Journal a prayer by rewriting the following verse and asking God to help you to stand tall in the faith: "All glory to God, who is able to keep you from falling away and will bring you with great joy into his glorious presence without a single fault" (Jude v. 24 NLT).

LEARN ABOUT ...

10 Light or Dark?

Jesus said, "If anyone walks in the day, he does not stumble.... But if one walks in the night, he stumbles, because the light is not in him" (John 11:9–10). Advance into the light, and you'll be sure-footed. March into darkness, and you're headed for a fall.

∘ ∘ • ∘ ∘

An article in the US Navy's *Proceedings* magazine told of two battleships that had been at sea in heavy weather for several days. The visibility was poor with patchy fog, so the watchful captain of one of the ships remained on the bridge. Shortly after dark, the lookout reported, "Steady light, bearing on the starboard bow!" A steady light meant their ships were on a dangerous collision course.

The captain then called out, "Signal that ship: 'We are on a collision course; advise you change course twenty degrees.'"

Back came the signal, "Advisable for you to change course twenty degrees."

The captain said, "Send: 'I'm a captain; change course twenty degrees.'"

"I'm a seaman second-class," came the reply. "You had better change your course twenty degrees."

By that time the captain was furious, "Send: 'I'm a battleship; change course twenty degrees.'"

Back came the flashing light, "I'm a lighthouse."

They immediately changed course. Smart move. A lighthouse has a few good characteristics: (1) warns of potential danger; (2) signals safe harbor; (3) is stronger than a storm; and (4) shines brightest in the fog.

God's Word is like a lighthouse. Some "teachers" challenge the veracity of God's lighthouse, taking their shipload of parishioners into dangerous waters. But wise teachers will chart a sure course, using the light of God's Word to guide their ships to safe harbor.

LISTEN TO ...

A teacher affects eternity; he can never tell where his influence stops.

—Henry Adams

DAY 2

Steering the Ship

On April 14, 1912, the unthinkable happened to the unsinkable *Titanic* on her maiden voyage. Near midnight the luxury liner struck an iceberg that ripped a three-hundred-foot hole through the hull, sinking her in just two and a half hours. *Titanic* had encountered no rough seas or bad weather; however, she had received urgent warnings of dangerous ice floes.

April 13: *Rappahannock* warns by signal lamp of heavy pack ice ahead and ice denting her bow and twisting her rudder.

April 14, 9:00 a.m.: *Coronia* reports "bergs, growlers, and field ice."

April 14, 1:42 p.m.: *Baltic* warns of "icebergs and large quantities of field ice" 250 miles ahead of *Titanic's* position.

April 14, 1:45 p.m.: *Titanic* intercepts message from *Amerika* reporting passing two icebergs and relays it to the US Hydrographic Office.

April 14, 7:30 p.m.: *Californian* warns of "three large bergs" only fifty miles ahead of *Titanic*. While communicating with Cape Race, *Titanic* tells the *Californian* to "shut up and get off" because the transmission was jamming his signals.

Finally, April 14, 9:40 p.m.: *Mesaba* reports "great number of large icebergs."[1]

The captain should have altered *Titanic's* course. But he failed to make the slight adjustment of turning the ship's relatively small rudder in order to avert a huge disaster.

Today the book of James warns that unless we get our "small rudders"—our tongues—under control, our "ships" are headed for destruction.

LIFT UP ..

Lord, I realize that many small things hold sway over me: small words of kindness make my day; sometimes my small thinking holds me back. Help me to remember that small things can make a big impact. In Jesus' name. Amen.

LEARN ABOUT ...

4 Rudder

A rudder is a broad, flat device used to direct a ship's course. A ship controlled by a rudder carries precious cargo to wonderful places. A tongue controlled by God will spread the good news wherever it goes. "Go therefore and make disciples of all the nations" (Matt. 28:19).

5 Pilot

Bits control the wild nature of horses; the rudder overcomes winds that drive ships astray. Therefore, a strong hand must control both. The tongue controlled by God's hand can be tamed. "Take control of what I say, O LORD, and guard my lips" (Ps. 141:3 NLT).

6 Mulish

David's refusal to repent resulted in his "groaning all the day long" (Ps. 32:3). God used this discomfort to rein in his mulish behavior: "Your hand was heavy upon me" (v. 4). Repentance restored his health and relationship to God: "I acknowledged my sin" (v. 5).

LOOK AT ...

James reminded his readers that not many should be teachers, warning that words can make others stumble. In today's passage, he used some comparisons to show the tongue's power.

READ JAMES 3:3–4.

Indeed, we put bits in horses' mouths that they may obey us, and we turn their whole body. Look also at ships: although they are so large and are driven by fierce winds, they are turned by a very small rudder wherever the pilot desires. James 3:3–4

1. James used natural illustrations to help us see the impact that small things have on large things. In the first illustration, what small instrument is put into the mouth of a large horse?

2. What two things result from the small bit?

3. Name the two things that make a ship difficult to maneuver.

4. What small thing turns the ship and keeps it on course?

5. Who is at the ship's controls?

LIVE OUT ...

6. a. In Psalm 32:8–9, David spoke of God bringing him to repentance after he had fallen into sin. Read these verses. What did God promise to do for David (v. 8)?

b. What did God warn David (and us) against (v. 9)?

c. What are the characteristics of these beasts (v. 9)?

7. The psalms are full of exhortations about our tongues turning toward right or wrong. Look up the verses, indicate which direction they went (Right or Wrong), and describe how they were used.

Scripture	R/W	Description
Psalm 10:7		
Psalm 12:2–4		
Psalm 15:2–3		
Psalm 52:2–5		
Psalm 66:16–17		
Psalm 119:172–173		

8. a. Think of your life as a ship. Do you allow God's Word to be your "rudder"? Are you consecrating your words to His glory and honor? Journal about a time when God helped you steer your tongue toward speech that is edifying. What did you say, and how did it make others feel?

b. Now journal of a time when you steered your tongue toward trouble. What did you say, and what were the consequences?

∘ ∘ • ∘ ∘

After nearly completing his first overseas cruise, a young ensign was given an opportunity to prepare for and take the ship out to sea. With a stream of commands, the decks were buzzing with men, and soon the ship was sailing out of the channel.

His efficiency established a new record for getting a destroyer under way, and he was not surprised when a seaman approached him with a message from the captain. He was surprised, though, to find that it was a radio message that read: "My personal congratulations upon completing your underway preparation exercise according to the book and with amazing speed. However, you overlooked one of the unwritten rules—make sure the captain is aboard before getting under way."

We may pilot our own ships, but we've discovered that we must follow the directions of our divine Captain. Our tongues are like rudders. When controlled by strong hands and good hearts, the tongue guides us to desired destinations. However, if held loosely and with wrong intentions, our tongues can do devastating damage, leaving us shipwrecked. If your tongue has taken you into uncharted waters and your hand is not strong enough to navigate the storm, don't forget the Captain. If you let Him, He'll steady your hand, curb your tongue, and quiet your heart. With God at the helm, you're headed for smooth sailing.

LISTEN TO ...

When Christ came into my life, I came about like a well-handled ship.

—*Robert Louis Stevenson*

DAY 3

Below Deck

To plan a honeymoon, you do some research on Carnival Cruise Lines and discover the "fun ship" *Ecstasy* offering exotic vacations from Miami to the Bahamas. This floating paradise offers a health club featuring state-of-the-art equipment and body and facial treatments; the Blue Sapphire Lounge showcasing Las Vegas–style venues; the Crystal Palace Casino with over two hundred slot machines and sixteen blackjack tables; three luxurious pools, one boasting a heart-pounding waterslide; a library lined with mahogany bookshelves stocked with classics and best sellers; and elegant meals in two dining rooms.

You immediately call your travel agent and book passage for the vacation of a lifetime. But two days into the cruise, there's trouble in paradise. You realize there's one place you should have checked before setting sail—the engine room! When a disastrous fire disables the engines, the ship is left crippled. You begin to swelter in your cabin: no air conditioning. The kitchens serve leftovers: no oven. The casino lights go dim and discotheques go silent: no electricity. The fire is extinguished as a tugboat pulls the ship back to Miami. Your dream vacation has become a nightmare.

Ships have powerful engines. But if even a small fire gets out of control, the power source can be damaged, and the whole ship can be crippled. James likened the tongue to fire. When our words rage out of control, others get burned and our lives go up in smoke.

Lift Up ...

Lord, this week I have become so aware of the power my tongue has to hurt others. Please purify my heart so that my words will be pure. In Jesus' name. Amen.

Look At ...

We've seen that our tongues can either bring smooth sailing or cause shipwrecks. Now we find that our words can cause great destruction below deck as well.

LEARN ABOUT ...

4 Defile

Defiled means "stained, contaminated." "The whole body" implies the entire vessel is permeated. Plutonium is good fuel on a nuclear submarine. But if it leaks, the whole ship is defiled with radiation. "The words you speak come from the heart—that's what defiles you" (Matt. 15:18 NLT).

5 Course

"Course of nature" in James 3:6 is also translated "your whole life" (NLT), and "the whole course of his life" (NIV). The destructive impact of ruinous speech burns and spreads to everyone we encounter throughout our lives. Our past, present, and future can be destroyed by a slip of the tongue.

7 Fire and Water

Fire out of control brings destruction, especially to dry places. If your spiritual life is dry, perhaps you have neglected your water source. Jesus said, "He who believes in Me, ... out of his heart will flow rivers of living water" (John 7:38).

READ JAMES 3:5–6.

Even so the tongue is a little member and boasts great things. See how great a forest a little fire kindles! And the tongue is a fire, a world of iniquity. The tongue is so set among our members that it defiles the whole body, and sets on fire the course of nature; and it is set on fire by hell. James 3:5–6

1. James drew his readers' attention to the tongue. Contrast what the tongue does in comparison to its size.

2. How is the tongue like a fire?

3. James built on the analogy of the forest fire to explain how dangerous a tongue out of control can be. What phrase describes how sinful the tongue can be?

4. What negative impact does the tongue have on the body?

5. How can the fire extend beyond the body?

6. Who did James imply was the originator of sins of the tongue?

LIVE OUT ...

7. a. The tongue can ignite a huge fire of trouble. In 2 Corinthians 12:20–21 (NIV), Paul described some tongue trouble. Reflecting upon your life, place a check in the space where you have the most trouble taming your tongue.

   ___ Quarreling
   ___ Slander

____ Factions

____ Outbursts of anger

____ Jealousy

____ Gossip

____ Disorder

____ Arrogance

b. Journal a prayer to God asking Him to extinguish the verbal flames you have ignited. If you have harmed others, ask Him to heal their wounds and restore their hearts.

8. James reminded believers that the tongue is a "world of iniquity"—full of sin. Proverbs 6:16–19 lists seven of the things God hates. Which of these things are or could result in sins of the tongue?

9. Though sins of the tongue are "set on fire by hell," there is a kind of speech set on fire by heaven. Acts 2 tells how, on the day of Pentecost, tongues of fire came upon the believers (see Acts 2:1–4). Read verses 38–39, then answer the following questions to discover what Peter spoke as a result of this heavenly fire.

a. What message did he speak (v. 38)?

b. What promise did he make (v. 38)?

c. Who did this promise include (v. 39)?

d. Who will you take this message to?

LEARN ABOUT …

8 Iniquity

The Bible often uses *iniquity* to describe evil, wickedness, unrighteousness, or lawlessness. Iniquity suggests different types of evil: transgressions of spiritual law; crimes against God; moral or legal wrongs; depravity; and sin in general. "Under his tongue is trouble and iniquity" (Ps. 10:7).

9 Heavenly Fire

Jesus came to "baptize you with the Holy Spirit and fire" (Matt. 3:11). According to Bible commentator Matthew Henry, "The Spirit, like fire, melts the heart, separates and burns up the dross, and kindles pious and devout affections in the soul…. This is that fire which Christ came to send upon the earth."

° ° • ° °

The summer of 1947 was an unseasonable scorcher in Brantford, Ontario. So when Roddie, his big brother, Dennis, and Mac went for a weenie roast in the forest, they had no problem finding scrub brush for kindling. With the wrappers from the buns placed on top of the pile, a mere strike of Roddie's match quickly ignited the pile. Sparks flew upward as the wind snatched up fragments of the burning plastic, then hurtled them back down like meteors all around the campsite. Dennis began huffing and puffing like the big bad wolf in an attempt to extinguish the fire. Instead, it fanned the flames. All three boys began stomping wildly on the burning embers, waving their arms in the air and screaming like Indians on the warpath. This billowed the flames even higher. Then the boys did what any twelve-year-old would have done—they ran for their lives! Looking back in horror, they saw the entire ten-acre woods going up in smoke.

My (Lenya) dad—fondly nicknamed "Hot Rod"—learned that it literally takes only a spark to get a forest fire burning. James warned that our fiery tongues can wreak havoc too. Angry accusations, contentious comments, or godless gossip can burn others, leaving lives in ruin. Remember that those who heat things up verbally are playing with hellfire: "As charcoal is to burning coals, and wood to fire, so is a contentious man to kindle strife" (Prov. 26:21).

LISTEN TO ...

Confine your tongue, lest it confine you.

—Proverb

DAY 4
Fire Torpedoes!

Most of us would agree that wielding weapons in public is not good for anyone's health. Yet most of us are carrying a potentially deadly weapon around with us all the time—a weapon that is not good for our spiritual or emotional health. The psalmist said that some people "sharpen their tongues like swords and aim their words like deadly arrows. They shoot from ambush at the innocent man" (Ps. 64:3–4 NIV). Spiteful words spewed from vengeful hearts can blow others away, critically wounding their spirits. But, the truth is, hateful words can backfire on us, hurting us as much as those we've attacked.

During World War II, the US submarine *Tang* surfaced under cover of darkness to fire on a large Japanese convoy off the coast of China. Since previous raids had left the American vessel with only eight torpedoes, the accuracy of every shot was absolutely essential. The first seven missiles were right on target; but when the eighth was launched, it suddenly deviated and headed right back at the submarine. The emergency alarm to submerge rang out, but it was too late. Within a matter of seconds, the US sub received a direct hit and sank almost instantly.

Instead of doing battle with the Enemy, Christians often use God's Word like a torpedo to attack one another. With precisely aimed missiles of criticism, contempt, or callousness, we can cripple the body of Christ, of which we are all members. You cannot sink someone else's end of the boat and still keep your own afloat.

Lift Up ...

Father, I know that the only antidote to an out-of-control tongue is Your Holy Spirit residing within me, Your Word guiding me, and Your Son forgiving me. Thank You for the remedy to help tame my tongue. In Jesus' name. Amen.

LEARN ABOUT ...

2 Tame

Tame means "to domesticate from a state of wildness to usefulness; to be made submissive; to humble or tone down." No animal—or tongue—willingly consents to being tamed; it goes against their nature. "Will the wild ox consent to being tamed?" (Job 39:9 NLT).

3 Unruly

Unruly means "undisciplined." The term describes someone not easily ruled and implies stubborn resistance to control. Believers have a responsibility to help control those whose words are out of control: "We exhort you, brethren, warn those who are unruly" (I Thess. 5:14).

6 Cage It!

We've caged the mighty lion, encased poisonous reptiles in terrariums, and placed the killer whale Shamu in a tank. God in His infinite wisdom placed our tongues in a cage of their own: behind two lips and surrounded by sharp teeth. If your tongue raises its ugly head—bite it.

LOOK AT ...

Yesterday we found that the tongue was described as a fire that is ignited by hell. Today we discover that the tongue can be full of deadly poison.

READ JAMES 3:7–8.

For every kind of beast and bird, of reptile and creature of the sea, is tamed and has been tamed by mankind. But no man can tame the tongue. It is an unruly evil, full of deadly poison. James 3:7–8

1. Name the four categories of animals James mentioned.

2. What phrase makes you think the animal kingdom has been subdued?

3. How is the tongue different from wild animals? Why?

4. What is the tongue full of?

5. Think back to yesterday's lesson concerning the force behind the sinful tongue. Relate this to the tongue full of poison—why is this an appropriate illustration?

LIVE OUT ...

6. James exhorted us to tame, or humble and tone down, our tongues. Using TAME as an acrostic, journal about some ways you can tone down your tongue.

T (*Example: talk without using sarcastic wit.*)

A

M

E

LEARN ABOUT ...

7 Good Words

Tongues produce a world of good when we pray, praise, or preach the gospel. "Love your enemies, bless those who curse you, ... and pray for those who spitefully use you and persecute you" (Matt. 5:44).

8 Antidote

People say, "My lips are sealed," pretending to lock the door and throw away the key, only to blab anyway. We can't control our tongues, but God can if we give Him the keys. "Take control of what I say, O LORD, and guard my lips" (Ps. 141:3 NLT).

7. Our unruly tongues need to be disciplined. Discipline includes both stopping bad habits and starting good ones. In other words, don't just bite your tongue; bless others with it instead. In the columns, record some biting words you've said in the past, then edit those words into a blessing.

BITING WORDS
(*Example: you're too old to wear that.*)

BLESSING WORDS
(*Example: you're so young at heart.*)

8. The tongue was described as "full of deadly poison." Below are some words that describe the symptoms of poisoning.

- Sweating
- Weakness
- Paralysis
- Increased pulse rate
- Pain
- Restricted breathing

Briefly journal about a time when poisonous words affected you in one of these ways.

· ° • ° °

Gossip can be one of the most potent poisons, infecting everyone who comes into contact with it. Here are some symptoms of gossip poisoning followed by the antidote guaranteed to neutralize this deadly venom.

SYMPTOMS OF GOSSIP POISONING

1. Dislike: Developing bitterness even though the person involved did not directly offend you.
2. Disapproval: Criticizing those involved. Acting as the judge in the matter while recruiting others to "your side."
3. Distortion: Searching out more gossip and using it to give the worst possible impression of others or to make yourself look spiritual.
4. Deception: Believing that such actions are actually accomplishing God's will and using prayer to spread the rumors further.

ANTIDOTES TO GOSSIP POISONING

1. Repentance: Ask God to cleanse your mind and to forgive you for poisoning others with gossip. *"If we confess our sins, He is faithful and just to forgive us our sins and to cleanse us from all unrighteousness"* (1 John 1:9).
2. Restoration: Pray for a genuine love for everyone involved. If you've sinned against someone, make it right. *"If you bring your gift to the altar, ... first be reconciled to your brother, and then come and offer your gift"* (Matt. 5:23–24).
3. Renewal: Be transformed by renewing your mind with truth instead of lies. God's Word is the antidote of the soul. *"You are already clean because of the word which I have spoken to you"* (John 15:3).

When you lose the urge to spread bad reports about others, have more compassion, and begin to genuinely care about the people involved, then God is working to cure the poison of gossip in your life and to build up a living faith.

LISTEN TO ...

Never believe anything bad about anybody unless you positively know it to be true; never tell even that unless you feel that it is absolutely necessary—and remember that God is listening while you tell it.

—*Henry van Dyke*

DAY 5

Gourmet Galley

Have you noticed how people inevitably gather in the kitchen? It doesn't matter that the living room is decorated beautifully or the den has a big-screen TV. These rooms simply don't have the magnetic pull of the kitchen. The kitchen just feels like home. It's the place where you can pour a cup of coffee as you pour your heart out and where homespun wisdom is offered with a pinch of love.

The same is true of a ship's galley. At all hours passengers can find a warm fire burning, savory soups simmering, and fresh bread baking. However, the galley can be a dangerous place when high seas cause hot broth to slosh from cauldrons or pitch the novice sailor against a hot grill. Sometimes, in the galley, people get burned. James reminded believers that words can be as inviting as a gourmet galley when they offer "A Little Something" known as a blessing, or they can be as scalding as a sea-tossed pot of stew when they spew curses.

LIFT UP ...

Lord, my heart's desire is to use my tongue to bless others. Change me from the inside out so that my words and actions bring blessing. In Jesus' name. Amen.

LOOK AT ...

This week's lesson has exposed the power of the tongue. Today we find that our tongues can quickly switch from gourmet to garbage.

READ JAMES 3:9–12.

With it [the tongue] we bless our God and Father, and with it we curse men, who have been made in the similitude of God. Out of the same mouth proceed blessing and cursing. My brethren, these things ought not to be so. Does a spring send forth fresh water and bitter from the same opening? Can a fig tree, my brethren, bear olives, or a grapevine bear figs? Thus no spring yields both salt water and fresh. James 3:9–12

Learn About ...

1 Bless God

Bless means "to speak well of or celebrate with praises." We bless God by praising His divine characteristics and expressing gratitude for His mercies. "I will bless the LORD at all times; His praise shall continually be in my mouth" (Ps. 34:1).

1. What good do we do with our tongue?

2. What evil do we do with our tongue?

3. Explain why cursing people is evil in God's sight.

3 Curse Others

A curse is a prayer for evil or misfortune on another. God made everyone in His image. "When God created human beings, he made them to be like himself ... and he blessed them" (Gen. 5:1–2 NLT). Those God has blessed, we have no right to curse.

4. Explain the hypocrisy some professing Christians exhibit with their mouths.

5. What strong warning did James give concerning this type of hypocrisy?

6. James used the natural imagery of water and fruit to demonstrate his point.

6 The Source

Water often speaks of the refreshing power of the Holy Spirit, and fruit often represents the love, joy, and peace the Spirit produces in our lives. This divine source of love will spill out of our hearts and lips to refresh others.

   a. What is a fresh spring unable to produce?

   b. What is a fig tree or grapevine unable to produce?

   c. What does this analogy teach you about the words you speak?

Live Out ...

7 Sing Psalms

Psalms are prayers, poems, and hymns that focus the worshipper's thoughts on God in praise and adoration. You don't have to be a songwriter to write a psalm; you simply need a heart of praise. "Sing psalms to Him; talk of all His wondrous works!" (Ps. 105:2).

7. a. Today we learned that one of our primary functions as believers is to bless God. Read Psalm 103:2–5, and list all the reasons we have to praise God.

8 Can't Curse

Balak, the king of Moab, hired Balaam to curse the Israelites. But God wouldn't allow him to speak curses; instead, He caused Balaam to bless them. "What have you done to me? I took you to curse my enemies, and look, you have blessed them bountifully!" (Num. 23:11).

---

9 Fresh Water

Without fresh water, there can be no life. Ninety-seven percent of the earth's water is salty, making it unusable for drinking or farming. Only 3 percent is fresh water. How does your speech compare with these statistics—mostly bitter and only a little bit refreshing?

b. Now journal a personal psalm of praise to God, thanking Him for one or more of these blessings in your life.

8. In the Old Testament, God warned His people against cursing others. Fill in the chart to learn about these warnings.

SCRIPTURE	DO NOT CURSE
Exodus 21:17	
Exodus 22:28	
Leviticus 19:14	
Ecclesiastes 10:20	

9. a. As believers, we are called to speak refreshing words, not words that are bitter or stinging. Think of a friend who might need to hear good words. Draw a cup and fill it to overflowing with words that will bless that person. (*Example: thank you; I love you; I appreciate your kindness.*)

b. Journal about how words of blessing have helped you, and then write when you will speak refreshing words to the person you named above.

° ° • ° °

Xanthus, the philosopher, once told his servant to prepare for dinner guests and get the best thing he could find in the market. The philosopher and his guests sat down the next day at the table. They had nothing but tongue—four or five courses of tongue cooked in this way and that. The philosopher finally lost his patience and said to his servant, "Didn't I tell you to get the best thing in the market?" The servant said, "I did get the best thing in the market. Isn't the tongue the organ of sociability, the organ of eloquence, the organ of kindness, the organ of worship?"

Then Xanthus the philosopher said, "Tomorrow I want you to get the worst thing in the market." And on the morrow the philosopher sat at the table, and there was nothing but tongue—four or five courses of it—in this shape and that. The philosopher lost his patience again and said, "Didn't I tell you to get the worst thing in the market?" The servant replied, "I did; for isn't the tongue the organ of blasphemy, the organ of defamation, the organ of lying?"

The tongue can be used for evil or for good, for blessing or for cursing. If the people in your life were asked what type of words you've served them, what would they say?

LISTEN TO ...

The great test of a [wo]man's character is [her] tongue.

—Oswald Chambers

LESSON EIGHT

The Moral of the Story Is ...
James 3:13–18

Everyone loves fables. The characters are usually animals that act like people, and the moral of each story is told at the end of the fable in the form of a wise proverb. Aesop, a Greek slave, was the father of fables. His tales illustrated the failings and virtues of human nature in a simple, humorous way.

James also wanted to impart wisdom to his readers, teaching them the difference between earthly and heavenly wisdom. This week, join us in rediscovering some of Aesop's fables that help illustrate the wisdom James wanted believers to develop.

THE ANT AND THE GRASSHOPPER

One summer day a Grasshopper was chirping to its heart's content. An Ant passed by bearing a heavy ear of corn to his nest. "Come chat with me," said the Grasshopper, "instead of toiling in that way."

"I am helping lay up food for the winter," said the Ant, "and so should you."

"Why bother about winter?" said the Grasshopper. "We've got plenty of food now." The Ant continued its toil anyway. When winter came the Grasshopper had no food and was starving to death, while the ants distributed grain from the stores they'd collected in the summer. The Grasshopper learned the hard way; it's best to prepare for days of necessity during days of plenty.

The Moral of the Story Is ... Wisdom is revealed by what you do with what you know.

Day 1: James 3:13   **WHAT YOU DO WITH WHAT YOU KNOW**

Day 2: James 3:14–15   **PRIDE COMES BEFORE THE FALL**

Day 3: James 3:16   **EVERY MAN FOR HIMSELF**

Day 4: James 3:17   **VIRTUES WORTH CULTIVATING**

Day 5: James 3:18   **ONLY GOD CAN CHANGE OUR NATURE**

DAY 1

What You Do with What You Know

LEARN ABOUT …

2 Understanding

Understanding literally means "to set together; to comprehend." It speaks of reflective thought, prudence, or discernment. It is sometimes translated as "mind." "We know that the Son of God has come, and he has given us understanding [mind] so that we can know the true God" (1 John 5:20 NLT).

LIFT UP …

Lord, to be truly wise I should model myself after You. Please help me put on Your attributes. Today help me learn what it means to be meek. In Jesus' name. Amen.

LOOK AT …

Last week we learned that what we say indicates the condition of our heart. This week we will learn that the kind of life a person lives reveals the kind of wisdom she possesses.

READ JAMES 3:13.

Who is wise and understanding among you? Let him show by good conduct that his works are done in the meekness of wisdom. James 3:13

1. Who was James looking for?

2. Fill in the following chart with the lessons you learn about understanding.

SCRIPTURE   **LESSONS ON UNDERSTANDING**

Deut. 1:13

LEARN ABOUT ...

3 Good Conduct

Good conduct means "manner of life," and isn't a one-time action but a consistent lifestyle. The NKJV says, "Only let your conduct be worthy of the gospel of Christ" (Phil. 1:27). The NLT translates, "You must live ... in a manner worthy of the Good News about Christ."

5 Get Wisdom!

Wisdom is the ability to judge correctly—taking the best course of action based on knowledge. The first principle of biblical wisdom is to humble ourselves before God in reverence and obedience to His commands. "Fear of the LORD is the beginning of wisdom" (Prov. 9:10 NLT).

7 Enlightenment

The Age of Enlightenment began in the 1600s when philosophers contrasted superstitious religion with scientific reason. True enlightenment begins with Jesus. "I am the light of the world. He who follows Me shall not walk in darkness, but have the light of life" (John 8:12).

1 Samuel 25:3

1 Kings 3:9

Psalm 111:10

Proverbs 1:5

3. According to James 3:13, what should a believer show?

4. What does this conduct produce?

5. Describe how these works should be done.

6. a. In Proverbs 2:2–7, Solomon gave advice concerning how to gain wisdom. What actions should we take to seek wisdom (vv. 2–4)?

   b. To what are wisdom and understanding likened (v. 4)?

   c. What does God promise if we take these actions (vv. 5–7)?

LIVE OUT ...

7. James sought people with wise understanding. Ephesians 1:18–19 speaks of people with enlightened understanding, while Ephesians 4:18–19 describes those with darkened understanding. List the characteristics of each.

ENLIGHTENED MIND	DARKENED UNDERSTANDING

8. Today we learned that good conduct is a lifestyle. Rather than the *Lifestyles of the Rich and Famous,* James commended the *Lifestyles of the Righteous and Faithful.* Using two words from the following list (or think of your own), name your lifestyle program. Then journal about how you've developed this manner of life.

   Righteous, meek, kind, faithful, humble, trustworthy, loving, stable, strong, quiet, gentle, funny, unpredictable, proud, shy, helpful, flamboyant, artistic, perfectionist, creative, athletic, scholarly, busy, lazy, loud, bossy, organized, chaotic

   Lifestyles of the _____ and _____.

9. Wisdom is the practical application of what we know. The following is a list of things a wise person must know and do. Place an ✗ beside the items you know but do not practice, and a ✔ beside those things you know and act upon.

   ___ Increases learning (Prov. 1:5)
   ___ Departs from evil (Prov. 14:16)
   ___ Increases in strength (Prov. 24:5)
   ___ Controls her feelings (Prov. 29:9)
   ___ Doesn't glory in wisdom (Jer. 9:23)
   ___ Hears and obeys Jesus (Matt. 7:24)
   ___ Settles disputes among Christians (1 Cor. 6:5)

∘ ∘ • ∘ ∘

LEARN ABOUT ...

8 Lifestyles

Imitation is the sincerest form of flattery. Christians are encouraged to follow their leaders' lifestyles. "Remember your leaders, who spoke the word of God to you. Consider the outcome of their way of life and imitate their faith" (Heb. 13:7 NIV). Whom do you model your life after?

9 Act Wisely

Wisdom not demonstrated in righteous acts is as useless as faith without works. To know something doesn't make you wise. You can be book smart but common-sense foolish if you never alter your actions based on your knowledge. When you act upon what you know, you are truly wise.

When a young man applied for a job as a farmhand, he listed one qualification: "I can sleep when the wind blows." The farmer was puzzled, but he'd taken a liking to the young man, so he hired him. A few days later, a violent storm awakened the farmer and his wife from a deep sleep. They jumped out of bed, and, to their surprise, they found the shutters securely fastened and a supply of logs neatly stacked beside the fireplace. The tools were placed in the shed so they wouldn't rust, the tractor was parked in the garage, and the barn was locked with the animals safely inside. All was well.

At that moment the farmer realized the meaning of the young man's claim, "I can sleep when the wind blows." Because the farmhand had conducted good works when the skies were clear, he was prepared for the storm when it broke. When the wind blew, he had no fear and could sleep peacefully.

This young man could have given the farmer a long list of skills when applying for the job. Instead he gave the farmer a humble statement backed by diligent actions. He showed he was truly wise by preparing for a rainy day when the sun was shining. In the same way, believers will display their wisdom by "good conduct ... done in the meekness of wisdom" (James 3:13).

Listen To ...

Wisdom comes privately from God as a by-product of right decisions, godly reactions, and the application of spiritual principles to daily circumstances [and] ... from being faithful to the small, obscure tasks few people ever see.

—*Charles R. Swindoll*

Pride Comes before the Fall

Godly wisdom is identifiable by an important attitude—meekness. James warned believers that there is another type of wisdom in opposition to this godly wisdom, which should be avoided at all costs. This pseudo-wisdom manifests itself with the attitudes of envy, egotism, and exaggeration.

THE JAY AND THE PEACOCK

A Jay venturing into a yard where Peacocks used to walk found a number of feathers, which had fallen from the Peacocks. He tied them all to his tail and strutted toward the Peacocks. When he came near them, they discovered the cheat and pecked at him until they plucked away his borrowed plumes. The Jay was forced to go back to the other Jays, who had watched his behavior. They were annoyed with him and said: "It is not only fine feathers that make fine birds."

Wisdom that is demonic envies, covets, and cunningly attempts to elevate itself to a place of prominence. This describes Satan's flaw that led to his ultimate fall. Ezekiel 28 says that before Satan landed in Eden, he was "the anointed cherub" who had access to the "holy mountain of God" (v. 14). He was "perfect" until one proud day "iniquity was found" in him (v. 15). His "heart was lifted up because of [his] beauty." Therefore God condemned him, saying, "You corrupted your wisdom for the sake of your splendor" (v. 17). And then God cast him to the ground.

The Moral of the Story Is ... Pride comes before the fall.

LEARN ABOUT ...

I Bitter Envy

Bitter means "pointed, sharp, prickly, or pungent." Envy, like jealousy, is a painful awareness of an advantage enjoyed by another coupled with a desire to possess that advantage. Bitter envy describes the worst type of envy, one that completely disregards the feelings and well-being of others.

---

3 Braggart

In this passage, James described an arrogant person. In modern society boasting and self-seeking are viewed as acceptable qualities. Boasting is rampant among politicians, sports figures, and celebrities. But a Christian who exhibits arrogance reveals a lack of divine wisdom.

---

5 Unholy Trinity

The three types of worldly wisdom correspond with our three enemies. *Earthly* symbolizes the world, *sensual* the flesh, and *demonic* the devil. "All that is in the world—the lust of the flesh, the lust of the eyes, and the pride of life—is not of the Father" (I John 2:16).

LIFT UP ...

Lord, please take my thoughts captive. Don't let my mind be consumed with selfish ambition or prideful arrogance. Keep me from the lies of the Enemy. In Jesus' name. Amen.

LOOK AT ...

We've seen that living faith possesses the meekness of wisdom manifested in good works. Now the book of James describes a wisdom that parades itself as heavenly but is, in fact, demonic.

READ JAMES 3:14–15.

But if you have bitter envy and self-seeking in your hearts, do not boast and lie against the truth. This wisdom does not descend from above, but is earthly, sensual, demonic. James 3:14–15

1. What are the first two sinful attitudes mentioned here?

2. Where do these attitudes originate?

3. What prideful behavior are we warned against?

4. When we boast because of envy and self-seeking, we are lying. Why is this a lie against the truth?

5. How did James describe this kind of wisdom?

LIVE OUT ...

6. Match the following scriptures with the corresponding characteristics of worldly wisdom.

    Philippians 3:18–19   Sensual

    2 Corinthians 11:13–14   Earthly

    Jude vv. 16–19   Demonic

7. James warned against bitter envy. This type of envy can wear three different faces. Below is a description of each. Journal about a time when your face was marked by these devilish displays of jealousy.

    • Saddened when others got ahead.

    • Gladdened when others fell behind.

    • Maddened when you didn't get all the credit.

8. Boasting in ourselves is lying against the truth because we are taking credit for something God has created. If you are beautiful, thank God for creating you that way. If you have a brilliant mind, honor God with your thoughts. Journal a prayer boasting in God alone by rewriting the following verse: "I will boast only in the LORD.... Come, let us tell of the LORD's greatness; let us exalt his name together" (Ps. 34:2–3 NLT).

9. Circle the three words in these verses that describe how God views worldly wisdom.

    For the wisdom of this world is foolishness with
    God. For it is written, "He catches the wise in their own

LEARN ABOUT ...

6 Demonic

Demonic means demon-like. Demons disseminate errors to seduce believers. One deception is the belief that through mediums people can converse with deceased humans, which is forbidden. "Do not defile yourselves by turning to mediums" (Lev. 19:31 NLT).

7 Jealousy

Bitter envy manifests itself in a striving jealousy that competes with others for attention. Jealousy originates with pride, displays itself in covetousness and evil desires, and ends in destruction. "A heart at peace gives life to the body, but envy rots the bones" (Prov. 14:30 NIV).

8 Boast

While the Bible teaches that we are not to boast in ourselves, we are encouraged to use our lips to boast about others. "Do not boast.... Let another man praise you, and not your own mouth; a stranger, and not your own lips" (Prov. 27:1–2).

LEARN ABOUT ...

9 Worldly

Worldliness is devotion to this world rather than spiritual affairs. Worldly people are so earthly minded they are no heavenly good. Worldliness can be seen in those who elevate ecology over theology and recycling over religion. "Set your mind on things above, not on things on the earth" (Col. 3:2).

craftiness"; and again, "The LORD knows the thoughts of the wise, that they are futile." (1 Cor. 3:19–20)

· · • · ·

Corrie ten Boom told the story of a proud woodpecker who was tapping away at a dead tree when the sky unexpectedly turned black and the thunder began to roll. Undaunted, he went right on working. Suddenly a bolt of lightning struck the old tree, splintering it into hundreds of pieces. Startled but unhurt, the haughty bird flew off, screeching to his feathered friends, "I didn't know there was such incredible power in my beak."[1]

That old woodpecker is a lot like people who think more highly of themselves than they ought. You know the ones—the ones who are so busy bragging about their achievements that they fail to recognize God as the source of those abilities. They suffer from spiritual delusions of grandeur.

James reminded his readers that godly wisdom will be humble—giving God the credit—while demonic wisdom will take all the credit. The next time you're tempted to brag or say, "Look at me!" remember: "This is what the LORD says: 'Don't let the wise boast in their wisdom, or the powerful boast in their power, or the rich boast in their riches. But those who wish to boast should boast in this alone: that they truly know me and understand that I am the LORD who demonstrates unfailing love, and who brings justice and righteousness to the earth, and that I delight in these things'" (Jer. 9:23–24 NLT).

LISTEN TO ...

To have a low opinion of our own merits and to think highly of others is itself an evidence of wisdom.

—Thomas à Kempis

DAY 3
Every Man for Himself

We have been strongly warned against the attitudes of envy and self-seeking based on worldly wisdom. Envy and self-seeking promote a lifestyle of "every man for himself." This lifestyle is completely contrary to Christ's command that we live with an attitude of sacrificial love. Jesus said, "A new commandment I give to you, that you love one another; as I have loved you" (John 13:34).

THE THREE TRADESMEN

A great city was besieged. The frightened inhabitants came together and consulted about the best way to protect their town from the enemy. A Bricklayer recommended bricks as the best material for resistance. A Carpenter proposed timber as a better method of defense. A Hunter said, "Sirs, I beg to differ. There is nothing so good as leather for protection." Because they were confused about which to choose, each man began setting up defenses as he saw fit. On one side of the city, a wall of brick was erected, on another side a wall of wood, and on a third side a wall of leather. But one side was left defenseless, and that's where the enemy came in and conquered the city.

The Moral of the Story Is ... Every man for himself brings destruction.

LIFT UP ...

I praise You, Father, that You are not the author of confusion but of peace. Keep me seeking after Your wisdom as You protect me from the Enemy of my soul. In Jesus' name. Amen.

LEARN ABOUT ...

1 Self-Seeking

Self-seeking can be translated "selfish ambition." The self-seeking person is selfish and loves to stirs up strife in order to get ahead. But God has harsh words for the selfish: "To those who are self-seeking ... [God will render] indignation and wrath, tribulation and anguish" (Rom. 2:8–9).

2 Confusion

The word translated *confusion* means "disorder" and speaks of instability, perplexity, and tumult. Since God is a God of order, His people are noted for their stability and confidence rather than chaotic disorder: "God is not the author of confusion but of peace" (I Cor. 14:33).

4 Every Evil

"Every evil thing" speaks broadly of the results of worldly wisdom. In one sense, *evil* means "worthless or futile." In another sense, it means "vile and contemptible." In other words, nothing good and everything bad are the results of envy and self-seeking.

LOOK AT ...

James showed how worldly wisdom is demonic and devoid of spiritual truth. Now his words show the consequences of living by self-gratification.

READ JAMES 3:16.

For where envy and self-seeking exist, confusion and every evil thing are there. James 3:16

1. List the two types of worldly wisdom repeated here.

2. What happens to the mind of the envious, self-seeking individual?

3. What things surround this type of person?

4. Why do you think envy and self-seeking lead to these results?

5. Early in biblical history, self-seeking people took an action that resulted in great confusion for the world. Read Genesis 11:4–9 to learn about this time.

   a. Explain what these people wanted to build and the self-seeking motive behind it (v. 4).

   b. Who came to inspect this endeavor? What problem did He foresee (vv. 5–6)?

   c. Describe the action taken by the Lord and the result (vv. 7–9).

6. Another story in Genesis tells about a time when envy brought about great evil. Read Genesis 4:1–8. Explain the role you think envy played in this evil event and why.

LIVE OUT ...

7. James strongly warned against self-seeking or selfish ambition. In Philippians 2:3 Paul gave the antidote to these evil attitudes: "Let nothing be done through selfish ambition or conceit, but in lowliness of mind let each esteem others better than himself." With this in mind, honestly examine your heart, then journal the following steps.

Step One: Name a position or attribute you are jealous of someone else possessing. (*Example: I'd be a better president of the PTA than Jane Doe.*)

Step Two: Journal a prayer asking God to give you a humble spirit, "lowliness of mind."

Step Three: In order to esteem others better than yourself, list the good qualities and qualifications of the person you are envious of.

8. One consequence of envy and self-seeking is confusion. People are confused because they think the things of the world—"the works of the flesh"—will satisfy them. Read about the specific works of the flesh found in Galatians 5:19–21, then describe how one of these fleshly works has brought confusion into your life. (*Example: I thought it was fine to watch a psychic on TV, but what she said did not match God's Word.*)

LEARN ABOUT ...

7 Esteem

The world promotes tearing others down. The Bible promotes building others up. When you esteem others, you will be esteemed. "Let not mercy and truth forsake you ... and so find favor and high esteem in the sight of God and man" (Prov. 3:3–4).

8 In the Flesh

The *flesh* refers to our carnal, earthly nature apart from God's divine influence. The flesh represents our evil lusts and desires. The flesh is prone to sin and opposed to God. "So then, those who are in the flesh cannot please God" (Rom. 8:8).

Learn About ...

9 Pardon

Evil is the failure of free beings to conform in character and conduct to the will of God, bringing about sin. However, God offers pardon to all who turn from their evil ways to Him. "You are God, ready to pardon, gracious and merciful" (Neh. 9:17).

9. James warned against allowing evil things to influence us. The prophet Isaiah taught that doing good is a personal choice. Read Isaiah 1:16–17, and explain how we can cease to do evil.

∘ ∘ • ∘ ∘

Imagine a few scenarios that depict the potential evil caused by jealous, self-seeking individuals. Think of the confusion on a football team if jealous guards tried to play quarterback instead of blocking. Serious harm could come to the unprotected quarterback. What if selfish ambition occurred on a commercial airliner? The passengers would be in extreme jeopardy if an ambitious but unqualified stewardess decided to pilot the plane. In politics, confusion and evil would abound if the legislative, executive, and judicial branches failed to carry out their constitutional tasks and seized one another's jobs in a power grab.

In the same way, serious evil can come to our relationships at home, work, or church if we allow envy and self-seeking to rule our life. A wife who doesn't think her husband is "keeping up with the Joneses" might willingly destroy her marriage. A coworker envious of another's promotion could easily obliterate a reputation through slanderous comments. A church member who feels overlooked might split a congregation by spreading seeds of discontent and criticism.

Not surprisingly, self-seeking and envy were the emotions that led to the crucifixion of Jesus Christ. Judas selfishly betrayed Jesus for thirty pieces of silver, and "it was out of envy that the chief priests had handed Jesus over" (Mark 15:10 NIV). But Christ showed a different way: "being in the form of God, ... [He took] the form of a bondservant, and ... humbled Himself and became obedient to the point of death" (Phil. 2:6–8). Let's follow the wisdom of Christ.

Listen To ...

One year of self-surrender will bring larger blessings than fourscore years of selfishness.

—*Henry van Dyke*

DAY 4
Virtues Worth Cultivating

After warning against cultivating worldly values that lead to lives of vice, the book of James turns our attention back to heavenly wisdom—godly actions and attitudes that result in godly virtues.

THE LION AND THE LITTLE MOUSE

A big Lion was awakened when a little Mouse began scurrying up and down his back. The Lion trapped the mouse in his huge paw and opened his jaws to swallow him. "Pardon, O King!" cried the little Mouse. "If you forgive me, I'll never forget it! Perhaps I can do you a good turn someday!" The Lion was so amused at the idea of the little Mouse helping him that he let the Mouse go in peace. Soon after, the Lion was caught in a trap. The hunters tied him to a tree while they searched for a wagon to carry him off. Just then the little Mouse happened to pass by. Seeing the sad plight of the Lion, the Mouse gnawed away the ropes that bound the King of the Beasts. "Was I not right?" said the little Mouse, "I *was* able to help you!" The moral? Little friends may prove great friends.

The Lion went against his nature by listening to the little Mouse and granting him mercy, and that is what saved him in the long run. The same is true for believers: We must stand against our sin nature and against worldly wisdom. When we do, we find heavenly rewards.

The Moral of the Story Is ... Godly virtues are worth cultivating.

LIFT UP ...

Father God, please fill me with Your Spirit and reveal to me the knowledge of Your ways that I might live a pure, holy, fruitful life for Your kingdom and Your glory. In Jesus' name. Amen.

LOOK AT ...

This week's lesson is a study in contrasts: the wisdom of the world as opposed to the wisdom from above. We have learned the dark truth that the world's wisdom results in confusion and every evil thing. Now we step into the light and discover that those who possess the wisdom from above demonstrate living faith through godly attributes.

READ JAMES 3:17.

But the wisdom that is from above is first pure, then peaceable, gentle, willing to yield, full of mercy and good fruits, without partiality and without hypocrisy. James 3:17

1. James used the word *but* to change our focus from wisdom that does not descend from above to wisdom that does come from above. What did James say is the first virtue of godly wisdom? How would you define this in your own words?

2. "Then" what is the second virtue of divine wisdom?

3. Name the next two qualities that are evident in heavenly wisdom.

4. Describe what wisdom from above is filled with.

5. What two vices does this wisdom *not* exhibit?

LEARN ABOUT ...

2 Peaceable

In almost every book of the New Testament, *peaceable* describes (a) harmony between people and nations; (b) freedom from molestation; (c) order in government or church; (d) harmonious relationship with God; (e) rest and contentment in Christ.

3 Yielding

Gentle means "moderate, meek, and mild." *Willing to yield* literally means "easily entreated or persuaded." One who is gentle will patiently listen and easily yield her will to follow God's will. But meek does not mean weak. A gentle believer will not yield to wrongdoing.

4 Fruitful

Fruit refers to deeds that show the power of the Holy Spirit working in believers who abide in Christ. This union generates "the fruit of the Spirit"—Christ's character reproduced in those who believe. Jesus said, "You will know them by their fruits" (Matt. 7:16).

Learn About ...

8 God's Will

The Spirit prays for us to do God's will: "The Spirit intercedes for the saints in accordance with God's will" (Rom. 8:27 NIV). Jesus also prays: "He always lives to make intercession for them" (Heb. 7:25). Won't you make it your prayer to do the will of the Father?

6. Remembering lessons 2 and 5 (James 2:1–13), define again *partiality* and *hypocrisy*.

   Partiality:

   Hypocrisy:

Live Out ...

7. a. The wisdom of God is peaceable, bringing harmony to relationships with both God and people. Name a relationship of yours, in the past or present, that has hit a sour note.

   b. Now journal a prayer to God by rewriting the following passage and asking Him to restore harmony:

   > May God, who gives this patience and encouragement, help you live in complete harmony with each other, as is fitting for followers of Christ Jesus. Then all of you can join together with one voice, giving praise and glory to God, the Father of our Lord Jesus Christ. (Rom. 15:5–6 NLT)

8. Another virtue that demonstrates godly wisdom is a willingness to yield to God's will. When we fail to yield in traffic, we are likely to have a collision. So, too, when we fail to yield to God's will, we are likely to wreck our lives. With this in mind, fill in the chart to discover God's will for you. Draw a yield sign beside the areas in which you have yielded.

SCRIPTURE

GOD'S WILL YIELDED?

Ephesians 6:5–6

1 Thessalonians 4:3

1 Thessalonians 5:18

1 Peter 2:15

2 Peter 3:9

LEARN ABOUT ...

9 Good Fruit

Root determines fruit. Jesus said, "I am the vine, you are the branches. He who abides in Me ... bears much fruit" (John 15:5). Since Jesus, our root and vine, is pure and peaceable, as branches we should yield purity and peace.

9. a. Today James urged us to be fruitful by allowing the Holy Spirit to reproduce Christ's character in us. Circle the virtues of heavenly wisdom you need most in your life right now.

Pure   Peaceable

Gentle   Willing to yield

Full of mercy   Full of good fruits

b. Based on your knowledge of Scripture, journal about a situation when Christ exhibited these virtues in His life. What do you learn from this?

° ° • ° °

We've all heard people say, "God loves you and has a wonderful plan for your life." Somehow we mistakenly conclude "God's will" brings only joy and allows no suffering. But that wasn't the case for Jesus, and it isn't the case for the rest of us.

God's plan included Jesus being born in a lowly stable; growing up in a blue-collar home; walking dusty roads with no place to lay His head; hearing the crowd shout, "Hosanna!" then yell, "Crucify!" God loved Jesus and had a wonderful plan for His life—His death. It wasn't always easy for Jesus to yield to the will of His Father. He struggled at Gethsemane, three times asking God to remove the cup of sorrow. But each time, He yielded to the Father's will: "Not as I will, but as You will" (Matt. 26:39). And so, Jesus was "first pure, then peaceable, gentle, willing to yield, full of mercy and good fruits, without partiality and without hypocrisy."

God loves *you*. He has a wonderful plan for your life—eternal life. But life on earth includes drinking from the cup of sorrow. A bad diagnosis, a rocky relationship, a prodigal child, financial struggles, or other difficulties make you plead as Jesus did, "Let this cup pass from Me!" (v. 39). But God's will won't ever lead you where His grace will not keep you. Therefore, *you* can confidently pray, "Your will be done on earth as it is in heaven" (Matt. 6:10).

LISTEN TO ...

God's will is not an itinerary but an attitude.

—*Andrew Dhuse*

Only God Can Change Our Nature

The book of James has taught us to think and act with godly wisdom. While it is far more natural to act with worldly wisdom, we gain wisdom from above when God dwells in our hearts and plants His character in our lives.

THE SCORPION AND THE LADYBUG

A Scorpion befriended a Ladybug, who became a loyal companion to him. A time came when the Ladybug struggled to cross a dangerous river, so the Scorpion offered to take her to the other side on his back. He had come to care for the Ladybug and had promised he would never harm her, so she accepted his offer of a ride. But, safely across the river, he stung her with his venomous tail. As she lay in greatest pain, she said, "But you promised you would never hurt me. Why did you?" He shrugged and said sadly, "Because it is my Nature." The moral of this story is: regardless of our wishes or intent, it is to our Nature alone that we inevitably succumb.

James reminds us that God wants to change our nature from the inside out, allowing us to make true peace with Him that leads to peace with others.

The Moral of the Story Is … Only God can change our nature.

LIFT UP …

Jesus, I praise You that You are my peace. Thank You for the rich relationship I enjoy with You today. Teach me to plant the fruit of peace in the lives of those You place in my path. In Your name. Amen.

LEARN ABOUT ...

1 Righteousness

Righteousness literally means "straightness." It conforms to the revealed will of God and obeys His Word. To bear the fruit of righteousness, believers will plant God's commands in their hearts, resulting in "fruit" such as giving, praying, fasting, and loving their neighbors.

3 Peace

Peace, literally "to join," implies reconciliation after strife, bringing about wholeness and well-being. Those reconciled to God experience spiritual peace and well-being. "God ... reconcile[d] to himself all things ... by making peace through his blood, shed on the cross" (Col. 1:19–20 NIV).

7 Abiding Fruit

Branches don't struggle to produce fruit; they stay connected to the vine. Likewise, Christians shouldn't strive to bear fruit; they should simply abide in Christ. "As the branch cannot bear fruit of itself, unless it abides in the vine, neither can you, unless you abide in Me" (John 15:4).

LOOK AT ...

The book of James now turns to an agricultural metaphor about righteous living. We discover that Christians who have God's wisdom planted in their hearts will sow a wonderful harvest.

READ JAMES 3:18.

Now the fruit of righteousness is sown in peace by those who make peace. James 3:18

1. What is the fruit or by-product of godly wisdom?

2. Read Hebrews 12:11, and explain how God cultivates the fruit of righteousness in His children.

3. According to James, how is this fruit sown?

4. Who sows (plants) the fruit of righteousness?

5. According to Matthew 5:9, why are peacemakers blessed?

6. a. Read 2 Corinthians 9:10. Who supplies the "seed" sown?

   b. In what two ways does He ensure that there is enough for everyone?

LIVE OUT ...

7. Today we discovered that Christians can bear "the fruit of righteousness." Fill in the chart to discover other fruits we can produce.

SCRIPTURE   **SPIRITUAL FRUIT**

John 4:35–36

Romans 6:22

Galatians 5:22–23

Colossians 1:10

Hebrews 13:15

LEARN ABOUT ...

8 Pruning

Pruning away branches is the method Jesus uses to increase fruitfulness. "He prunes the branches that do bear fruit so they will produce even more" (John 15:2 NLT). God often uses His Word, His Spirit, and providential circumstances to "prune" or help His children become more productive.

9 Reconciliation

Reconcile means to "restore to friendship, harmony, or communion." God desires us to be reconciled to Him and to other human beings. "God ... has reconciled us to Himself through Jesus Christ, and has given us the ministry of reconciliation" (2 Cor. 5:18).

8. Sometimes trees are pruned to produce more fruit. Christians, too, are chastened and disciplined to yield righteous fruit. Using PRUNE as an acrostic, list some unfruitful behaviors God has cut away in your life, helping you reap a harvest of righteousness.

P (*Example: pride*)

R

U

N

E

9. We have learned that peace is not a state of mind or the absence of war. Instead, peace carries the idea of reconciliation between conflicting parties. With this in mind, journal through the steps found in Matthew 5.

Step One: Write about one of your relationships that has been severed through strife: "If you bring your gift to the altar, and there remember that your brother has something against you ..." (v. 23).

Step Two: Write about what you'll do *today* to make things right with that person: "Leave your gift there before the altar, and go your way. First be reconciled to your brother" (v. 24).

Step Three: Write a prayer thanking God for making you a peacemaker: "Then come and offer your gift" (v. 24).

∘ ∘ ● ∘ ∘

Charles Dickens, the great English novelist whose works include *A Christmas Carol*, *Oliver Twist*, and *A Tale of Two Cities*, and another great writer of the Victorian age, William Makepeace Thackeray, the author of *Vanity Fair*, both loved to write about London and its often inequitable social structure. The two had been friendly rivals until they quarreled over an unknown matter.

Just before Christmas in 1863, they happened to meet in London but passed quickly by, refusing to speak to one another. Unhappy at their estrangement, Thackeray turned back to his old and dear friend, seized his hand, and told him he couldn't bear the coldness that existed between them. Dickens was so touched by the gesture that his anger and bitterness faded away. The two men were friends once again. On Christmas Eve, Thackeray died suddenly of an aneurysm. Dickens was one of the illustrious people to attend the funeral at Westminster Abbey. Sir Thomas Martin, who had been with the men that wintry day in London, said, "I saw Dickens … standing at the grave of his rival. He must have rejoiced, I thought, that he had shaken hands so warmly a few days before." Nearly seven years later, Dickens himself was buried at Westminster Abbey.

William Thackeray lived up to his middle name "Makepeace" and went to his grave at peace with his friend. And Charles Dickens could say along with his famous character Tiny Tim, "God bless us every one!"

LISTEN TO …

Sowing seeds of peace is like sowing beans. You don't know why it works; you just know it does. Seeds are planted, and topsoils of hurt are shoved away.

—*Max Lucado*

LESSON NINE

War of the Worlds!
James 4:1–10

"War is hell." I (Penny) know this adage is true because my father is a Korean War veteran. As a young girl, I would hear him scream in the middle of the night and anxiously listen as my mom soothed him back to sleep. In those days we hadn't heard of post-traumatic stress disorder (PTSD). However, there's no denying the long-term effects the war had on my dad.

PTSD is triggered by exposure to terrifying events. It often occurs among soldiers who have been in combat situations. Many people with PTSD experience flashbacks and night-mares. They also experience emotional numbness, sleep disturbances, depression, anxiety, irritability, or outbursts of anger. The effects of war are physical and emotional, long lasting and far reaching. War shapes the lives of those who have gone into battle and impacts their families and friends as well.

There are other kinds of wars that are just as traumatic as military conflict. They, too, cause adverse side effects. In the book of James, we have read about the war of the worlds—the kingdom of God against the kingdoms of men. This conflict had many battlefronts: war of words, class war, and spiritual warfare. The church was in the trenches, and it was tough going!

But while war is hell, peace is heavenly. If you are suffering the trauma of kingdom war-fare, look up! Jesus said, "In Me you may have peace. In the world you will have tribulation; but be of good cheer, I have overcome the world" (John 16:33).

Day 1: James 4:1–2	DECLARATION OF WAR
Day 2: James 4:3–4	ENEMIES OF GOD
Day 3: James 4:5–6	PSYCHOLOGICAL WARFARE
Day 4: James 4:7–9a	RESISTANCE MOVEMENT
Day 5: James 4:9b–10	UNCONDITIONAL SURRENDER

DAY 1

Declaration of War

LEARN ABOUT ...

1 Wars

Fights lead to war; wars are serious disputes resulting in combat. James used these words as metaphors for personal relationships in the church, which had become combative in nature. "His words are as smooth as butter, but in his heart is war" (Ps. 55:21 NLT).

LIFT UP ...

Father, there is war without and war within. I am so thankful that You have sent the Prince of Peace to overcome my flesh and the world. Teach me to walk in peace with my brothers and sisters in Christ. In Jesus' name. Amen.

LOOK AT ...

Last week we learned that worldly wisdom causes conflict while godly wisdom promotes peace. Now we examine more closely the source of conflicts among people.

READ JAMES 4:1–2.

Where do wars and fights come from among you? Do they not come from your desires for pleasure that war in your members? You lust and do not have. You murder and covet and cannot obtain. You fight and war. Yet you do not have because you do not ask. James 4:1–2

1. What was the first hypothetical question James asked?

2. Why do you think James felt compelled to address the issue of wars and fights among the people?

LEARN ABOUT ...

3 Pleasure

The Greek word translated *pleasure* stems from the word *hedonon*, from which we get the English words *hedonist* and *hedonism*. It conveys the idea of pursuing sensual desire and passion. God made us with a capacity for pleasure. Yet, uncontrolled desires for pleasure—hedonism—cause great conflict.

---

5 Lust

Lust is desire for the forbidden or an obsessive sexual craving. Although there are legitimate desires for which God makes provision, lust is desiring things that are contrary to God's will. "Make no provision for the flesh, to fulfill its lusts" (Rom. 13:14).

---

6 Covetous

To *covet* is to wish for what one does not have; also translated "greed." Covetousness lies in discontentment with what one has. "Take heed and beware of covetousness, for one's life does not consist in the abundance of the things he possesses" (Luke 12:15).

3. James answered his first question with another question. According to the second question, where do wars and fights come from?

4. Where is the battle waged?

5. James gave a list of desires that lead to conflict. Fill in the chart to show what you do and why you do it.

WHAT YOU DO	WHY YOU DO IT

6. a. James said that wars begin with lust and covetousness. Read Genesis 26:12–22. In what three ways did the Philistines respond to Isaac's prosperity?

   v. 14 _____

   v. 15 _____

   v. 16 _____

   b. How did their quarrel continue to escalate, and how did it finally end (vv. 17–22)?

7. According to the last phrase in James 4:2, what is one reason we don't have what we desire?

LIVE OUT ...

8. a. Wars begin with "desires for pleasure." *Merriam-Webster's Collegiate Dictionary* gives three different definitions for pleasure. After each definition list some things that you find pleasurable.

Sensual gratification:

Frivolous amusement:

Source of delight or joy:

b. Our pleasures can turn to poison when they become excessive, obsessive, or aggressive. Journal about a situation when your desire for pleasure became poisonous. (*Example: my desire for amusement at the movies took away my discernment to abstain from watching unscriptural sex and unbridled obscenities.*)

9. James warned that lust leads to conflict. Paul said, "Walk in the Spirit, and you shall not fulfill the lust of the flesh" (Gal. 5:16). The following are Paul's lists of fleshly and spiritual behaviors. Circle the ways you've indulged in the flesh, then underline the fruit of the Spirit you've displayed.

Lust of the Flesh: "Sexual immorality, impurity, lustful pleasures, idolatry, sorcery … quarreling, jealousy, outbursts of anger, selfish ambition, dissension, division, envy, drunkenness" (Gal. 5:19–21 NLT).

Fruit of the Spirit: "Love, joy, peace, patience, kindness, goodness, faithfulness, gentleness, and self-control" (Gal. 5:22–23 NLT).

10. Today we discovered that conflicts escalate because of prayerlessness—"you do not have because you do not ask." Make a short list of the things you don't have but wish you did. Beside each item, journal a prayer asking God to be your provider.

LEARN ABOUT …

9 Selfless

Human beings have three favorite words: *I, me,* and *mine.* Lust and covetousness are rooted in selfishness, but godliness has its roots in selflessness. "Because He laid down His life for us, … we also ought to lay down our lives for the brethren" (1 John 3:16).

10 Provider

Too often God's children look for provision in all the wrong places, when God has a storehouse of supplies to match every need. "My God shall supply all your need according to His riches in glory by Christ Jesus" (Phil. 4:19).

° ° • ° °

Sibling rivalry is as old as Cain and Abel. So it's no surprise that the tug of war between my (Lenya) sister, Suzanne, and me began the day I was born. It started with a fight for our parents' attention. She thought Dad liked me best, and I felt that Mom favored her. Our conflict moved from relationships to possessions. One Christmas Grandma gave us matching baby dolls: hers was blue and mine was pink. But one day Suzanne discovered the blue doll's hair was missing and insisted that *hers* was the pink doll. I was left crying, clutching the bald blue doll. Thankfully we grew out of our animosity and now are the best of friends, unlike the sisters in the following story.

Two spinster sisters lived together. Because of an argument, they stopped speaking to each other. Unwilling to move out of their house, they used the same rooms, ate at the same table, and slept in the same bedroom. A chalk line divided their areas into two halves. Each could come and go, cook and eat, sew and read without ever crossing over into her sister's domain.

God's children can experience sibling rivalry too. Instead of dividing homes, they divide churches because of jealousy, envy, and strife. Paul pleads with God's kids, "Brothers and sisters … live in harmony with each other. Let there be no divisions in the church. Rather, be of one mind" (1 Cor. 1:10 NLT).

LISTEN TO ...

The wars that rage within the world are a reflection of the wars that rage inside people.

—*Leighton Ford*

DAY 2

Enemies of God

We entered the world just one week apart that cold wintry December in 1957. She was to be born breech but flipped during delivery and came out headfirst. I (Lenya) was headed in the right direction but at birth changed my mind and came out backwards. We are both left-handed and five-foot-seven and have ash-blonde hair and hazel eyes. That's why my cousin Valerie and I named ourselves "twin cousins." We were inseparable—until Gretchen moved into the neighborhood.

Gretchen was a doctor's daughter and had all the cool toys, *Mystery Date* being the most coveted game of all. Everyone wanted to be her friend. But Gretchen liked to play favorites and develop exclusive friendships. If Valerie was "in," then I was "out," and vice versa. The one who was Gretchen's friend was forced to treat the other cousin like a foe—no verbal exchanges allowed. We'd even walk on the opposite side of the street to avoid the enemy. But one bright day, Valerie and I realized that blood *is* thicker than water. Reunited we proclaimed, "Who needs Gretchen and her toys anyway?"

In our passage this week, James declared that some friendships just don't mix. Like oil and water, God and this world are not compatible. We must make a choice: will we be God's friend or His foe? The sacrifice of Jesus has made us members of God's family, and His blood is thicker than any friendship this world has to offer.

LIFT UP ...

Jesus, I am so grateful that You are my best friend. Please keep me from friendship with the world and draw me ever closer to You. In Your name. Amen.

LOOK AT ...

Yesterday we discovered that conflicts and wars begin with selfish desires. Today we discover that lustful desires also result in a declaration of war against God.

Learn About ...

2 Amiss

Amiss means "off target" in a physical or moral sense. Prayers go amiss—off target—because of wrong motives. But our Father hits the bull's-eye every time. God doesn't always give us what we want; He gives us what we need. He'll say no to keep us on target.

3 Adultery

James was speaking metaphorically about spiritual, not sexual, infidelity. When people disobeyed God or practiced idolatry, the prophets accused them of spiritual adultery. The Living Bible interprets this verse, "You are like an unfaithful wife who loves her husband's enemies."

4 The World

The world does not refer to planet Earth, but to the spiritual reality of the humanistic, Satan-inspired value system opposed to God. The world system will entice us to be unfaithful to God. "He shall judge the world with righteousness, and the peoples with His truth" (Ps. 96:13).

7 On Target

Prayer doesn't change God's mind, but it changes our hearts. When we pray for passing pleasure, our motives are wrong. When we pray for God's glory, our motives are on target.

Read James 4:3–4.

You ask and do not receive, because you ask amiss, that you may spend it on your pleasures. Adulterers and adulteresses! Do you not know that friendship with the world is enmity with God? Whoever therefore wants to be a friend of the world makes himself an enemy of God. James 4:3–4

1. How does God respond to some of our requests? Why?

2. What impure motive hinders our prayers?

3. What startling label did James give those consumed by the pursuit of pleasure?

4. If you become the world's friend, how does that affect your relationship to God?

5. What phrase revealed that this is something James's readers should have already known?

6. Therefore, what conclusion did James reach? To whom did this apply?

Live Out ...

7. Sometimes our prayers go amiss because we pray with impure motives. Draw a line connecting the scriptures with the actions that will get our prayers back on target.

Mark 11:24	Keep commandments
Mark 11:25	Ask in Jesus' name
John 14:13	Forgive
John 15:7	Believe
1 John 3:22	Abide in Christ

8. a. James said that Christians who get too friendly with the world are committing spiritual adultery. Read Jeremiah 3:6–14. How did Israel and Judah commit spiritual adultery (vv. 6–8)?

   b. What two options did these adulterous people face (vv. 8, 12, 14)?

   c. Based on what you've learned today, are you being faithful or faithless toward God?

9. a. *Idolatry* is putting anyone or anything before your devotion to God. Describe a potential area in your life that could turn into idolatry. (*Example: I always put my children first. If their sporting events are on Sunday, we skip church. I'm so busy with their schedules that I don't have time to read my Bible and pray.*)

   b. Journal a prayer to God by rewriting the following verse; let Him know that you will choose Him first: "No one can serve two masters. For you will hate one and love the other; you will devoted to one and despise the other. You cannot serve both God and [anything else, including] money" (Matt. 6:24 NLT).

LEARN ABOUT …

8 Idolatry

In the Old Testament, idolatry is the worship of something created instead of the Creator Himself. In the New Testament, idolatry is the replacement of God in the mind of the worshipper. Therefore, anything that comes between God and us is an idol.

9 God's Friend

Obey God, and you'll be His friend. Jesus said, "You are my friends if you do what I command. I no longer call you slaves, because a master doesn't confide in his slaves. Now you are my friends, since I have told you everything the Father told me" (John 15:14–15 NLT).

○ ○ ● ○ ○

History is full of traitors, from Judas to Benedict Arnold. What makes traitors so grievous is that they are people we trusted. They are our friends, our neighbors, and our countrymen.

John Walker Lindh seemed like an all-American boy on a quest for truth. But when the US Army found him consorting with the enemy in an Afghani prison camp, it was apparent that he had succumbed to wicked lies. His motto changed from, "In God we trust" to "In Osama we hope." CNN reports that Walker Lindh even received personal thanks from Osama bin Laden for "taking part in jihad." He went from being a tourist to a terrorist who is now serving a twenty-year prison sentence for providing services to the Taliban and carrying a weapon. No one knows what caused this misguided youth to become a malcontented coconspirator. Was it his early health problems? His parents' divorce? Or maybe he got in over his head, as his lawyer suggested. The truth is that most people with health problems and unstable families are loyal citizens.

Some things are black and white. You're either a patriot or a traitor. You're either God's friend or His enemy. Jesus said, "He who is not with Me is against Me, and he who does not gather with Me scatters abroad" (Matt. 12:30). God wants to know—are you His friend or foe?

LISTEN TO ...

Man draws the nearer to God as he withdraws further from the consolations of this world.... Oh, how swiftly the glory of the world passes away!

—*Thomas à Kempis*

DAY 3

Psychological Warfare

"Capture their minds, and their hearts and souls will follow" is the PSYOP motto. Psychological operations (known as PSYOP in the United States) are military tactics that convey selected information to enemy audiences to influence their emotions and reasoning. PSYOP employ two key tactics: (1) diminish morale or the will to resist; (2) give opponents a "carrot and stick" approach—cooperate and be rewarded; resist and face the consequences. Here are some examples.

During World War II, Toyko Rose's radio broadcasts became a major means of disseminating pro-Japanese propaganda to demoralize the Allied troops. During the Gulf War, the Allied coalition flew loudspeaker aerial missions around Faylaka Island, broadcasting the message to surrender. The next day 1,405 Iraqis surrendered to the US Marines. In the recent war on terrorism, US planes dropped the leaflet "Taliban Reign of Fear" over Afghanistan. On it Muslim leader Osama bin Laden's face was transformed into a fearful snarling Jinn. The *Koran* identifies the Jinn as creatures that practice deceit to do evil. Associating the Jinn with al-Qaeda and the Taliban was meant to capture the minds of the Afghans and show that these oppressive leaders had turned toward evil.

God knows that those who have rejected Him have made themselves His enemies, and He desires to capture their hearts, minds, and souls. Paul said, "Let God transform you into a new person by changing the way you think" (Rom. 12:2 NLT). God even uses the "carrot and stick" approach—draw near to Him and be rewarded, or reject Him and meet resistance.

LIFT UP ...

Father, I am grateful for Your grace. I'm so undeserving of the many benefits You've blessed me with, yet You promise even "more grace." Your grace is amazing! In Jesus' name. Amen.

LEARN ABOUT ...

3 Godly Jealousy

Jealousy involves vigilance in guarding someone we love. A spouse who is jealous takes great care to guard the relationship from interlopers. In the same way, God guards His relationship with His bride—the church—to ensure that our affections are for Him alone.

5 Amazing Grace

Grace is undeserved favor. It is amazing that God would sign a peace treaty with wretched sinners like us. Yet, when you accept Jesus as your Lord and Savior, God pours out more grace than you could ever imagine. "Where sin abounded, grace abounded much more" (Rom. 5:20).

6 Attitude?

Pride says, "I don't need God." Humility says, "I can't live without God." Pride pushes God away; humility reaches up to God and out to others. Human pride in the garden of Eden brought death; God's humility in the garden of Gethsemane brought eternal life.

LOOK AT ...

This week we've learned that selfishness leads to wars with others and ultimately with God. Today we learn that God jealously desires for us to surrender to Him in a spirit of humility.

READ JAMES 4:5–6.

Or do you think that the Scripture says in vain, "The Spirit who dwells in us yearns jealously"? But He gives more grace. Therefore He says: "God resists the proud, but gives grace to the humble." James 4:5–6

1. Is it possible for the Scripture to say things "in vain"? Explain.

2. Where does God's Spirit live?

3. How does He respond to spiritual infidelity?

4. James said that God's Spirit lives in us. Read 1 Corinthians 6:15–20.

   a. What phrases reveal the believer's intimate relationship with God (vv. 15, 17, 19)?

   b. What does this passage add to our understanding of why God hates spiritual adultery?

5. According to James, what is God willing to give instead of condemnation? How much is He willing to give?

6. How did James say your attitude affects God's response to you?

LIVE OUT ...

7. a. Most people think jealousy is a negative trait. But in James we find that God yearns jealously for us in a positive way. The apostle Paul also yearned for the early church to stay pure and faithful: "I am jealous for you with godly jealousy. For I have betrothed you to one husband, that I may present you as a chaste virgin to Christ" (2 Cor. 11:2). Name someone whom you long to see stay spiritually pure.

   b. Journal a prayer, based on 2 Corinthians 11:2, asking God to keep that person's faith unsullied by the world.

8. Many people associate grace with salvation alone. But we have learned that God gives *more* grace. Check the ways in which you need more grace.

   ____ Grace for "different gifts" (Rom. 12:6 NIV)
   ____ Grace "for every good work" (2 Cor. 9:8)
   ____ Grace "sufficient for you … in weakness" (2 Cor. 12:9)
   ____ Grace for "eternal encouragement and good hope" (2 Thess. 2:16 NIV)
   ____ Grace "to help us when we need it" (Heb. 4:16 NLT)

9. The prideful meet resistance while the humble find grace. Read 2 Chronicles 7:14 to learn how to humble yourself before God and what will result.

   a. What three things must we do to humble ourselves?

   b. What three things does God promise to those who humble themselves?

LEARN ABOUT ...

7 Yearning

Yearn means "to experience longing or craving; feel tenderness and compassion." After a lengthy separation, Joseph "yearned for his brother; … and sought somewhere to weep" (Gen. 43:30). A woman facing the loss of her child "yearned with compassion for her son" (1 Kings 3:26).

8 Abundant Grace

God has an "abundance of grace" (Rom. 5:17). In other words, no matter what situation you may find yourself in, God has more than enough grace to help. "The LORD will give grace and glory; no good thing will He withhold from those who walk uprightly" (Ps. 84:11).

9 Humility

Greek philosophers despised humility, for it implied weakness. But biblical humility grows out of the recognition that all we have and are comes from God. Jesus was the supreme example of humility: "being found in appearance as a man, He humbled Himself" (Phil. 2:8).

c. Journal about a situation where your stubborn pride has met God's resistance. Then write a prayer to God humbling yourself and asking for His blessings.

∘ ˙ • ˙ ∘

Giovanni Bernardone was born in Italy to a wealthy cloth merchant. His father, Pietro, was furious that Giovanni's mother had named the boy in honor of John the Baptist; thus, Pietro renamed the child Francesco, or Francis. Francis led a pampered and frivolous life, dreaming of heroic exploits. During adolescence he joined the militia and was captured during his first battle. He endured a year in prison. Upon his release, Francis encountered a poor leper and reconsidered his religious beliefs. Imitating Christ, he renounced all his belongings, including the clothes he was wearing, and accepted total poverty. Now we know him as Saint Francis of Assisi, the founder of the Franciscans, who devote themselves to preaching and caring for the poor and sick.

Someone once asked Saint Francis how he was able to accomplish so much. He replied, "The Lord looked down from heaven … and said, 'Where can I find the weakest, the littlest, the poorest man on the face of the earth?' Then He saw me and said, 'Now I've found him, and will work through him. He won't be proud of it. He'll see that I am only using him because of his … insignificance.'"

James said that God resists the proud but gives grace to the humble. Because of his wealth and position, Francis started out as a proud young man seeking only adventure and acclaim. By humbling himself, he was given great grace to change and live a life that counted for eternity.

Listen To …

Pride is spiritual cancer; it eats the very possibility of love or contentment, or even common sense.

—*C. S. Lewis*

Resistance Movement

Why do humans resist authority? The Pilgrims on the *Mayflower* resisted the oppressive demands of the church and government by fleeing Europe. The early American colonists resisted England's taxation without representation by dumping tea into Boston Harbor. Rather than submit to India's Salt Acts, which forced impoverished citizens to buy salt at exorbitant prices from the government, Mahatma Gandhi protested by walking to the sea to make salt from seawater. In the 1960s, the hippies, whose resistance anthem was "Make Love Not War," orchestrated "sit-ins" and picketed college campuses. In every household, on a daily basis, children resist their parents' authority.

The original resistance movement was when Satan attempted to stage a coup against God's authority in heaven. He said, "I will ascend above the heights of the clouds, I will be like the Most High" (Isa. 14:14). It is believed that he enlisted one-third of the angels to join his ranks. But it didn't work, and "that serpent of old, called the Devil and Satan, who deceives the whole world; he was cast to the earth, and his angels were cast out with him" (Rev. 12:9).

Though he was cast out, his resistance movement of sin continues. Satan entices humanity to resist God using every trick in the book. Today the book of James reminds us that God, our ultimate authority figure, wants us to learn how to resist the resistor.

LIFT UP ...

Lord, my desire is to draw near to You. I mourn over the times I have been resistant and disobedient. I rejoice that You are willing to forgive me. In Jesus' name. Amen.

LOOK AT ...

Yesterday we learned that in order to make peace with God, we must wage war against ourselves—humble ourselves before God. Today we learn other steps toward peace with God.

LEARN ABOUT ...

1 Submit

Submission speaks of lowering, humbling, or being compliant. This military term means to yield oneself to the authority or will of another. A person with living faith willingly submits to God in the same way that a private willingly submits to a general.

2 Resist

Another military term, *resist*, means to battle against, set oneself against, exert opposition. People who have made themselves friends with God have become Satan's enemies. "Your enemy the devil prowls around like a roaring lion looking for someone to devour" (1 Pet. 5:8 NIV).

7 Lament and Repent

Repentance is turning away from sin and turning back to God. It includes a change of mind and feelings of "godly sorrow" for sin. "Godly sorrow brings repentance that leads to salvation and leaves no regret" (2 Cor. 7:10 NIV).

8 Rebel

To *rebel* is "to oppose or disobey authority." Rebellion can be open defiance or subversive resistance. God ranks spiritual rebellion among one of the worst sins. "Rebellion is as sinful as witchcraft, and stubbornness as bad as worshiping idols" (1 Sam. 15:23 NLT).

READ JAMES 4:7–9A.

Therefore submit to God. Resist the devil and he will flee from you. Draw near to God and He will draw near to you. Cleanse your hands, you sinners; and purify your hearts, you double-minded. Lament and mourn and weep! James 4:7–9a

1. Yesterday we learned that God gives more grace. "Therefore" James exhorted his readers to do what two things?

2. What does God promise those who resist the Devil?

3. Skim Matthew 4:1–11. What "weapon" did Christ use to resist Satan?

4. It is not enough to "resist the devil." What else must we do to make peace with God?

5. What does God promise if we do this?

6. Explain what sinners and double-minded people need to do.

7. With what attitude should we repent?

8. James encouraged believers to submit themselves to God. Submission is an attitude of yielding to one in authority. Using SUBMIT as an acrostic, list some of the areas in your life that need to be yielded to God.

S

U

B

M

I

T

9. We have been exhorted to resist Satan. Think of an area in your life where you have had difficulty resisting Satan. First Peter 5:8–9 (NLT) gives three practical steps to stand in opposition to the enemy. Journal about how these steps can help you resist Satan more effectively in the future.

"Watch out for your great enemy, the devil."

"Stand firm against him."

"Be strong in your faith."

10. We have learned that repentance is not just feeling sorry for yourself but being sorry that you've sinned against God. It is not regret for getting caught but remorse that brings change. Fill in the chart to discover more.

SCRIPTURE	REPENTANCE INCLUDES
Job 42:6	
Ezekiel 18:30–32	
Mark 1:15	
Acts 26:20	

LEARN ABOUT ...

9 Armor

Christians battle against a great Enemy. However, God is more powerful than our foe. He provides impenetrable armor to protect us. "Put on all of God's armor so that you will be able to stand firm against all strategies of the devil" (Eph. 6:11 NLT).

10 Repentance

James spoke of both inward and outward repentance: "cleanse your hands" and "purify your hearts." Jesus told pretentious religious leaders that repentance begins in the heart: "Outwardly you look like righteous people, but inwardly your hearts are filled with hypocrisy and lawlessness" (Matt. 23:28 NLT).

○ ○ ● ○ ○

A teacher asked, "What does the word *repent* mean?" A little boy responded, "It's being sorry for your sins." Then a little girl raised her hand and added, "It's being sorry enough to quit." I experienced both of these aspects of repentance after a sad experience at the happiest place on earth.

During the summer of 1978, I (Lenya) was an "almost Christian," attending church and reading my Bible. But I had not yet repented of all my sins. Believe it or not, I was unsure whether smoking marijuana was sinful. A misguided churchgoer had advised me that God gave us all the herbs on earth for our enjoyment.

When my friends pulled out a joint on the gondola ride at Disneyland, I didn't participate, but I didn't disapprove of their behavior either. As our gondola reached the Matterhorn, the Disneyland police were waiting for us. They held me guilty by association. After calling our parents, they kicked us out of the park. I was not only sorry we were caught; I felt genuine repentance for not being a better witness. From this event I learned that submitting to God means not only changing our actions but also changing our minds about sin.

LISTEN TO ...

True repentance has a double aspect; it looks upon things past with a weeping eye, and upon the future with a watchful eye.

—*Robert Smith*

DAY 5

Unconditional Surrender

I (Penny) was miserable. I thought I wanted out of my marriage, so I gave my husband, Kerry, an ultimatum: "Go to church, pay more attention to the family, or I'm out of here." Amazingly, he did everything I asked. Soon he surrendered to God and accepted Jesus as his Savior.

But the problems didn't end. I harbored bitterness. We had financial struggles that seemed insurmountable. Though I was attending a Bible study and trying to be a godly wife and mother, I was despondent. One night I told Kerry "I don't trust this change in you. I'm completely unhappy." He replied, "I'm committed to making things work. I don't know how we'll get out of this mess, but I love you and the kids."

Our evening devotion had been, "Humble yourselves under the mighty hand of God, that He may exalt you in due time, casting all your care upon Him, for He cares for you" (1 Pet. 5:6–7). In desperation I said, "Maybe we haven't really humbled ourselves before God. Let's confess our fears and doubts." And we did. We cried tears of sorrow and confessed the ways we had failed God and one another. I don't know how long we lay there, praying and crying. Finally we rose and looked deep into each other's eyes. I knew then that we would make it. We had surrendered our lives unconditionally to God. I trust Him to work things out. And He does.

LIFT UP ...

Holy Father, sometimes there are so many battles going on in my heart that I don't know whether to laugh or cry. Let me know the joy of humbly repenting and surrendering all to You. In Jesus' name. Amen.

LEARN ABOUT ...

I Laugh or Cry?

There is a time to weep and a time to laugh. The wise woman knows the appropriate time for each. Sinners should cry; repenters can celebrate. "[There is] a time to weep, and a time to laugh; a time to mourn, and a time to dance" (Eccles. 3:4).

3 Now or Later?

Laugh now, and you'll cry later: "The angels will come ... and cast [the wicked] into the furnace of fire. There will be wailing and gnashing of teeth" (Matt. 13:49–50). Cry now and you'll laugh later: "Blessed are you who weep now, for you shall laugh" (Luke 6:21).

5 Up or Down?

The way down is the way up. Humble yourself and let God lift you up, or lift yourself up and let God take you down. "For the day of the LORD of hosts shall come upon everything proud and lofty, upon everything lifted up—and it shall be brought low" (Isa. 2:12).

LOOK AT ...

We have found that submitting to God brings true repentance. Now we discover that submitting to God also means humbling ourselves before Him.

READ JAMES 4:9B–10.

Let your laughter be turned to mourning and your joy to gloom. Humble yourselves in the sight of the Lord, and He will lift you up. James 4:9b–10

1. What is the difference between the Christian and non-Christian response to sin?

2. Read Proverbs 14:9, 12–13. Explain the difference between the foolish and upright person.

3. James encouraged us to mourn over our sin. Fill in the following chart to discover how God blesses those who mourn and weep.

SCRIPTURE	BLESSINGS OF MOURNING
Psalm 6:8	
Psalm 30:5	
Psalm 126:6	

4. Instead of laughing, what should we do? Before whom?

5. What does God promise those who humble themselves?

Live Out ...

6. a. Today we learned that laughter can be good or bad, depending on what you think is funny. Check off the following situations that make you laugh.

    ____ A dirty joke

    ____ The calamity of others

    ____ Answered prayer

    ____ My husband's sense of humor

    ____ With my friends

    ____ Because I was nervous

    ____ When I was tickled

    ____ Behind someone's back

    ____ At a funny movie

    ____ At my friends

    b. Journal about a time when you laughed at an inappropriate situation. How did it make you or others feel later?

7. God comforts those who mourn over sin. Isaiah 61:1–3 reveals God's exchange program for the truly repentant. Read this passage and list the evidence of godly sorrow and God's response.

    Godly Sorrow
    (*Example: poor in spirit*)

    God's Response
    (*Example: preach glad tidings*)

8. This week the message of humility has been repeated. When Scripture repeats something, it is intended to get our attention and is God's way of emphasizing a point. Peter closely repeated James's exhortation about humility. Using 1 Peter 5:5 as a template,

Learn About ...

6 Sympathetic

It has been said, "Laugh and the world laughs with you; cry and you cry alone." A Christian will laugh and cry with others. We are to be sympathetic. "Be happy with those who are happy, and weep with those who weep" (Rom. 12:15 NLT).

7 Comfort

God comforts us with motherly tenderness and fatherly compassion. Motherly? "As a mother comforts her child, so will I comfort you" (Isa. 66:13 NIV). Fatherly? "The Father of compassion and the God of all comfort, who comforts us in all our troubles" (2 Cor. 1:3–4 NIV).

8 Humiliation

There's a difference between humility and humiliation. The humble person willingly lowers herself to positions of service, like Jesus, who became a man that He might serve. Humiliation means to be reduced to a lower position in others' eyes. You have a choice: will you be humble or be humiliated?

journal a prayer to God asking Him to strip you of pride and then clothe you with humility: "Be clothed with humility, for 'God resists the proud, but gives grace to the humble.'"

○ ○ ● ○ ○

A cocky seminary graduate was given the opportunity to try out for the pastorate in a simple country church. The week before his big debut, he purchased a new suit to dazzle the congregation and had his hair styled in the latest fashion. The day of his first sermon, he strutted up to the pulpit full of self-confidence. He pulled out his copious notes full of wit and wisdom and began to deliver his message. But suddenly he was struck with stage fright and began to stutter. The words simply would not come out. Finally, he burst into tears and rushed off the platform in utter humiliation.

There sitting in the front row were two elderly no-nonsense farm wives. They had watched in silence as the young man made his grand entrance. But when he slunk from the stage, one remarked to the other, "If he would have come in the way he went out, he would have gone out the way he came in." It was her way of saying two very profound things. First, "Pride comes before the fall," and second, "The humble will be exalted."

Each of us faces the same opportunity as this young preacher: humble ourselves or be humiliated. If we trust in ourselves, our talents, or our abilities, we're headed downhill fast. But when we humbly offer ourselves to God, acknowledging our utter dependence upon Him, and give Him credit for the gifts He has given, we are on our way up.

LISTEN TO ...

It is not to the humiliated but the humble that God gives grace. But he is humble who turns humiliation into humility.... For it is the possession of a joyful and genuine humility that alone enables us to receive grace.

—*Bernard of Clairvaux*

What You Don't Know Can Hurt You

James 4:11–17

Some clichés make sense. "A place for everything, and everything in its place" is a great way of saying, "Get organized." "Absence makes the heart grow fonder" means what it says: we miss those who are out of sight but not out of mind.

But some catch phrases just don't ring true. The 1960s movie *Love Story* propagated the lamest sentiment ever uttered: "Love means never having to say you're sorry." Picture actress Ali MacGraw batting her eyelashes as she spoke those heartfelt but completely absurd words. If, as the saying goes, "You always hurt the ones you love," then you probably need to tell them you're sorry.

Another untrue adage is, "What you don't know can't hurt you." Really? If you don't know you've got cancer, does that mean you won't die? Does not knowing your bank account is empty stop the checks from bouncing? Ignorance is *not* bliss. James wanted his readers to know that what you don't know *can* hurt you! Some members of the early church judged one another, assuming they knew the motives of others. Some were making grand plans for a future they could not predict. Still others assumed they knew God's will when, in fact, they had no clue. We will learn that the worst ignorance is a lack of knowing ourselves—thinking we're something we are not. This week discover that what you don't know really *can* hurt you.

Day 1: James 4:11–12	**YOU DON'T KNOW ANOTHER'S HEART**
Day 2: James 4:13–14	**YOU DON'T KNOW WHAT'S GOOD FOR YOU**
Day 3: James 4:15	**YOU DON'T KNOW GOD'S WILL**
Day 4: James 4:16	**YOU DON'T KNOW YOURSELF**
Day 5: James 4:17	**YOU DO KNOW RIGHT FROM WRONG**

DAY I
You Don't Know
Another's Heart

LEARN ABOUT ...

I Evil Speaking

Speaking evil means to slander another person. This sin of the tongue includes thoughtless, critical, derogatory, or untrue speech against others. "Let your speech always be with grace, seasoned with salt, that you may know how you ought to answer each one" (Col. 4:6).

LIFT UP ...

Father, I am glad that You alone can judge because You alone are just. Thank You for combining mercy with judgment. Help me to extend mercy instead of judging others. In Jesus' name. Amen.

LOOK AT ...

In last week's lesson, we learned how to make peace with God by humbling ourselves and repenting of sin. As James continued his faithful teaching on living faith, he focused on some things we really need to know about how we speak and think of our brothers and sisters in Christ.

READ JAMES 4:11–12.

Do not speak evil of one another, brethren. He who speaks evil of a brother and judges his brother, speaks evil of the law and judges the law. But if you judge the law, you are not a doer of the law but a judge. There is one Lawgiver, who is able to save and to destroy. Who are you to judge another? James 4:11–12

1. What did James warn the believers against?

Learn About ...

2 Judge

The word *judge* here does not refer to evaluation but to condemnation. Thus, when we judge others, we are really saying they deserve to be condemned. Jesus said that judging others has consequences: "With what judgment you judge, you will be judged" (Matt. 7:2).

---

6 Lawgiver

John said the law was given through Moses, but Moses merely transcribed God's words. "For the LORD is our Judge, the LORD is our Lawgiver" (Isa. 33:22). To criticize the law is to usurp God's authority, presuming to enact a better law.

---

8 Slander

Slander means "to make false charges; to misrepresent in order to damage another's reputation." Slander is like dirt thrown against a clean wall: it may not stick, but it will leave a mark. Once you have dirtied someone else's reputation, it takes God's love to clean it up.

2. Explain what is at the root of badmouthing fellow Christians.

3. One who speaks evil of and judges a believer also speaks against what?

4. Read Matthew 22:36–39. According to this passage, what two commands reveal the heart of God's law?

5. What indictment did James make against those who judge the law?

6. Who is the only One who has the right to judge? Why?

7. Write your answer to James's ironic concluding question.

Live Out ...

8. a. James warned us against speaking evil of others. Ephesians 4:31–32 describes the various forms of evil speaking and then gives a remedy. Record something you've said that reflects each form of evil speech.

   Bitterness: (*Example: she's such a backstabber; I'm glad she finally got what she deserved.*)
   Anger:
   Harsh Words:
   Slander:
   Malice:

   b. Journal a prayer asking God to replace your evil speech with a tender heart. Use the following verse: "Be kind to each other, tenderhearted, forgiving one another, just as God through Christ has forgiven you" (Eph. 4:32 NLT).

9. Instead of evil speech, Paul exhorted, "Let no corrupt word proceed out of your mouth, but what is good for necessary edification" (Eph. 4:29). Transform your five hurtful statements in question 8 into words of edification by using EDIFY as an acrostic.

E (*Example: even though she did wrong, I pray God will forgive her and make things right.*)

D

I

F

Y

10. Today we learned that God is the ultimate lawgiver. Fill in the following chart to discover some of the reasons God has given us His laws.

SCRIPTURE	REASON FOR LAW
Romans 7:7	
Galatians 3:24	
Galatians 5:14	
1 Timothy 1:8–9	
Hebrews 9:28–10:1	

∘ ∘ • ∘ ∘

My (Lenya) mother always said, "If you can't say something nice, don't say anything at all." It takes just one rumor to devastate someone's life. In high school a dirty secret spread throughout my school: "Rachel

---

LEARN ABOUT . . .

9 Edification

Edify means "to build up"; therefore a building is called an edifice. Strengthening believers in the faith is appropriate edification. Christians are built up by good speech. "Encourage each other and build each other up, just as you are already doing" (I Thess. 5:II NLT).

---

10 Law Rejected

God's laws make humans aware of their sinfulness: "Through the law we become conscious of sin" (Rom. 3:20 NIV). Without speed limits it would not be wrong to drive 150 mph. The law is the great equalizer—we're all guilty. "For everyone has sinned; we all fall short of God's glorious standard" (Rom. 3:23 NLT).

Rodriquez was raped." No one could verify it, but nobody denied it either. That summer Rachel went from all-American girl to pot-smoking hippie chick. She was so humiliated by the gossip mill that she just checked out. I wish my classmates could have attended the following summer camp.

At this church camp, an ugly rumor about two counselors quickly became the talk of the camp. At morning prayer the youth leader retold the story of how Jesus refused to condemn the woman caught in adultery, saying, "If any one of you is without sin, let him be the first to throw a stone at her" (John 8:7 NIV). So one by one the accusers walked away. Then the leader passed around a bucket of stones, insisting each person carry one in his or her pocket until camp ended. Any time the campers felt like criticizing someone else, talking behind another's back, or passing on an ugly rumor, they were told, "Reach into your pocket, touch the stone, and ask yourselves if you are without sin."

It's so easy to judge others, but only God knows a person's heart. Let's try an experiment. Find a small stone to carry in your pocket or purse as a reminder that we are not to judge others, and pray, "Lord, keep me from casting stones."

Listen To ...

He who flings dirt upon another dirties himself more.

—Proverb

DAY 2
You Don't Know What's Good for You

Left to our own devices, most of us would be living in a world of hurt. What seems good to us now isn't necessarily good later. The all-you-can-eat buffet on Sunday means an extra two pounds on Monday. Smoking cigarettes may make you look cool now, but you'll look pitiful later pulling an oxygen tank behind you. Short-term gratifications rarely have long-term benefits. That's why for generations parents have been warning their children, "You don't know what's good for you!"

For instance, when my (Lenya's) son, Nathan, was a child, he didn't understand that a penny saved is a penny earned. Each Friday as we handed him his allowance, it began burning a hole in his pocket. On the way home from the bank, if we stopped at the gas station, he'd go in and squander his money on junk food. Inevitably, Saturday morning as we were shopping in Target, he didn't have enough money to buy the latest music CD. As he gazed longingly at the display case, the words I said Friday would echo in his ears: "You just don't know what's good for you!"

God's children can be clueless too. They often think they are in control of their futures. Sometimes they squander the resources God has given them on the stock market, the lottery, or shady business deals. The book of James reminds us that when we make our plans without asking God about His plans, we will inevitably come up short. While we may not know what's good for us, our heavenly Father really does know best.

LIFT UP ...

Father, though I don't know the future, You do. I find comfort knowing You have a plan for me. Don't let me take for granted the time You have provided as I seek to understand Your will. In Jesus' name. Amen.

LEARN ABOUT ...

2 Godless Plans

In business and life, it is wise to plan and have a strategy for future goals. Planning is not sinful. The problem occurs when God is left out and His will is not considered. When God is not part of the agenda, planning is foolish and sinful.

---

3 Presumptuous

To be *presumptuous* is to overstep your bounds or take liberties; to expect or assume an outcome. The psalmist prayed, "Keep back Your servant also from presumptuous sins; let them not have dominion over me. Then I ... shall be innocent of great transgression" (Ps. 19:13).

---

6 Unpredictable

When James described life as unpredictable and a vapor, he revealed two reasons why it's foolish to plan without God: (1) ignorance of the future and (2) the brevity of life. "An entire lifetime is just a moment to you [God]; at best, each of us is but a breath" (Ps. 39:5 NLT).

LOOK AT ...

We have found that we must not slander or judge others because we don't know their hearts. Now we learn that sometimes we make plans without knowing what God has in store for us.

READ JAMES 4:13–14.

Come now, you who say, "Today or tomorrow we will go to such and such a city, spend a year there, buy and sell, and make a profit," whereas you do not know what will happen tomorrow. For what is your life? It is even a vapor that appears for a little time and then vanishes away. James 4:13–14

1. What two words did James use to get his readers' attention?

2. Who was James addressing here?

3. These people made five presumptions that excluded God. What plans did they make for themselves apart from God?

    Time:
    Location:
    Duration of business:
    Purpose of travel/enterprise:
    Ultimate goal:

4. In making their plans, what could they not know?

5. What rhetorical question did James ask?

6. Restate in your own words the answer James gave to this question.

LIVE OUT ...

7. a. Jesus told a parable about a man who sinned presumptuously. Read Luke 12:16–21. How had this man prospered (v. 16)?

    b. What did he plan to do with his profits (vv. 17–19)?

    c. What was really in his future (v. 20)?

    d. What is the main message of this parable (v. 21)?

8. Examine your own life. Do you have your own agenda? Do you pray before you make decisions, or do you assume that it is your choice? When making business decisions, does the goal of making a profit take precedence over pleasing God? Journal about the areas in your life in which you do not consult God. Then journal a prayer asking Him for His advice.

9. As Christians, we have the privilege of making our plans according to God's will and for His glory. God gives us the resources that we need in order to please Him. Fill in the chart to discover what benefits there are in consulting God.

SCRIPTURE	BENEFIT OF CONSULTING GOD
Psalm 37:3–6	
Proverbs 3:5–6	
Jeremiah 29:11–13	
Romans 8:28	

LEARN ABOUT ...

7 Success

Failing to consult God ultimately leads to failure. Humbly submitting your plans to God will lead to success—if not here, then in the hereafter. "Commit your actions to the LORD, and your plans will succeed" (Prov. 16:3 NLT). Include God in all your plans.

8 Seek God First

It has been said, "Keep the main thing, the main thing." To believe in God, yet not consult Him, reveals that He is not your main thing. Instead, "Seek first the kingdom of God and His righteousness, and all these things shall be added to you" (Matt. 6:33).

9 God's Plans

It is utter folly to make your own plans apart from God because ultimately He will supersede them. God is the sovereign ruler of the universe and the master of your fate. "In his heart a man plans his course, but the LORD determines his steps" (Prov. 16:9 NIV).

∘ ∘ • ∘ ∘

Isn't it amazing the time and money people spend on plans that may never come true? I've (Lenya) always loved thinking about future space flight. My favorite childhood cartoon was *The Jetsons*, a show about a family that traveled by spacecraft, had robots clean their home, and received piping hot meals at the push of a button. I thought that living on the moon or even Mars would be possible in my lifetime.

I found out that I wasn't alone. There was a planetarium that needed money, so its director dreamed up a gimmick that preyed upon future-oriented, hopeful yet gullible people like me. He printed brochures that offered one-thousand-acre lots on the planet Mars for only twenty dollars. "This land still features pink skies, unlimited rock gardens, and not one but two moons. So peaceful, quiet, and romantic—even the natives are friendly," the literature promised. "At one-sixth the gravity of Earth, your golf game will improve immensely—drives will be six times longer. Mars will provide a world of adventure for the entire family." The gag was surprisingly successful. People across the country sent in their money for a deed.

James reminded us that making life plans without praying and seeking God is just as foolish as buying land on Mars. I may not know what the future holds, but I know Who holds my future. Because God holds eternity in His hands, isn't it a good idea to trust Him with all your tomorrows?

LISTEN TO ...

The future has a habit of suddenly and dramatically becoming the present.

—*Roger Babson*

DAY 3
You Don't Know God's Will

The million-dollar question is, "What is God's will for my life?" If I possessed a miraculous way of discerning God's exact plans for individuals on a personal basis, I'd put every psychic on this planet out of business. There is a market out there for inquiring minds who desperately need to know, "What is God's will?"

My (Lenya) friend Kent Bagdasar is a public relations and marketing genius who has a finger on the pulse of what Americans want. Several years ago Kent, then on a church staff, was asked to fill in for the church's pastor, who had a thriving recorded tape ministry. Kent was concerned that tape sales would plummet once people saw his name on the package instead of the beloved pastor's name. So when the secretary asked for the title of his message he said, "Knowing God's Will," insisting, "I'd spend two dollars to find out what God's will is, wouldn't you?" But when it came to preparing his message, Kent realized that discovering God's will is much more complicated than buying a two-dollar tape. He decided to teach on something else, but unfortunately the labels had already been printed. The tape became a best seller at the time, even though it did not reveal how to know God's will.

James realized the necessity of not only discovering the will of God but also obeying it. He assumed that God's will is not that difficult to discern. Today we will gain insight into what Scripture has to say about knowing the will of God.

LIFT UP ...

Lord, I praise You that Your plans are always good. Show me Your good and perfect will for my life, and help me obey You. In Jesus' name. Amen

LOOK AT ...

We have found that it is unwise to make plans without asking God to reveal His plan to us. Now we discover the blessings of acknowledging God and obeying His will.

LEARN ABOUT ...

1 God's Will

God's will is found in God's Word. Understanding God's general will leads to knowing His specific will. For instance, Scripture teaches that God hates divorce. Unless your spouse is unfaithful, it's not God's will for you to separate. "Do not be unwise, but understand what the will of the Lord is" (Eph. 5:17).

4 Do His Will

It's one thing to know God's will and another thing to do it. "Do the will of God with all your heart" (Eph. 6:6 NLT). And we should do good! "It is God's will that by doing good you should silence ... foolish men" (1 Pet. 2:15 NIV).

6 In His Will?

What is the proof of knowing God's will? Ceasing to copy the world and starting to imitate God. "Do not be conformed to this world, but be transformed by the renewing of your mind, that you may prove what is that ... perfect will of God" (Rom. 12:2).

7 Willful?

God promises eternal life to those who do His will and loss for those who don't. "This world is fading away.... But anyone who does what pleases God will live forever" (1 John 2:17 NLT). Your will determines how He will respond to you!

READ JAMES 4:15.

Instead you ought to say, "If the Lord wills, we shall live and do this or that." James 4:15

1. What did James encourage believers to say when making plans?

2. How does this differ from what they said before (see v. 13)?

3. What do you think the word *if* implies here?

4. What issues did James say are included in God's will?

5. What do you think is meant by "this or that"?

LIVE OUT ...

6. a. Read Colossians 1:9–12 to discover more about God's will. What was Paul's prayer for the Colossians (v. 9)?

   b. List four ways you can fulfill God's will (v. 10).

   c. Describe the results of walking in God's will (v. 11).

   d. How should you respond (v. 12)?

7. Today we learned that God's will is discovered in God's Word. Fill in the chart to discover some aspects of God's will for you.

SCRIPTURE	GOD'S WILL
John 7:17	

Romans 12:2

Ephesians 6:6–8

Hebrews 10:6–7

LEARN ABOUT ...

8. We have a choice: to accept or reject God's will as revealed in His Word. Luke 7:30 reveals that the "Pharisees and lawyers rejected the will of God for themselves, not having been baptized by him." With this in mind, check off the ways you are not living up to God's known will in these areas.

8 In His Will?

When Christians conform to the will of God, they reveal that they are part of His family. Jesus taught, "Anyone who does God's will is my brother and sister and mother" (Mark 3:35 NLT). Obedience strengthens relationship. The more we do the will of God, the more we resemble Him.

____ Receive salvation.   ____ Be thankful in all things.

____ Be separate from the world.____ Be a worshipper of God.

____ Be baptized.   ____ Stay sexually pure.

____ Do good works.   ____ Develop a transformed mind.

____ Pray according to His will. ____ Tithe.

9 Willing?

Some don't do God's will because they don't know what it is. Others don't obey because they're not willing. If you are unwilling to obey, ask God to help make you willing. "It is God who works in you both to will and to do for His good pleasure" (Phil. 2:13).

9. The writer of Hebrews said that not only does God want you *to know* His will, but He also completely equips you *to do* His will. Journal a prayer to God by rewriting the following verse and asking Him to help you both know and do His will:

Now may the God of peace who brought up our Lord Jesus from the dead, that great Shepherd of the sheep, through the blood of the everlasting covenant, make you complete in every good work to do His will, working in you what is well pleasing in His sight, through Jesus Christ, to whom be glory forever and ever. Amen. (Heb. 13:20–21)

∘ ∘ • ∘ ∘

A girlfriend once confided in me (Penny), "I'm scared to pray 'Thy will be done' because I am afraid God will want me to go to Africa. Or maybe my husband or daughter will get cancer!"

I hugged her and said, "Imagine your daughter telling you, 'I want to do whatever you want today, Mommy.' You wouldn't think, *Now's my chance to make her do all the chores I hate to do. I'll make things hard for her and won't allow her to play!*"

"Of course not," said the woman. "I'd try to give her the best day ever."

"So why would you think that God is less loving than you?" I asked.

I reminded her of a time when Jesus corrected His disciples' wrong thinking about their heavenly Father. In the book of Matthew, we read, "What man is there among you who, if his son asks for bread, will give him a stone? Or if he asks for a fish, will he give him a serpent? If you then, being evil, know how to give good gifts to your children, how much more will your Father who is in heaven give good things to those who ask Him!" (Matt. 7:9–11).

Although we may not always know God's specific will, we can always know His heart: "'For I know the plans I have for you,' says the LORD. 'They are plans for good and not for disaster, to give you a future and a hope'" (Jer. 29:11 NLT).

LISTEN TO ...

I find the doing of the will of God leaves me no time for disputing about His plans.

—*George MacDonald*

DAY 4
You Don't Know Yourself

"I am the master of my fate: I am the captain of my soul." These chilling words were quoted as part of Timothy McVeigh's last statement before he died by lethal injection June 11, 2001. McVeigh was executed for his actions in the 1995 Oklahoma City bombing that killed 168 people and injured more than five hundred. Until the 9/11 attacks, it was the most destructive terrorist act committed on US soil.

McVeigh's biographer said, "If ... you didn't know his history and you began chatting with him, ... you'd find him a very affable, knowledgeable young man." Yet his downfall appeared to be his arrogance. McVeigh not only confessed to the crime, but he also took pride in being responsible for the bombing. He put himself in the position of judge, jury, and executioner for the alleged crimes of the US government. Convincing himself that he was on a soldier's mission, Timothy described the civilian deaths as "collateral damage."[1]

A self-described agnostic, he appeared to be unrepentant to the end. Paul Howell, who lost his daughter, Karan Howell Shepherd, in the vicious attack said, "I was hoping ... we could see some kind of maybe, 'I'm sorry,' you know, something like that," Howell recalled.[2]

Timothy McVeigh's boastful and arrogant attitude led him to commit an act of incredible evil. Today we discover that those who arrogantly follow their own self-serving agenda are, in fact, rejecting God's authority. Because they don't know God, they don't really know themselves either.

LIFT UP ...

Lord, give me wisdom and insight into the areas of my heart that do not please You. Help me to be humble and not proud. If I boast, let it be in You and Your goodness. In Your name. Amen.

LEARN ABOUT ...

1 Boasting

Boasting can express valid joy, or it can parade one's own accomplishments. Boasting in this text refers to pretentious or presumptuous bragging. Solomon warned, "Do not boast about tomorrow, for you do not know what a day may bring forth" (Prov. 27:1).

---

2 Arrogance

Arrogance is a feeling of superiority shown in presumptuous claims. Hannah proclaimed, "Talk no more so very proudly; let no arrogance come from your mouth, for the LORD is the God of knowledge; and by Him actions are weighed" (1 Sam. 2:3).

---

6 Our Boast

Not all boasting is wrong. Boasting in the Lord is very right. "My soul shall make its boast in the LORD; the humble shall hear of it and be glad. Oh, magnify the LORD with me, and let us exalt His name together" (Ps. 34:2–3).

LOOK AT ...

James taught us that seeking God's will is wise. Now we discover that it is not God's will for us to be boastful or arrogant.

READ JAMES 4:16.

But now you boast in your arrogance. All such boasting is evil. James 4:16

1. What type of speech did James consider here?

2. What underlying attitude does this speech reveal?

3. How did James classify boasting?

4. Why do you think arrogant boasting is evil?

5. Fill in the following chart to discover more about evil boasting.

SCRIPTURE	EVIL BOASTING
Psalm 5:5–6	
Psalm 49:5–6	
Psalm 94:4	
Psalm 97:7	

6. Boasting in our pride and arrogance is evil. The apostle Paul spoke of proper boasting. Fill in the chart to learn more.

SCRIPTURE	PROPER BOASTING
2 Corinthians 1:12	
2 Corinthians 7:4	
2 Corinthians 10:13	
2 Corinthians 11:30	

LIVE OUT ...

7. Arrogant boasting takes personal credit for what God has done. The prophet Isaiah revealed the absurdity of this by using the imagery of the potter and the clay. Read Isaiah 29:16. Journal about a time when you, the clay, took credit when it should have been given to God, the Potter.

8. List the seven things from Proverbs 6:16–19 that the Lord hates. What tops His list?

9. a. Rather than being boastful, believers are to be humble. Place an (H) beside the humble attributes and a (B) beside the boastful attitudes.

   ____ Admits when wrong

   ____ Says "I'm sorry"

   ____ Name drops

   ____ Serves others without recognition

   ____ Proclaims his or her good deeds loudly

   ____ Dominates conversations

   ____ Looks down on others

   ____ Gives God the glory

   ____ Always seeks the limelight

   ____ Thinks he or she is always right

   ____ Elevates others

   ____ Team player

   b. Journal about which of the humble attributes you will develop in your life.

LEARN ABOUT ...

7 Giving Credit

How does it feel when someone takes credit for something you did? Give credit where credit is due. "But now, O LORD, You are our Father; we are the clay, and You our potter; and all we are the work of Your hand" (Isa. 64:8).

8 Haughty

Murder? Sin! Stealing? Sin! Lookin' cool? Sin! Did you realize that a haughty look, "looking cool" in modern vernacular, is a sin? The next time teenagers try to strut their stuff, remind them, "A haughty look, a proud heart, and the plowing of the wicked are sin" (Prov. 21:4).

9 Boast Not

The mark of a true believer is to hate what God hates. Since God hates boasting, you should too. If you hate it, you won't do it. "All who fear the LORD will hate evil. That is why I hate pride, arrogance, corruption, and perverse speech" (Prov. 8:13 NLT).

° ° • ° °

Mongolian folklore recounts this little tale of a boastful frog. Two geese were headed south on their annual autumn migration when they were entreated by a frog to take him along. The geese were willing to carry him if a means of transportation could be devised. The quick-witted frog produced a long stalk of grass and told the two geese to hold one end while he clung to the middle with his mouth. The three friends were soaring along, enjoying their journey, when some men noticed them from below.

The men shouted their admiration for the device and called out, "Who was clever enough to figure that out?" When the vainglorious frog opened his mouth to say, "It was I!" he lost his hold, fell to the earth, and was dashed to pieces.

I don't know about you, but we're feeling a bit bruised by all this ego bashing. Time and again, the book of James has reminded us: humility—good! Pride—bad! But James was not the only harbinger of this message. The entire Bible is rife with verses that warn against pride and promote humility. Moses taught it, the Old Testament prophets proclaimed it, the psalmists sang it, Jesus exemplified it, and the apostles preached it. If by now you haven't humbled yourself before God, you must have a will of iron. Isn't it time to give your pride the final deathblow and humbly say "Uncle!" to the Lord?

LISTEN TO ...

Arrogance has its own built-in misery. The arrogant person may offend others, but he hurts himself more.

—*Billy Graham*

DAY 5

You Do Know Right from Wrong

In the middle of a recurring nightmare, I (Penny) awoke in a cold sweat. The apocalypse had come. The world was in utter chaos—fires raging, sirens screaming, people running around in panic. Suddenly a bright light shone from heaven. The arms of God reached out to rescue His children. Looking up, I watched my family rising to meet Him in the clouds. I was left behind.

I was raised in the buckle of the "Bible Belt"—the southern part of America where conservative Christianity is part of the culture. I attended church every Sunday and asked Jesus into my heart in the fourth grade. I was a good Christian girl until high school. I turned from reading the Bible to reading trashy novels; from partaking of the Living Water to drinking beer; from fellowship with believers to party hopping. Knowing better, I had the same bad dream night after night.

This week's lesson has revealed three kinds of people: (1) those who presumptuously ignore God's will, living as if God and His will do not exist; (2) those who acknowledge that God exists but arrogantly reject His will in favor of their own goals; (3) those who believe God exists, acknowledge that His will is best, then proceed to disobey it. Today we discover that the third type of person is the worst of all. Doing what's wrong when you know what is right reveals that "You *Do* Know Right from Wrong."

LIFT UP ...

Father, please help me to hear Your voice and avoid evil. I am Your servant; protect me as I follow You. In Jesus' name. Amen.

LOOK AT ...

James exhorted us to not boast about tomorrow. As we come to the end of James 4, we see he warned again that a living faith is a doing faith.

LEARN ABOUT ...

2 Knowing Good

Knowing and doing good should go together in a persistent lifestyle. God "will give eternal life to those who keep on doing good" (Rom. 2:7 NLT). If helping the poor is good today, it will be good tomorrow. Doing good is the gift that keeps on giving.

---

4 Doing Wrong

Knowing God's will but choosing to disobey expresses the sin of willful pride. It's saying, "I know what You want, God, but You can't make me do it." "The words of his mouth are wickedness and deceit; he has ceased to be wise and to do good" (Ps. 36:3).

---

7 Just Do It!

God's will is not a "take it or leave it" proposition. We are obligated to just do it! With knowledge comes responsibility. "Someone who does not know, and then does something wrong, will be punished only lightly. When someone has been given much, much will be required in return" (Luke 12:48 NLT).

READ JAMES 4:17.

Therefore, to him who knows to do good and does not do it, to him it is sin. James 4:17

1. James linked what he said previously with what he was about to say. What do you think the "therefore" is there for?

2. Did those James was addressing know what was good and right? How do you know?

3. How did the people respond to this knowledge?

4. What did James conclude?

5. Jesus told the chief priests and elders a parable contrasting what two sons did with what they knew. Read Matthew 21:28–31.

   a. Explain what the father asked the first son and the son's response (vv. 28–29).

   b. Explain what the father requested of the second son and his response (v. 30).

   c. Explain what the religious leaders learned from this parable (v. 31).

6. James said it is sinful to know the truth and not do it. Look up each passage and briefly explain the consequence of willful disobedience.

   Romans 1:21–22

Hebrews 10:26–27

2 Peter 2:20–21

7. Based on James 4:17, what did James imply we should do in order to avoid sin?

LIVE OUT ...

8. We have found that doing good means persisting in a lifestyle of good deeds. Journal about something good you have done in the past. How will you continue to repeat that in the future?

9. We can usually find excuses for not doing something we know is right. Check the spaces that indicate something you've failed to do, and then write the excuse beside it.

GOOD DEED   **BAD EXCUSE**

____ Help the oppressed (Isa. 1:17).

____ Pray for enemies (Matt. 5:44).

____ Help other believers (Gal. 6:10).

____ Be willing to share (1 Tim. 6:18).

____ Pursue peace (1 Pet. 3:11).

10. a. An obedient believer both knows and does what God asks. From the following list, circle the ways God has let you know what He wants you to do.

Prayer   Bible reading

Sound biblical teaching   Conversations with believers

Godly counsel   Providential circumstances

LEARN ABOUT ...

8 Persistence

Persist means "to resolutely continue despite opposition." "At Joppa there was a certain disciple named ... Dorcas. This woman was full of good works and charitable deeds which she did" (Acts 9:36). For Dorcas to be "full of good works," she must have continued them throughout her lifetime.

9 No Excuse

The Bible clearly shows what we should and should not do, so there's really no excuse for failing to do good. Jesus said, "They would not be guilty if I had not come and spoken to them. But now they have no excuse for their sin" (John 15:22 NLT).

10 Disobedience

Disobedient means "to refuse to hear; to be insubordinate." Passively avoiding doing what's right is as disobedient as actively doing something wrong. "They profess to know God, but in works they deny Him, being abominable, disobedient, and disqualified for every good work" (Titus 1:16).

b. Now journal about a time you failed to do what God asked even though you knew better. What was the result?

· · · · ·

Before sixteen-year-olds can drive, they must get a license, and my (Lenya's) son, Nathan, was no exception. We enrolled him in the McGinnis School of Driving, where he had to fulfill certain requirements before receiving his license: thirty-three hours of classroom instruction, including a written test and eye exam; seven hours driving with a certified instructor; forty-three hours driving with a licensed adult; and passing the state driving test. With all of this preparation, Nathan and all drivers should know the rules of the road. But knowing and obeying are two different things. People who detour from the law make excuses like this list provided by a car insurance company:

"The other car collided with mine without giving warning of its intentions."

"A pedestrian hit me and went under my car."

"Coming home I drove into the wrong house and collided with a tree I don't have."

"I glanced at my mother-in-law and headed over the embankment."

"The pedestrian had no idea which direction to run, so I ran over him."

While these excuses are humorous, they show how prone we are to evade responsibility for our wrong actions. James told his readers that, like errant drivers, Christians who do not obey the Bible are full of excuses. But there is really no good excuse for doing something wrong when you know what is right.

Listen To …

Our human nature tends toward both good and evil…. You possess free choice to move in the direction you wish.

—*Pseudo-Macarius*

While You Wait
James 5:7–12

In 1942 during World War II, General Douglas MacArthur was ordered to leave the Philippines prior to the takeover by the invading Japanese army. Before General MacArthur left the islands, he spoke the famous words, "I will return." Two years later, as supreme commander of the Southwest Pacific for the Allies, he stood again on the Philippine Islands and said, "This is the voice of freedom. People of the Philippines, I have returned."

As we have learned throughout the book of James, Christians live in a state of emotional, physical, and spiritual warfare. What, then, is our hope amidst the suffering, persecution, trials, and tribulations of life? Our hope is this: *the* Supreme Commander, Jesus Christ, will return to establish His perfect kingdom. Biblical prophecy confirms this steadfast hope in Christ's return. Both the Old and New Testaments overflow with references to the second coming of Christ. It has been estimated that in the Old Testament there are nearly two thousand references to Christ's second coming. In the New Testament there are over three hundred references to the second advent of Christ—one out of thirty verses.

General MacArthur was a trustworthy man who kept his promise to return. How much more is Jesus Christ, the perfect God-man, able to keep His promise to return and put an end to the wars that rage within and without? This week the book of James gives us insight into what we should do "While We Wait" for His return.

Day 1: James 5:7	I WILL RETURN
Day 2: James 5:8	YOU'D BETTER WATCH OUT
Day 3: James 5:9	WAIT TILL YOUR FATHER GETS HOME
Day 4: James 5:10–11	IN THE WAITING ROOM
Day 5: James 5:12	WAITING WITH INTEGRITY

DAY 1
I Will Return

LIFT UP ...

Jesus, the more I experience the sorrow in the world, the more I long for Your return. Please give me patience to live faithfully and confidence to wait expectantly until You come. In Your name. Amen.

LOOK AT ...

In lesson 2 we studied the first part of James 5, which spoke against the corruption of the wicked rich, and how much better it is to trust God than gold. As we move forward in chapter 5, we see that James continued his no-nonsense teaching to believers in the early church. Remember that they were suffering persecution for their faith and had been scattered to different places throughout the Roman world. James reminded them, and us, to trust in God's promise that Christ will come again. Until then, we must be patient.

READ JAMES 5:7.

Therefore be patient, brethren, until the coming of the Lord. See how the farmer waits for the precious fruit of the earth, waiting patiently for it until it receives the early and latter rain. James 5:7

1. James was drawing his letter to a close. "Therefore," what did he exhort the brethren to be?

2. What did James urge them to patiently await?

LEARN ABOUT ...

1 Patience

Patience is the ability to endure pain and hardship without complaint; the ability to persevere without losing heart. James used patience as bookends to his letter. He began by encouraging the persecuted believers to be patient in trials. At the end, he encouraged them to wait patiently for the Lord's return.

2 His Coming

"The coming of the Lord" speaks of Christ's future return to the earth. This next historical event on God's calendar is the climax of His plan to redeem humanity. "They will see the Son of Man coming on the clouds of heaven with power and great glory" (Matt. 24:30).

LEARN ABOUT ...

5 Heavenly Rain

Early rains were the first autumn showers and latter rains were the last spring showers. Early rains prepared the soil for seed; latter rains prepared the crops for the harvest. "He will cause the rain to come down for you—the former rain, and the latter rain" (Joel 2:23).

---

8 No Complaint

No matter what situation God places you in, one thing you must never do is complain. "Do everything without complaining or arguing, so that you may become blameless and pure, children of God" (Phil. 2:14–15 NIV). Complaining Christians are a bad witness.

3. Like Jesus, James often used natural illustrations to make spiritual applications. Who did James use as an example of patience?

4. For what does that person wait?

5. What must the fruit of the earth receive in order to grow properly?

6. James's first readers would have been familiar with farming illustrations. Read Deuteronomy 11:10–14.

   a. How were the crops in Egypt watered (v. 10)?

   b. Explain how the crops in the Promised Land were watered and why (vv. 11–12).

   c. What spiritual conditions did the Lord set for cultivating a fruitful harvest (v. 13)?

   d. What physical blessings did God provide (v. 14)?

7. Read Hosea 6:3. How did Hosea symbolically connect the coming of the Lord with the rains?

LIVE OUT ...

8. *Patience* is the ability to endure pain, difficulties, and hardship without complaining or losing heart. Write about three situations that have tried your patience, and indicate whether or not you complained or lost heart.

SITUATION	COMPLAINED?	LOST HEART?
Painful:	__ yes __ no	__ yes __ no
Difficult:	__ yes __ no	__ yes __ no
Hardship:	__ yes __ no	__ yes __ no

9. James exhorted us to be like spiritual farmers who patiently wait for a fruitful harvest. In the columns, list something you have waited for, how long you waited, and whether the wait was worth it.

WAITED	FOR HOW LONG?	WORTH IT?

10. Today we learned that the early and latter rain could refer to the two advents of Jesus Christ. Journal about how you have responded to Christ's first coming. How does that make you feel about His second coming?

○ ° ● ° ○

An atheist farmer ridiculed people who believed in God. He wrote this letter to the local newspaper: "I plowed on Sunday, planted on Sunday, cultivated on Sunday, hauled in my crops on Sunday; but I never went to church on Sunday. Yet I harvested more bushels than any of those God-fearing Christians." The editor printed the letter and then added this remark: "God doesn't always settle His accounts in October."

The psalmist has a name for someone who lives as though God doesn't exist—fool! "Only fools say in their hearts, 'There is no God'" (Ps. 14:1 NLT). Foolish suppositions lead to foolish lifestyles. The foolish farmer did not believe that God existed and hence believed there would not be any consequences for ignoring Him. But the wise editor knew

LEARN ABOUT ...

9 Can't Wait

In today's world of instant gratification, patience is not always seen as a virtue. But there are some things worth waiting for: dessert after a meal, sex in marriage, God's perfect timing. The one thing most worth waiting for is Jesus Christ's return. Can't wait!

10 Promised Rain

The Old Testament speaks often of the Messiah coming to rule and reign on the earth. Solomon said of the Lord's coming: "He shall come down like rain upon the grass before mowing, like showers that water the earth. In His days the righteous shall flourish" (Ps. 72:6–7).

that the story isn't over until Jesus returns. At that time many people will be surprised by what happens.

In Matthew 24 Jesus revealed that when He comes, it will be "as the days of Noah" (v. 37). People will be going about their normal business, eating meals and getting married. But when He comes, "two men will be in the field: one will be taken and the other left" (v. 40). While no one knows the day or time of Christ's return, the truly wise will go about their business with an attitude of patient expectancy, waiting for their Savior to take them to their heavenly home.

LISTEN TO ...

The second advent is possible any day, impossible no day.

—*Richard Trench*

You'd Better Watch Out

The word *Christmas* fills my (Lenya's) heart with anticipation that something special is about to happen. As a child, after Thanksgiving I'd count the days, hours, minutes until Christmas. Every store window, twinkling light, and song on the radio reminded me that "Santa Claus is coming to town." The song said, "You'd better watch out," so I knew I should be on my best behavior. I can still remember hanging my stocking on the mantle with care, "in hopes that St. Nicolas soon would be there." I could hardly sleep and would wake long before everyone else.

As a mother, I was still the first one up. I'd turn on Christmas carols really loud, so Skip and Nathan would get up. Nathan would walk down the stairs saying, "Mom, it's Christmas!"

The tragedy of Christmas is that some people teach their children to anticipate the return of the jolly man in the red suit, not the babe in the manger. We ascribe to Santa the attributes of Christ: he sees all, knows all, keeps track of bad and good, and rewards accordingly. If children can exude such enthusiasm over the return of a mythical character, shouldn't Christians be ecstatic over the reality of Jesus Christ's return? Perhaps we could use some childlike faith. Jesus said, "Unless you … become as little children, you will by no means enter the kingdom of heaven" (Matt. 18:3). We mature Christians could use a dose of wonder, excitement, and anticipation as we await the Lord's coming.

LIFT UP …

Father, when I am weak, You give me strength; when it is hard to stand, You prop me up. I praise You for using the trials in my life to strengthen and establish my heart. In Jesus' name. Amen.

LEARN ABOUT ...

I Establish

Establish means "to strengthen, cause to stand, prop up." James urged those ready to collapse under trials and persecution to be bolstered by the hope of Christ's return. "Now to Him who is able to establish you according to my gospel and the preaching of Jesus Christ" (Rom. 16:25).

3 Coming

Coming carries the dual idea of arrival and presence. "The coming of the Lord" means Christ will arrive and bless us with His presence. "For what is our hope? ... Is it not even you in the presence of our Lord Jesus Christ at His coming?" (I Thess. 2:19).

5 While Waiting

Patience is not just passive; it is also active. While you wait for the Lord's return, don't just twiddle your thumbs, but get busy doing those things that will establish your heart. "Do not become sluggish, but imitate those who through faith and patience inherit the promises" (Heb. 6:12).

LOOK AT ...

We have learned that as believers we must patiently wait for Jesus to return. Now we explore another attribute we should adopt as we wait.

READ JAMES 5:8.

You also be patient. Establish your hearts, for the coming of the Lord is at hand. James 5:8

1. In addition to being patient, what else did James encourage the believers to do? How would you put this in your own words?

2. Psalm 27:14 says "Wait on the LORD; be of good courage, and He shall strengthen your heart." From this, explain how you can cultivate a strong heart and how God promises to help.

3. Why should we establish our hearts, according to James?

4. What phrase did James use to say that Christ could return at any moment?

5. Since Christ's resurrection, believers have gained strength in the imminence, or nearness, of His return. Fill in the table with phrases that describe Christ's imminent return and how we should live in light of His return.

SCRIPTURE	CHRIST'S RETURN	HOW TO LIVE
Romans 13:12		
Hebrews 10:25		
1 Peter 4:7		
Revelation 22:7		

6. According to 2 Peter 3:9, why is Christ patiently waiting to return?

Live Out ...

7. In today's passage, James exhorted us to establish our hearts. The psalmist said that trust strengthens hearts while fear weakens them: "His heart is steadfast, trusting in the LORD. His heart is established; he will not be afraid" (Ps. 112:7–8). Using FEARS and TRUST as acrostics, list the things you fear, then explain how to trust God instead.

```
F                    T
E                    R
A                    U
R                    S
S                    T
```

8. a. The coming of the Lord offers the promise of His physical presence. Until then Jesus has left us with the promise of His spiritual presence: "Be sure of this: I am with you always, even to the end of the age" (Matt. 28:20 NLT). Journal about a time you felt very alone. How would someone's company have brought you comfort at that time?

   b. Now imagine Jesus being with you during that time of need. How does that make you feel? Journal a prayer thanking God for being "a very present help in trouble" (Ps. 46:1).

9. We've gained valuable insight into *how* to live while we wait. Review the chart in question 5 concerning "How to Live." Which

Learn About ...

7 Fear Not

There's no need to fear; God is always near! "Don't be afraid, for I am with you. Don't be discouraged, for I am your God. I will strengthen you and help you. I will uphold you with my victorious right hand" (Isa. 41:10 NLT).

8 Who Moved?

Driving home from their anniversary party, a couple reminisced about their honeymoon. The wife said, "Remember we sat so close you could hardly drive? Now we're on opposite sides of the car." The husband lovingly replied, "I never moved." If you don't feel close to God, guess who moved?

9 At Hand

At hand means "approaching imminently, drawing near, or coming soon." Believers in every age should live with the hope that Jesus could come at any moment, in the twinkling of an eye. "'Surely I am coming quickly.' Amen. Even so, come, Lord Jesus!" (Rev. 22:20).

of these areas needs to be strengthened or established in your life? What will you do to grow stronger in this area?

· · • · ·

For nearly two centuries the poem *'Twas the Night before Christmas* has told of the wondrous visit of Saint Nick. For nearly two millennia, the church has been waiting for the second coming of Jesus Christ. Here's what that night might look like:

'Twas the night before Jesus came and all through the house
Not a creature was praying, not even this louse.
Our Bibles were lying on the shelf without care
In hopes that Christ Jesus would not come there.
The children were dressing to crawl into bed,
Not once ever kneeling or bowing a head.
And Mom in her rocker with babe on her lap
Was watching the *Late Show* while I took a nap.
When out of the east there arose such a clatter,
I sprang to my feet to see what was the matter.
Away to the window I flew like a flash
Tore open the shutters and threw up the sash!
When what to my wondering eyes should appear
But angels proclaiming that Jesus was here.
With a light like the sun sending forth a bright ray
I knew in a moment this must be THE DAY!
I fell to my knees, but it was too late;
I had waited too long and thus sealed my fate.
I stood and I cried as saints rose out of sight;
Oh, if only I had been ready tonight!

—*Anonymous*

LISTEN TO ...

The only way to wait for the Second Coming is to watch that you do what you should do, so that when he comes is a matter of indifference. It is the attitude of a child, certain that God knows what he is about.

—*Oswald Chambers*

Wait Till Your Father Gets Home

I (Penny) grew up with two brothers, so life could be miserable sometimes. They were "snips and snails and puppy dog tails," while I was "sugar and spice and everything nice." Sometimes their adventures got way out of hand, like the time they snuck into my room and stole my Barbies. First they cut off the dolls' hair. Then they dressed them in G. I. Joe combat gear and took them out to the mesa to play war. Finally they buried them where I could never find them. I was sitting in my room, crying my eyes out, while my brothers taunted me with the information that my Barbies had been taken as prisoners of war. Then Mom walked in. "What's wrong, honey?"

"The boys are being mean to me!" I answered with my standard whine. Chris and Pat weren't laughing anymore. They knew they were in *big* trouble. My mom sent them to their rooms and said, "Just wait till your father gets home!"

Apparently in James's day, God's children were having some trouble getting along too. We've learned that they were treating some of the rich members with partiality, there were fights occurring among the congregations, and they were talking trash about one another. As he drew his letter to a close, James reminded the brethren that they should be one big happy family. But if they continued to contend with one another, he warned, "Wait until your heavenly Father gets home!"

LIFT UP ...

Father, my grumbling reveals my impatience with You and with the people in my life. Please turn my contentious words to words of contentment. In Jesus' name. Amen.

LOOK AT ...

Yesterday we discovered that by strengthening our hearts, we gain patience. Today we discover that we must live with contentment rather than contention until Christ comes.

READ JAMES 5:9.

Do not grumble against one another, brethren, lest you be condemned. Behold, the Judge is standing at the door! James 5:9

1. What sin of the tongue did James warn the brethren against?

2. The King James Version reads slightly differently: "Grudge not one against another." We've learned that the tongue only speaks what is in the heart. Based on this translation, what sin do you think a grumbler harbors in his heart?

3. Against whom were the brethren sinning in this manner?

4. What is the consequence of this sin?

5. What title did James give Jesus?

6. What phrase reminds believers that Christ's return is imminent?

7. In His first appearance, Jesus said, "I did not come to judge the world but to save the world" (John 12:47). However, today we discover that when Jesus returns, He will come in judgment. What qualities and characteristics do you think Christ possesses that make Him qualified to judge the world?

LIVE OUT ...

8. Instead of grumbling, we are to love one another. With this in mind, complete the following steps.

LEARN ABOUT ...

2 Grumble

Grumble means "to bear a grudge; to mutter or mumble something in a low or hushed tone." It can sound like a growl or a rumble. "Do not seek revenge or bear a grudge against a fellow Israelite, but love your neighbor as yourself. I am the LORD" (Lev. 19:18 NLT).

4 Condemned

Condemn means "to declare to be wrong; to pronounce judgment; or to convict." James warned believers that if they hold grudges against others, they themselves will be judged as wrongdoers. "For by your words you will be justified, and by your words you will be condemned" (Matt. 12:37).

7 Judge

A judge is one who weighs and pronounces a verdict after questioning and deliberation. He is a public official that gives an authoritative opinion. God has given all authority to the Son: "For the Father judges no one, but has committed all judgment to the Son" (John 5:22).

Learn About ...

8 Discontent

Grumbling is usually a sign of a deeper problem—discontentment with our lot in life. When others receive more attention, possessions, friendships, or honors, we hold it against them or against God, thinking He gives more to others. "Be hospitable to one another without grumbling" (1 Pet. 4:9).

---

9 Jealousy

A jealous person is hostile, suspicious, or envious of one believed to enjoy an advantage. Jealous people constantly compare themselves to others, especially those who seemingly enjoy a privileged life. "Wrath is like a flood, but jealousy is even more dangerous" (Prov. 27:4 NLT).

---

10 Eavesdropping

When God eavesdrops at your door, does He hear grumbling or glorifying? "Those who feared the LORD spoke with each other, and the LORD listened to what they said. In his presence, a scroll of remembrance was written to record the names of those who feared him" (Mal. 3:16 NLT).

Step One: Name someone you've grumbled about or are holding a grudge against.

Step Two: Trace the cause of your grudge. Journal about how it began. (*Example: perhaps the person has more than you; hasn't paid attention to you.*)

Step Three: Journal a prayer of forgiveness for the person you hold a grudge against. Ask Christ to help you speak words of love rather than complaint.

9. a. Murmuring has its roots in jealousy and discontentment. In Matthew 20:1–16 Jesus told the parable of the workers in the vineyard. At what times of day did the landowner hire workers, and what did he promise them (vv. 1–7)?

   b. In what order did the landowner pay the workers, and how much did each receive (vv. 8–10)?

   c. How did the "first" respond to this process (vv. 11–12), and how did the landowner answer (vv. 13–15)?

   d. What is the moral to this story (v. 16)?

10. James reminded us that the Judge is standing at the door. This imagery almost makes one feel that God is eavesdropping on our lives. Journal about how you might live differently knowing that God is listening in on your conversations, the music you play, and the shows you watch.

∘ ∘ • ∘ ∘

"You kids be quiet and go to sleep now," Dad called from the living room where he was watching the news. But my sister and I (Lenya) just couldn't keep silent. We were telling each other stories and had gotten ourselves into a laughing jag. The more we tried to shut up, the more we started to crack up. That's when Dad sneaked down the hall and silently stood outside our room. As we were quietly whispering, he placed his ear against the door, eavesdropping on us. After several minutes of whispers and giggles, he burst into the room with a shout that scared us half to death! If we had known that the judge was standing at the door, we would have done what he said.

Jesus told John, the revelator, "Behold, I stand at the door" (Rev. 3:20). Jesus is watching and waiting to return for His own and to judge the unfaithful. Sometimes we live as though He is far away and unaware of what we're doing and saying. But the truth is He is AT THE DOOR! When He bursts through the clouds like lightning out of the east, will you be caught in the act or caught up in the air? Jesus warned that when He returns, "Two men will be in the field: one will be taken and the other left.… Watch … for you do not know what hour your Lord is coming" (Matt. 24:40, 42).

LISTEN TO …

Some people are always grumbling because roses have thorns; I am thankful that thorns have roses.

—*Alphonse Karr*

In the Waiting Room

I (Penny) sat looking through a magazine, but none of the words made any sense. I restlessly shifted in the uncomfortable chair and looked over at my mother. She was staring into space. Every few minutes I'd look at my watch. *How long have we been sitting in this waiting room?* An hour passed, then two. *The surgery shouldn't take this long, should it?* Finally, I looked down the sterile hallway and saw the doctor walking toward us with his head down. *This can't be good news.* We gathered as he said in a somber voice, "It was malignant. I got as much as I could, but she has a long road ahead of her." I realized then that I would be in the waiting room many more times in the future.

Though my grandmother suffered a great deal in her final days on earth, I now realize that our waiting room was her birthing room. In God's mercy and compassion, she was delivered into a kingdom where He would wipe away every tear.

In one sense all of life is a waiting room. Earth isn't our final destination; it's the place where we sojourn for a time. Sometimes in the waiting room of life, there's birth with all its joy—and other times, death with all its sorrow. The early church was in the waiting room of sorrow, suffering intense persecution and experiencing great trials. But James wanted them to know that this isn't all there is. There's a better world coming.

LIFT UP ...

Father, I thank You for Your Word, which is alive and speaks to me personally. Thank You for the examples of real people who encourage me to live a godly life until Your Son returns. In Jesus' name. Amen.

LOOK AT ...

Thus far we have learned to be patient, strong-hearted, and content until Christ returns. Now we discover that another key to living faith is to be comforted by Scripture.

READ JAMES 5:10–11.

My brethren, take the prophets, who spoke in the name of the Lord, as an example of suffering and patience. Indeed we count them blessed who endure. You have heard of the perseverance of Job and seen the end intended by the Lord—that the Lord is very compassionate and merciful. James 5:10–11

1. James asked believers to look to the prophets for inspiration. What was their job description?

2. What are the prophets examples of?

3. Read Luke 13:34. What did biblical prophets often have to suffer and endure?

4. How did James view the prophets who endured?

5. James moved from the prophets in general to Job in particular. How did he describe Job?

6. What phrase lets you know that God had a purpose in allowing Job's suffering?

7. In what two ways will God show His love to those who are undergoing trials?

LEARN ABOUT …

3 Prophet's Call

A prophet was a person who spoke for God and who communicated His message courageously to the nation of Israel. Since James was writing to the twelve tribes, they would understand this simple reference. "Remember, the ancient prophets were persecuted in the same way" (Matt. 5:12 NLT).

5 Perseverance

Persevere means "to persist steadfastly despite counter influences, opposition, or discouragement." You cannot persevere unless you face difficulties; you can't experience triumph without tragedy. To receive the blessing, you must bear the burden.

6 Job

You've heard the expression "he (or she) has the patience of Job." Job lost his children, his property, and his health, yet, "in all this Job did not sin nor charge God with wrong" (Job 1:22). He was truly an example of perseverance amidst trials.

LEARN ABOUT ...

8 Prophet's Pain

The accounts of biblical prophets inspire us as we endure suffering: (1) they prove that we can be in the will of God and still suffer; (2) they show us that sometimes we suffer because we are in God's will; and (3) they remind us that God cares for us when we suffer.

---

9 Suffering

It's not just prophets who suffer. If you're human, you'll suffer too. Take heart from Jesus, our suffering Savior: "He was despised and rejected—a man of sorrows, acquainted with deepest grief. We turned our backs on him and looked the other way" (Isa. 53:3 NLT).

---

10 So Blessed!

Blessed can mean "to bestow prosperity or happiness, or to protect and preserve." Though Job lost much, God preserved his life for future blessing. If you're in a season of suffering, patiently endure until the springtime of blessing.

LIVE OUT ...

8. James reminded believers that the prophets were examples of those who endured suffering. Fill in the chart to discover who some of the prophets were and how they suffered.

SCRIPTURE	PROPHET	HOW SUFFERED
1 Kings 18:4		
Jeremiah 37:15–16		
Daniel 6:16–17		
Hebrews 11:36–38		

9. We saw that the prophets received God's blessing because they patiently suffered. Journal about a situation you are facing or have faced in which God is using suffering to teach you patience.

10. Read Job 42:12–17. How did God show His mercy and compassion to Job in his "latter days"? Journal about how this gives you hope in your situation of suffering.

° ° • ° °

Everyone thinks they would rather have sunshine than showers. But what would the earth look like if it never rained again? Franklin Elmer Jr. found the answer in northern Chile. He described the desolate region where rain never falls lodged between the Andes Mountains and the Pacific Ocean. He wrote, "Morning after morning the sun rises brilliantly over the tall mountains to the east; each noon it shines brightly down from overhead; evening brings a picturesque sunset. Although storms are often seen raging high in the mountains, and heavy fog banks are observed far out over the sea, the sun continues to shine on this favored and protected strip of land…. It is a sterile and desolate desert. There are no streams of water, and nothing grows there."

When the storm clouds darken our path, we long for sunshine and joy. We plead with God to bring a halt to the downpour of suffering. A wise Arabian proverb says, "All sunshine makes the desert." Deserts, like this sunny part of Chile, are infertile and desolate places. So, too, life without trials leads to life void of depth, beauty, and character. God knows we need both sunshine and showers to make us fruitful. The prophets realized that the blessings found in suffering far outweighed their temporal pain. We, too, must recognize that in God's wise design and under His sovereign control, times of sorrow actually bring showers of blessing.

LISTEN TO …

Suffering is, of all things God can give us, the best gift. He gives it only to his chosen friends.

—Therese of Lisieux

DAY 5

Waiting with Integrity

"God, if You get me through tonight, I promise at dawn I'll give all my money to the poor." These kind of bargains made with God during desperate situations are called "foxhole confessions."

Jephthah, an Old Testament warrior, made a hasty vow to God and lived to regret it. Before engaging in battle with the Ammonites, Jephthah pledged, "If you give me victory over the Ammonites, I will give to the LORD the first thing coming out of my house to meet me when I return in triumph. I will sacrifice it as a burnt offering" (Judges 11:30–31 NLT). Victoriously returning from battle, Jephthah looked up to see his only daughter emerging from the house, dancing to celebrate his triumph. "When he saw her, he tore his clothes in anguish. 'Oh, my daughter!' he cried out. 'You have completely destroyed me! You've brought disaster on me! For I have made a vow to the LORD, and I cannot take it back'" (Judges 11:35 NLT). Right or wrong, Jephthah fulfilled his vow.

James warned against making such foolish vows, especially if we have no intention of keeping them. While we may not make vows like Jephthah today, we have a modern equivalent: the New Year's Resolution. In January, we resolve to give up sugar. By Easter, we're caught eating chocolate bunnies and regretting our weakness. The book of James reminds us that instead of making promises, we should let our yes be yes and our no be no.

Lift Up ...

Father, I know that You desire truth in my inner heart. I also know that You require my words and deeds to match. Help me to walk with inward and outward integrity until Your Son comes. In Jesus' name. Amen.

LOOK AT ...

We have learned some valuable lessons concerning how to live until Christ comes. Now we discover the importance of living with integrity.

READ JAMES 5:12.

But above all, my brethren, do not swear, either by heaven or by earth or with any other oath. But let your "Yes" be "Yes," and your "No," "No," lest you fall into judgment. James 5:12

1. What does "But above all" signify?

2. What phrase lets you know that no oath is appropriate?

3. Why do you think James told his readers not to swear oaths?

4. What did James instruct believers to do instead of taking an oath?

5. What is the result of failing to keep our word?

6. a. James took this instruction directly from Jesus' teaching in the Sermon on the Mount. Read Matthew 5:33–37. Why should we not swear by heaven (v. 34)?

    b. Why should we not swear by earth (v. 35)?

    c. What other things did Jesus warn against swearing by? What reasons did He give (vv. 35–36)?

    d. Who is the power behind unnecessary, untruthful oaths (v. 37)?

LEARN ABOUT ...

2 "I Swear"

To *swear* is to take an oath. Herod swore foolishly to Salome when her dancing pleased him. "He also swore to her, 'Whatever you ask me, I will give you'" (Mark 6:23). Salome's mother took advantage of the situation and told her to request the head of John the Baptist.

---

3 An Oath

Oaths were promises to fulfill verbal agreements. To make an oath testified that one's word was true and invoked consequences for not fulfilling it. We might say, "Cross my heart and hope to die" to prove our sincerity.

---

4 Yes! or No!

Instead of swearing, promising, or making an oath, we are told to be true to our word. We don't need to swear by any created thing to prove our sincerity; we prove our sincerity by acting with integrity. Actions do speak louder than words!

LEARN ABOUT ...

7 "I Promise"

A *promise* is a declaration that you will or will not do something. In other words, a promise is simply keeping your word. It means that you will say it, mean it, and do it. People who keep their word don't have to make promises.

---

8 Liars

There's no such thing as a little white lie. When we say we'll do something and fail to do it, we are liars. We live in a world of lies promoted by Satan, "for he is a liar and the father of lies" (John 8:44 NIV).

---

9 Best Things

If you are a *yes* person, remember that *no* can be a positive word. It's all right to say no to one thing so that you can say yes to a better thing. A good thing can be bad if it keeps you from the best thing.

LIVE OUT ...

7. This passage in James tells us to say what we mean, mean what we say, and do what we say we'll do. In which of the following ways have you failed to keep your word?

_____ Said to a friend, "I'll pray for you," then neglected to pray

_____ Said to a child, "I'll play in a minute," then never found the time

_____ Said to God, "I won't ever do that again," but did it anyway

_____ Said to my boss, "I'll get it done," then neglected my duty

_____ Said to myself, "I'll stop that bad habit," but couldn't kick it

_____ Said to God, "I'll make time for You," then got distracted by life

8. a. We often lie to others and to ourselves by saying one thing and doing another. Sometimes we say yes when we should have said no, and we end up breaking a promise. Journal about something you've said yes to this week that you should have said no to. (*Example: you said yes to a phone call when you should have been doing Bible study.*)

   b. Journal about how this action prevented you from keeping your word. (*Example: you didn't get your lesson done and were unable to keep your promise to participate in your small group.*)

9. In order to keep our word we must prioritize. Looking at your calendar, write a list of things you'll say yes or no to this week to maintain integrity.

YES	**NO**
(*Example: quiet time with the Lord*)	(*Example: watching morning TV shows*)

∘ ∘ • ∘ ∘

The Festival of Lying, where lying in all its forms is celebrated and debated, began at the Grizedale Theatre in Cumbria, England. The festival offers a diverse curriculum, including courses offered by professionals and professors on Internet hoaxes, techniques used by magicians and fake psychics, and discussions on lying, behavior, and conspiracy theories. Each year in November, a contest awards the title of "The Biggest Liar in the World" to the person worthy of following in Will Ritson's footsteps.

Will Ritson was a famous nineteenth-century Cumbrian who lived in the English Lake District. Will regaled his customers with regional folklore. He insisted that all his tall tales were fact—like the story about his foxhound who mated with a golden eagle: the hound's pups sprouted wings that allowed them to leap over the Lake District's stone walls more easily. Since that time, according to Will, the region had experienced little trouble with foxes.

If someone examined your life and your words, could you be invited to this festival? Do you tell distorted details to cover up promises you haven't kept, such as blaming traffic for being late when really you lingered too long in the mall? A half truth is a whole lie.

LISTEN TO ...

A [wo]man of words and not of deeds is like a garden full of weeds.

—English Proverb

Powerful Prayer
James 5:13–20

As a new Christian, the only "prayer" I (Lenya) knew was, "Now I lay me down to sleep …" I had no idea that prayer was simply talking to God, nor did I understand the power unleashed when a believer practices intercessory prayer. My first pastor, Chuck Smith, taught that intercessory prayer is real labor and real battle against Satan.

"Suppose that someone attacked you on a dark street and started wrestling with you," Chuck suggested. "If he were to pull a knife, the whole battle would suddenly be centered on one thing—control of the knife. All of a sudden, you'd forget about punching him in the nose. You'd be grabbing for his wrist and trying to knock that knife, the deciding factor in this battle, out of his hand. Satan knows that prayer brings victory and spells his defeat. He knows it's the deciding factor in this spiritual warfare. That's why he concentrates all his efforts against prayer. He'll do all he can to upset you and keep you from praying."

No matter what situation we face, praying is the most important thing we can do. Our "Powerful Prayers" may be the deciding factor in an unseen battle. As we come to the end of the book of James, we are encouraged again to put feet on our faith and act on what we believe. James knew the power of prayer, and he reminded believers to pray for the suffering, the sick, the sinner, the saint, and the straying.

Day 1: James 5:13	PRAYER FOR THE SUFFERING
Day 2: James 5:14–15	PRAYER FOR THE SICK
Day 3: James 5:16	PRAYER FOR THE SINNER
Day 4: James 5:17–18	PRAYER OF A SAINT
Day 5: James 5:19–20	PRAYER FOR THE STRAYING

DAY 1

Prayer for the Suffering

LEARN ABOUT ...

1 They Suffered

The word for *suffering* here refers to ill treatment from others. James addressed those who are persecuted, abused, or treated unfairly, not those who are sick. "This is commendable, if because of conscience toward God one endures grief, suffering wrongfully" (1 Pet. 2:19).

LIFT UP ...

God, You are an awesome God and worthy of our praise. Whether I'm sad and suffering or happy and well, help me to praise You with my whole heart. In Jesus' name. Amen.

LOOK AT ...

We've been challenged to be doers of the Word, to not be partial to the rich, to tame our tongues, to humbly submit to God, and to patiently wait for the Lord's return. In this week's passage, we read James's conclusion to his teaching on living faith with a firm call to prayer.

2 He Suffered

We follow a suffering Savior. Jesus never promised Christians life without sorrow, but He did offer peace along the way! "You may have peace in me. Here on earth you will have many trials and sorrows. But take heart, because I have overcome the world" (John 16:33 NLT).

READ JAMES 5:13.

Is anyone among you suffering? Let him pray. Is anyone cheerful? Let him sing psalms. James 5:13

1. What did James first ask the scattered Jewish believers?

2. a. Read 1 Peter 4:12–16 to learn more about suffering in the early church. How did some believers in the early church view suffering (v. 12)?

    b. How did Peter want them to respond to suffering? Why (vv. 13–14)?

LEARN ABOUT ...

3 Keep Praying

The word James used for *prayer* suggests an ongoing pleading. It could be translated, "keep on praying." Suffering can last for more than a moment; therefore, prayer must be continuous. "Never stop praying. Be thankful in all circumstances, for this is God's will for you who belong to Christ Jesus" (1 Thess. 5:17–18 NLT).

---

7 We Suffer

Beyond ill treatment, *suffering* means "affliction or distress that includes intense pain or sorrow." Suffering has been part of the human experience since the fall. Some suffering is the result of sin; some suffering serves to refine God's children. It can demonstrate God's power and help believers identify with Christ.

c. What kind of suffering did he exhort them to avoid (v. 15)?

d. What type of suffering did he commend? Why (v. 16)?

3. According to James 5:13, what action should the suffering believer take?

4. What is the second question James asked?

5. What should the cheerful believer do?

6. Review James 1:17. Why should we sing songs of praise to God?

LIVE OUT ...

7. a. From earlier lessons we know that the believers were persecuted because of their faith. Listed below are some of the ways the early believers suffered. Check the ways that parallel how believers suffer today.

____ Job discrimination

____ Family division

____ Government persecution

____ Dissension among believers

____ Persecution from other religions

____ Other_____

b. Think of some ways you have experienced similar suffering. Journal a prayer telling your heavenly Father about your pain by rewriting the following psalm: "O God, listen to my cry! Hear my prayer! From the ends of the earth, I will cry to you for help when my heart is overwhelmed. Lead me to the towering rock of safety, for you are my safe refuge, a fortress where my enemies cannot reach me" (Ps. 61:1–3 NLT).

8. Fill in the chart to discover some of the ways God helps us in our suffering when we go to Him in prayer.

SCRIPTURE   GOD'S HELP
Psalm 118:5–7
Psalm 138:3
2 Corinthians 12:7–9
Philippians 4:6–7

9. Throughout the book of James, we've learned that we can be cheerful despite our suffering. Write a list of things you can praise God for despite your circumstances.

LEARN ABOUT ...

8 Present Help

God does not always choose to remove our suffering, but He does promise to hear our prayers and help us through our suffering. Without suffering we tend to become self-sufficient and think we don't need God. Suffering reminds us that God is "a very present help in trouble" (Ps. 46:1).

9 Praise

We don't always praise God for our circumstances, but we can always praise Him for who He is in the midst of suffering. That takes living faith! Though beaten and imprisoned, "at midnight Paul and Silas were praying and singing hymns to God" (Acts 16:25).

You've heard it said, "Prayer changes things." In this beautiful poem written by an unknown Confederate soldier, we unearth the truth behind the old adage:

I asked God for strength, that I might achieve.
I was made weak, that I might learn humbly to obey.
I asked God for health that I might do greater things.
I was given infirmity, that I might do better things.
I asked for riches, that I might be happy.

I was given poverty, that I might be wise.

I asked for power, that I might have the praise of men.

I was given weakness, that I might feel the need of God.

I asked for all things, that I might enjoy life.

I was given life, that I might enjoy all things.

I got nothing that I asked for but everything I had hoped for.

Almost despite myself, my unspoken prayers were answered.

I am, among all men, most richly blessed.

It is natural to ask and hope for things from God, especially when we are suffering. Yet we've learned from James that we often "ask amiss." Thankfully, God doesn't always give us what we want; He gives us what we need to grow in spiritual maturity. Does this mean we shouldn't pray because God gives us what He wants anyway? Absolutely not! God wants us to pray with power, with purpose, and in His will—He delights to answer the prayers of His people. Whether we're going through a rough time or feeling especially joyful, it's always the right time to pray.

LISTEN TO ...

Don't ask God for what you think is good; ask Him for what He thinks is good for you.

—*Anonymous*

DAY 2

Prayer for the Sick

According to a study published in the 1988 *Southern Medical Journal*, prayer for recovery may help the healing process. This scientific study found that hospitalized heart patients had fewer complications when born-again Christians prayed for them. The study found that patients in the group being prayed for were less likely to experience congestive heart failure or cardiac arrest, as well as less likely to need antibiotics, diuretics, or the insertion of tubes for feeding or breathing.[1]

Sir Thomas Browne, a seventeenth-century physician, dedicated his life to prayer:

> I have resolved to pray more and pray always, to pray in all places
> where quietness inviteth, in the house, on the highway, and on the street;
> and to know no street or passage in this city that may not witness that I
> have not forgotten God. I purpose … to pray for my sick patients and
> for the patients of other physicians; at my entrance into any home to say,
> "May the peace of God abide here" … to pray God to give them wholeness
> of soul, and by and by to give them the beauty of the resurrection.[2]

James instructed believers to pray for the sick, not just for their physical healing but, more importantly, for their spiritual healing. Again we must remember that all prayers should be prayed in God's will. It may not be God's will to physically heal an ailing brother or sister in Christ; but it is *always* His will to bring spiritual healing and wholeness. Is anyone sick? Pray for them—body, mind, and spirit!

LIFT UP …

Father, my greatest need is forgiveness. I ask that You forgive me of my sins. I ask You to heal me according to Your will: body, mind, and spirit. In Jesus' name. Amen.

LEARN ABOUT ...

2 Elder

An *elder* is an overseer. The term literally means "aged person," not necessarily referring to years but rather to one's experience of walking with the Lord in prayer and study of the Word. Elders are to rule, teach, guard the truth from perversion and error, and shepherd the flock.

3 Anointing

The Greek word *anointing* is a medicinal term that could be translated "massaging." In the New Testament, anointing oil was frequently used in connection with healing—it was therapeutically applied to soothe wounds, refresh tired bodies, and stimulate muscles. Thus, the act was compassionate as well as ceremonial. James was clear that prayer, not potions, were responsible for healing.

6 Whose Faith?

Notice that it is not the faith of the sick person but the faith of the elders that brings healing. Today many "faith healers" lay blame for sickness at the feet of the victim. Instead, the burden sits squarely on the shoulders of the one doing the praying.

LOOK AT ...

We have learned that we should pray when suffering and praise when cheerful. We also found that true living faith praises even in pain. Now we learn to ask others to pray for us.

READ JAMES 5:14–15.

Is anyone among you sick? Let him call for the elders of the church, and let them pray over him, anointing him with oil in the name of the Lord. And the prayer of faith will save the sick, and the Lord will raise him up. And if he has committed sins, he will be forgiven. James 5:14–15

1. What was James's next question?

2. What action should the sick person take?

3. Describe what the elders of the church should do for the sick person.

4. In whose name are the elders to pray?

5. Describe how the elders should pray, and what will result.

6. Who receives the credit for this?

7. James first focused on the physical condition of the sick. Next he focused on their spiritual condition. Besides healing, what can you infer the sick person and the elders should ask for in prayer?

8. What did God promise concerning sin?

LIVE OUT ...

9. The elders should provide spiritual maturity and leadership. In which of the following ways have you sought help from the elders or deacons of your church?

____ Dealing with a sinning Christian (Matt. 18:15–16)

____ Resolving a dispute (Acts 15:2)

____ Commissioning for ministry (Acts 15:22)

____ Giving updates on ministry (Acts 21:18–19)

____ Learning sound doctrine (Titus 1:9)

____ Prayer and anointing for illness (James 5:14)

10. James encouraged the sick to go to the elders and be anointed for healing. Fill in the following chart to discover other types of anointing and the reason for them.

SCRIPTURE	ANOINTED & WHY?
Exodus 40:12–15	
Numbers 7:1	
1 Samuel 10:1, 24	
Luke 4:18	

11. More important than physical healing is spiritual healing. James taught that *all* who pray to be healed from the disease of sin will be forgiven. Journal a personal prayer by rewording Psalm 25:16–18, asking God to forgive you of your sins:

Turn Yourself to me, and have mercy on me, for I am desolate and afflicted. The troubles of my heart have enlarged; bring me out of my distresses! Look on my affliction and my pain, and forgive all my sins.

LEARN ABOUT ...

9 Honorable

Elders have the job of recognizing the gifted, helping the struggling, rebuking the rebellious, and praying for the weak. They deserve to be honored. "Let the elders who rule well be counted worthy of double honor, especially those who labor in the word and doctrine" (1 Tim. 5:17).

10 Set Apart

In ancient Israel, anointing was performed to set apart a person for a particular work or service. Anointing symbolized that the person belonged to God in a special sense. Prophets, priests, and kings were anointed with oil that was poured on their heads.

11 Forgiven

Sin can cause physical sickness: promiscuous sex causes STDs; a guilty conscience triggers ulcers. When the Corinthians partook of the Lord's Supper unworthily, Paul said, "For this reason many are weak and sick among you" (1 Cor. 11:30). Since humanity's greatest disease is sin, the greatest cure is forgiveness.

∘ ∘ • ∘ ∘

Some people blame God for not answering prayers the way they desire. Ted Turner, self-made millionaire and founder of CNN broadcasting network, once received the *Humanist of the Year* award. In his acceptance speech, he shared a very emotional story revealing that he had been raised in a God-fearing family. His sister became ill, and as her illness progressed, her condition became critical. Ted desperately prayed to the Lord to heal her and spare her life. She died. From that time on, Ted chose to believe there is no God. He would not believe in a loving God who allowed his sister to suffer and die. Ted insisted that he would live his life depending on himself, not on an unfeeling, phantom being who did not exist. The audience applauded wildly.

Simply because God does not answer our prayers for physical healing does not mean we should give up on our faith in Him. I (Penny) have suffered from severe migraines for many years. I've gone to the elders for prayer and anointing. I've asked God to heal me. I've confessed my sins. I've consulted doctors. Yet I still have headaches. Through it all I have learned, with Paul, that God's grace is sufficient for me. I've experienced God's love and power in amazing ways through my suffering. I know with absolute certainty that God will answer my prayer for healing either on earth or in heaven, and I trust Him to know which is the right choice for me.

LISTEN TO ...

I have prayed hundreds, if not thousands, of times for the Lord to heal me—and he finally healed me of the need to be healed.

—*Tim Hansel*

Prayer for the Sinner

You've heard it said that confession is good for the soul. Dietrich Bonhoeffer agreed: "A man who confesses his sins in the presence of a brother knows that he is no longer alone with himself; he experiences the presence of God in the reality of the other person. As long as I am by myself in the confession of my sins everything remains in the dark, but in the presence of a brother the sin has to be brought into the light."[3]

Satan had found a foothold in my past that was hindering the present. Although I (Lenya) had recited "the sinner's prayer," I still felt ashamed of certain sins I had committed and felt unworthy to be used by God. I was convinced that if any of my Christian friends knew how *bad* I really was, they'd avoid me. At a summer retreat, the youth pastor taught on this text in James, saying, "If Satan is continually reminding you of sins you've already confessed, if you feel stuck in the past, then confessing your sins to another could break the cycle." I was terrified but felt compelled to confess the untold story of my past to my friends. Instead of condemnation, they offered compassion. Instead of pointing fingers, they laid hands on me and asked God to heal my wounds. From that time on, the cycle of guilt and shame was broken, and the light of God flooded my soul.

Today the book of James offers hope to all believers: confessing our sins to one another and praying for each other brings God's healing touch.

LIFT UP ...

Father, thank You for the intimate relationships You have given me. Thank You for my sisters and brothers in the Lord who pray for me and hold me accountable. In Jesus' name. Amen.

LEARN ABOUT ...

I Confess

Confess means "to say the same thing." Confession openly admits sin, declaring oneself guilty of what one is accused. We must confess our sins to the Lord and to those who've been affected by them. James didn't say confess to a priest but to one another.

2 Trespass

Trespass here means "to miss the mark, to err morally, or to sin." The Old Testament describes it as acting unfaithfully. It carries the idea of a person who knows better but sins against another and God anyway. The apostle Paul wrote: "And you He made alive, who were dead in trespasses and sins" (Eph. 2:1).

4 Healed

Healing is not necessarily physical—it also includes spiritual restoration. James used the word *healed* in the context of a repentant believer becoming spiritually whole again. Confessing our sins to fellow believers will cure the sin-sick soul and bring restoration.

LOOK AT ...

This week we have learned to pray for the suffering and the sick. Today's passage discusses the value of intimate, confessional prayer between brothers and sisters in Christ.

READ JAMES 5:16.

Confess your trespasses to one another, and pray for one another, that you may be healed. The effective, fervent prayer of a righteous man avails much. James 5:16

1. What is the first thing we are commanded to do with one another?

2. Read Galatians 6:1–3. How should we deal with another person's trespasses?

3. According to James, what should we do for one another after confession?

4. What does God promise will result from prayer and confession?

5. Describe the attitude with which we should pray.

6. What kind of person offers dynamic prayers?

7. What is the effect of fervent prayers?

LIVE OUT ...

8. a. James admonished believers to confess sins to one another. Have you ever obeyed this command?

    Yes!   No!

    b. If your answer is yes, journal about a time you confessed a sin, whom you confessed it to, and how you were healed.

    c. If your answer is no, journal about whom you'll ask to become your accountability–prayer partner and what you'd like to confess to that person.

9. a. James said the prayers of a righteous person will be effective. Read Matthew 5:23–24. Describe the situation that interrupted prayer (v. 23).

    b. List the three steps required to restore the effectiveness of your prayers (v. 24).

10. A righteous person's prayers will be both fervent and effective. Based on the definitions provided, evaluate your own prayer life.

    a. The Greek term translated *effective* comes from a word meaning *energy* and speaks of "putting forth power or putting into action." Effective prayers are full of energy and get the job done.

    1   2   3   4   5   6   7   8   9   10
    powerless   powerful

LEARN ABOUT ...

8 Prayer Partner

Everyone needs a prayer partner or confidante. Choose a person of the same sex whom you trust. Things shared in these relationships (1) should be completely confidential; (2) should be prayed over, not just talked about; and (3) should never be held up for ridicule or scorn.

9 Righteous

Righteousness is the action that promotes the peace and well-being of people in their relationships with one another and with God. "The mouth of the righteous speaks wisdom.... The law of his God is in his heart; none of his steps shall slide" (Ps. 37:30–31).

10 Good Company

Powerless prayers turn passionate when others join in: "If two of you agree on earth concerning anything that they ask, it will be done for them.... Where two or three are gathered together in My name, I am there" (Matt. 18:19–20). When you pray with others, God participates too.

b. The Greek term translated *fervent* means "to be hot or boil; to have zeal." Fervent prayers are so passionate they heat things up.

1	2	3	4	5	6	7	8	9	10
ice cold									red hot

· · • · ·

Two dangers threaten confession: too little and too much. Richard Owen Roberts said, "Beware lest your concern for propriety and pride keep you from confessing those sins the public deserves to hear about. Likewise, beware that your earnestness in making all things right before God does not play into the hands of the great deceiver who would love to turn your confession of sin into an inducement for another to sin."

Joy Dawson told a story about confessing too much that rings like a warning signal. A pastor was struggling in his flesh, consumed with lust for his beautiful secretary. As the two worked side by side, his desire grew. One day the pastor foolishly confessed his attraction to his young assistant. This opened the door for Satan to gain a foothold. The secretary was harboring the same feelings. They began an extramarital affair that divided two families and an entire church. Instead of confessing to one another, they could have consulted their spouses, their accountability partners, or a spiritual advisor from another church.

Before confessing your sins to another, ask yourself:

Why am I confessing? To make myself *feel* better or to ruthlessly deal with sin?

What am I confessing? My own sins and not someone else's shortcomings?

Who is the right person to confess the sin to? Will it cause the hearer to stumble, or will this person help stabilize my walk with the Lord?

How should I confess? Publicly or privately? If you sinned publicly, confess in public; if you sinned in private, confess privately.

LISTEN TO ...

For him who confesses, shams are over and realities have begun.

—*William James*

DAY 4

Prayer of a Saint

Miracles in Black by John C. Wengatz tells of an African convert named Joao Mbaxi who became a missionary to a cannibal tribe. He came to the village during a drought, but the tribe was sure tropical rains would come soon. However, months passed without even a hint of rain. Everyone in the tribe was suffering and facing starvation. They complained to Joao that in the years they had worshipped their idols, it had always rained. They ordered Joao to leave—and to take "the white man's God" with him. When the brave missionary refused to leave, the angry chief warned, "If your God is as good as you say and so powerful that He rules the sky, why doesn't He send us the needed showers? If it doesn't rain by sunrise tomorrow, we will drink your blood and eat your flesh!"

Remembering the prophet Elijah, Joao went to his hut and urgently prayed for God's help. The members of the tribe waited for the dawn, when the Christian would become their victim. But as daylight approached, they heard the distant roar of thunder and saw lightning streak across the sky—and rain poured across the land. The fervent prayer warrior was able to continue his work for Christ for many years.[4]

The book of James brings Elijah to our attention as an example of a righteous man with a powerful prayer life. As we examine the prayers of this saint, ask yourself if you have the living faith to pray as he did.

LIFT UP ...

Father, I thank You for listening and responding to my prayers. In Jesus' name. Amen.

LOOK AT ...

Yesterday we discovered that fervent prayer yields results. Now we look at an example of one righteous man's effective prayer.

LEARN ABOUT ...

1 Elijah

Elijah was an influential prophet during the ninth century BC. Emphasizing the need for unconditional loyalty to God, he opposed accepted standards of his day, which included belief in many gods. He served as God's instrument of judgment on wayward Israel because of the people's widespread idolatry.

---

3 Pray the Word

God honors the prayers of those who are obedient to His Word. Elijah interceded earnestly because he prayed according to the Word of God and the will of God. The Word of God and prayer must go hand in hand, for His Word gives us the promises to claim when we pray.

---

5 Intercede

Elijah interceded for Israel, first for drought so they would return to God: "A drought on her waters! ... For it is a land of idols" (Jer. 50:38 NIV). Next he prayed for rain so God would shower blessings on His repentant people: "There shall be showers of blessing" (Ezek. 34:26).

READ JAMES 5:17–18.

Elijah was a man with a nature like ours, and he prayed earnestly that it would not rain; and it did not rain on the land for three years and six months. And he prayed again, and the heaven gave rain, and the earth produced its fruit. James 5:17–18

1. What Old Testament figure did James refer to, and how did he describe this person?

2. How did this person pray? What were the results?

3. To better understand the basis for Elijah's prayers, read Deuteronomy 11:13–17, and discover how God used the weather to reward or punish his people.

   Blessed with rain because (vv. 13–14):

   Cursed with drought because (vv. 16–17):

4. Describe how God responded to Elijah's next prayer and how it blessed others.

5. Look up the following passages to discover why Elijah prayed the way he did.

   a. First Kings 16:33: Describe the condition of the nation of Israel based on Ahab's leadership.

   b. First Kings 17:1: How did Elijah predict God would respond?

c. First Kings 18:17–18: Contrast whom Ahab and Elijah blamed for the drought.

d. First Kings 18:36–37: What did Elijah pray for the nation?

e. First Kings 18:38–39, 45: How did God answer Elijah's prayer?

LIVE OUT ...

6. James said that Elijah was a man with a nature just like the rest of us. From a study of Elijah's life, check off the ways you are like Elijah.

___ Self-righteous	___ Obedient to God
___ Fearful	___ Spoke God's Word
___ Complained to God	___ Depressed
___ Hungry	___ Prayed for others
___ Thirsty	___ Discipled others

7. James encouraged us to pray earnestly. Fill in the chart to learn about some biblical figures who prayed and what they prayed for.

SCRIPTURE	EARNEST PRAYER
1 Samuel 1:9–11	
Mark 5:22–23	
Luke 22:42–44	
Colossians 4:12	

8. a. Today we learned through Elijah's example to pray for our nation. With this in mind, write out some things you earnestly believe your nation needs prayer for.

LEARN ABOUT ...

6 Ordinary?

God empowers ordinary people to do extraordinary tasks. Moses, a murderer with a speech impediment, was used to deliver the children of Israel from bondage. Mary, a teenager pregnant out of wedlock, delivered the Savior to the world. When common people surrender to an uncommon God, miracles happen.

7 Earnest

Earnest prayer refers to prayer that is immediate, intense, and continuous. This type of prayer recognizes a need and turns to God for the solution. It does not give up but continues to pray intently. "Continue earnestly in prayer, being vigilant in it with thanksgiving" (Col. 4:2).

8 Intercession

Intercession is the "act of petitioning God or praying on behalf of another person or group." The sinful nature of this world separates human beings from God. However, it is the privilege and duty of all Christians to pray for others to be reconciled to God.

b. Journal an intercessory prayer to God for your nation using the following verse: "If My people who are called by My name will humble themselves, and pray and seek My face, and turn from their wicked ways, then I will hear from heaven, and will forgive their sin and heal their land" (2 Chron. 7:14).

° ° ● ° °

Elijah's prayers brought spiritual revival to the nation of Israel during wicked King Ahab's reign. God's miraculous answers to Elijah's prayers caused the people to take notice and return to worshipping the one true God. It's astounding to realize that the prayers of one person can impact an entire nation.

President Abraham Lincoln asked an entire nation to join him in prayer, proclaiming April 30, 1863, a National Day of Fasting, Humiliation, and Prayer:

> We have been the recipients of the choicest bounties of Heaven; we have been preserved these many years in peace and prosperity; we have grown in numbers, wealth, and power as no other nation has ever grown. But we have forgotten God. We have forgotten the gracious hand which preserved us in peace and multiplied and enriched and strengthened us, and we have vainly imagined, in the deceitfulness of our hearts, that all these blessings were produced by some superior wisdom and virtue of our own. Intoxicated with unbroken success, we have become too self-sufficient to feel the necessity of redeeming and preserving grace, too proud to pray to God that made us.
>
> It behooves us, then to humble ourselves before the offended Power, to confess our national sins, and to pray for clemency and forgiveness.[5]

Abraham Lincoln saw the abolition of slavery and the reuniting of a nation. Perhaps God is waiting for *you* to intercede for your country so the nation will return to Him.

LISTEN TO ...

An intercessor means one who is in such vital contact with God and with his fellowmen that he is like a live wire closing the gap between the saving power of God and the sinful men who have been cut off from that power.

—*Hannah Hurnard*

DAY 5

Prayer for the Straying

Some Christians have been known to shoot their wounded. When a believer falls into sin, it's easy to criticize and condemn the offender. However, God offers a better approach to restoring those who have strayed from the path: comfort and consolation.

A pastor's child learned this valuable lesson from an experience that made a deep impression upon him. His father received a call saying that a well-known Christian had been found drunk on the sidewalk. Immediately his father sent his chauffeured limousine to pick the man up, while his mother prepared the best guest room. The boy watched wide-eyed as the beautiful comforter was turned down on the exquisite, four-poster bed, revealing the finest monogrammed sheets.

"But mother," the young man protested, "he's drunk. He might even get sick!"

His mother replied kindly, "I know. But this man has slipped and fallen. When he comes to, he will be so ashamed. He will need all the prayer and loving encouragement we can give him." It was a lesson the son never forgot.

In his closing words, James offered a similar lesson of compassion that we must never forget. As believers we must come alongside those who have wandered from the truth. We are admonished to restore them by revealing to them the error of their ways and concealing from others the way they have erred.

LIFT UP ...

Father, when I stray, thank You for always bringing me back to the right path. Give me eyes to see those who are wandering and help me to turn them back toward You. In Jesus' name. Amen.

Look At ...

As James concluded his letter, he reminded those with living faith to pray for those wandering from the faith.

Read James 5:19–20.

Brethren, if anyone among you wanders from the truth, and someone turns him back, let him know that he who turns a sinner from the error of his way will save a soul from death and cover a multitude of sins. James 5:19–20

1. What final problem did James address among the brethren?

2. Explain the responsibility of the believers to those among them who wander.

3. Jesus talked about wandering "sheep." Read the parable in Matthew 18:12–14. Summarize how God responds to straying sheep and how He feels about sinners who return to Him.

4. James described the wanderer's sin as "the error of his way." How is sin an error of one's way or path?

5. Where will the wrong path eventually end?

6. What two things will the brethren accomplish in their rescue operation?

7. Read 1 Peter 4:8. What attitude should the brethren have when bringing people to repentance?

Learn About ...

1 Wander

Wander means "to roam from safety, truth, or virtue." In this instance it means to roam from obedience to God's Word, to gradually move away from the will of God. Wandering from the truth to sin can lead to chastening and premature death.

2 Turn Back

Turn back means "to repent—turn away from sin and toward God." The church helps the backslider by praying and promoting scriptural truth. "All Scripture is given by inspiration of God, and is profitable for doctrine, for reproof, for correction, for instruction in righteousness" (2 Tim. 3:16).

6 Cover

To *cover* means "to hide or veil." Once a sinner has repented of backsliding, God promises to cover his or her sins. This does not mean that believers should sweep sin under a carpet; it does mean that once sin has been forgiven, it should also be forgotten.

LEARN ABOUT ...

8 On Track

How to stay on track? Pray for God's help, and ponder God's Word. "Let me not wander from Your commandments! Your word I have hidden in my heart, that I might not sin against You" (Ps. 119:10–11). Trusting God helps avoid detours. Meditating on His truth exposes errors.

---

9 Backsliding

What the New Testament calls *wandering*, the Old Testament defines as *backsliding*, which means reverting to sin or lapsing morally. This term is found mainly in Jeremiah (see Jer. 3) and refers to the lapse of the nation of Israel into paganism and idolatry.

---

10 Restoration

God is the God of second chances. He delights to restore broken things. If you've strayed from Him, restoration is just a prayer away. "When he prays to God, he will be accepted. And God will receive him with joy and restore him to good standing" (Job 33:26 NLT).

LIVE OUT ...

8. James warned that some believers in the church had wandered from the truth to error. Using TRUTH and ERROR as acrostics, list some of the truths in God's Word and some ways people wander into error.

T (*Example: telling the truth*)	E (*Example: exaggerating the situation*)
R	R
U	R
T	O
H	R

9. a. We are told that when believers turn from the truth, it is our duty to pursue them that they might turn back to God. Journal about someone you know who has backslidden from the truth. What lies does this person believe? What road is he or she on?

   b. Journal a prayer asking God to bring this person back to the truth. Tell God you will be willing to be used by Him as a messenger of repentance and forgiveness.

10. Even the most well-intentioned believers can find themselves straying from God, and the apostle Peter is no exception.

   a. Read Matthew 26:69–75. Describe how Peter strayed from the truth.

   b. Read John 21:15–17. How and by whom was Peter turned back to God?

11. James taught us what having living faith really means. In closing, journal about some of the ways you have been challenged to live out what you believe. How has your faith increased through this study?

∘ ∘ • ∘ ∘

Many of us stray from the truth when life gets hard. If God doesn't answer our prayers in the way or in the time we expected, we are tempted to take matters into our own hands and wander from the truth. However, the book of James reminds us that living faith is a confident belief in God and an unwavering commitment to His promises.

Abraham trusted God's promise of fruitfulness despite infertility. He believed God could resurrect the dead while relinquishing his son Isaac on the altar of sacrifice. Paul said, "[Abraham] did not waver at the promise of God through unbelief, but was strengthened in faith, giving glory to God, and being fully convinced that what He had promised He was also able to perform" (Rom. 4:20–21). *Living faith believes God's promises regardless of circumstances, and living faith acts on God's Word.*

Lost something or someone precious? Faith believes God is good!

Depressed, lonely, or afraid? Faith believes God is light!

Marriage falling apart? Faith believes God is love!

Health waning and you are weak? Faith believes God is strong!

In World War II, these words were found scrawled on a cellar wall destroyed by bombing: "I believe in the sun even when it is not shining; I believe in love even when I do not feel it; I believe in God even when He is silent." Whether you are sick or straying, a sinner or a saint, will you turn to God in living faith and believe that His promises are true?

LISTEN TO ...

Fold the arms of thy Faith and wait in quietness until the light goes up in thy darkness. Fold the arms of thy Faith, I say, but not of thy Action: bethink thee of something that thou oughtest to do, and go and do it.... Heed not thy feelings: Do thy work.

—George MacDonald

Bibliography

The authors have used the following books and electronic sources in preparing the illustrations and sidebar material for this book.

"Aesop's Fables Online Collection," http://aesopfables.com. Most fables were translated into English by Rev. George Fyler Townsend (1814–1900) and Ambrose Bierce (1842–1914); the rest are derived from Jean De La Fontaine's French translation and have were translated to English by anonymous Internet sources. The site is maintained by John Long.

The American Heritage® Dictionary of the English Language, 4th ed.

Bible Illustrator for Windows, version 3.0F. Parsons Technology, 1998. Illustrations copyright © 1998 by Christianity Today, Inc.

Blanchard, Kenneth, and Norman Vincent Peale, *The Power of Ethical Management*. New York: William Morrow, 1988.

Blue Letter Bible, www.blueletterbible.org.

Bonhoeffer, Dietrich. *Life Together*. New York: Harper, 1954.

Bounds, Edward McKendree. *Purpose in Prayer*. New York: Fleming H. Revell, 1920.

Bromiley, Geoffrey W. *International Standard Bible Encyclopedia*. Vol. 2. Grand Rapids: Eerdmans, 1982.

Chesteron, G. K. *The Napoleon of Notting Hill*. West Valley City, UT: Waking Lion Press, 2006.

Craughwell, Thomas J. *Urban Legends: 666 Absolutely True Stories that Happened to a Friend … of a Friend … of a Friend*. New York: Barnes and Noble, 2002.

Easton's Bible Dictionary. In *PC Study Bible*. Seattle, Biblesoft: 2003, 2006.

Encyclopædia Britannica Online. Encyclopædia Britannica, 2011.

Farrar, Steve. *Family Survival in the American Jungle*. Sisters, OR: Multnomah, 1991.

Fausset's Bible Dictionary. Electronic Database. Seattle: Biblesoft, 1998, 2003, 2006.

Freeman, James M. *The New Manners and Customs of the Bible*. Alachua, FL: Bridge-Logos, 1998.

Henry, Matthew. *Matthew Henry's Commentary on the Whole Bible: One Volume Edition, Complete and Unabridged.* Peabody, MA: Hendrickson, 1991.

Hewett, James. *Illustrations Unlimited.* Carol Stream, IL: Tyndale, 1988.

INFOsearch™. Illustrations data and database. The Communicator's Companion™. P.O. Box 171749, Arlington, TX 76003. www.infosearch.com.

International Standard Bible Encyclopaedia. Electronic Database. Seattle: Biblesoft, 1996.

Keener, Craig S. *IVP Bible Background Commentary: New Testament.* Downers Grove, IL: InterVarsity Press, 1993.

Lockyer, Herbert. *All the Doctrines of the Bible.* Grand Rapids: Zondervan, 1964.

Luther, Martin. *The Letters of Martin Luther.* Translated by Margaret A. Currie. London, Macmillan and Co., 1908.

MacArthur, John. *The MacArthur New Testament Commentary: James.* Chicago: Moody, 1998.

———. *The MacArthur New Testament Commentary: Matthew 8–15.* Chicago: Moody Publishers, 1987.

———. *The MacArthur Study Bible.* Nashville: Thomas Nelson, 1997.

Marx, Karl. *The Karl Marx Library.* Volume 5. Translated by Saul K. Padover. New York: McGraw-Hill, 1972.

McClintock and Strong Encyclopedia. Electronic Database. Seattle: Biblesoft, 2000.

Merriam-Webster's Collegiate Dictionary, 11th ed.

Moody Monthly. Chicago: Moody, June 1988.

Nelson's Illustrated Bible Dictionary. Nashville: Thomas Nelson, 1986. (Out of print, but appears in *The PC Study Bible for Windows.*)

Nelson's Quick Reference Topical Bible Index. Nashville: Thomas Nelson, 1996.

The Nelson Study Bible. Nashville: Thomas Nelson, 1997.

New Exhaustive Strong's Numbers and Concordance with Expanded Greek-Hebrew Dictionary. Seattle: Biblesoft and International Bible Translators, Inc., 1994.

Peloubet, F. N. and M. A., eds. *Nelson's Illustrated Bible Dictionary.* In *PC Study Bible,* version 4.2b. Seattle: Biblesoft, 2004.

Post, Emily. *Etiquette.* New York: Cosimo, 2007.

The PC Study Bible for Windows. Biblesoft, version 3.0. Seattle: Jim Gilbertson, 1999.

Salt for Sermons, http://www.saltforsermons.org.uk.

SermonCentral.com, www.sermoncentral.com.

"Sermon Illustrations," Net Bible, www.sabda.org/netbible5/illustration.php.

Sermon Illustrations, www.sermonillustrations.com.

Smith, Chuck. *Effective Prayer Life.* Costa Mesa, CA: Maranatha, 1979.

Steel Jr., Richard A., and Evelyn Stoner. *Bible Illustrations, Book 3: Practical Bible Illustrations from Yesterday and Today.* Chattanooga, TN: AMG Publishers, 1996.

Strong, James H., ed. *Strong's Complete Word Study Concordance.* Chattanooga, TN: AMG, 2004.

———. *Strong's Concordance of the Bible.* Grand Rapids, MI: Baker, 1992. From *The PC Study Bible for Windows.*

ten Boom, Corrie. *I Stand at the Door and Knock.* Grand Rapids, MI: Zondervan, 2008.

Trumbull, H. C. *The Biblical Illustrator.* Seattle: Ages Software and Biblesoft, 2006.

Unger, Merrill F., and R. K. Harrison, eds. *The New Unger's Bible Dictionary.* Chicago: Moody Press, 1988.

———. *The Unger's Bible Dictionary.* In *PC Study Bible,* version 4.2b. Seattle: Biblesoft, 2004.

Vine, W. E. *Vine's Expository Dictionary of New Testament Words.* In *PC Study Bible,* version 4.2b. Seattle: Biblesoft, 2004.

———, Merrill F. Unger, and William White Jr. *Vine's Complete Expository Dictionary of Old and New Testament Words.* Nashville: Thomas Nelson, 1984, 1996.

Walvoord, John F., and Roy B. Zuck. *The Bible Knowledge Commentary: New Testament.* Colorado Springs: David C Cook, 1983.

Wengatz, John C. *Miracles in Black.* Nicholasville, KY: Schmul, 1987.

White, John. *The Fight: A Practical Handbook for Christian Living.* Downers Grove, IL: InterVarsity Press, 1976.

Wiersbe, Warren. *The Bible Exposition Commentary: New Testament, Volume 1.* Colorado Springs: David C Cook, 2001.

Youngblood, Ronald F. *Nelson's Bible Dictionary.* In *PC Study Bible,* version 4.2b. Seattle: Biblesoft, 2004.

notes

INTRODUCTION

1. G. K. Chesteron, *The Napoleon of Notting Hill* (West Valley City, UT: Waking Lion Press, 2006), 3.

LESSON ONE: A+ FAITH

1. "U.S. Religious Knowledge Survey," *The Pew Forum on Religion and Public Life*, September 28, 2010, www.pewforum.org/U-S-Religious-Knowledge-Survey.aspx, accessed February 20, 2012.
2. Adapted from Kenneth Blanchard and Norman Vincent Peale, *The Power of Ethical Management* (New York: William Morrow, 1988), 39–40.
3. Thomas J. Craughwell, *Urban Legends: 666 Absolutely True Stories That Happened to a Friend…of a Friend…of a Friend* (New York: Barnes and Noble, 2002), 295.
4. Karl Marx, "The Union of the Faithful with Christ," *The Karl Marx Library*, Vol. 5, translated by Saul K. Padover (New York: McGraw-Hill, 1972), 4.

LESSON TWO: IN GOD WE TRUST?

1. "'Garbage Mary' Is Really Millionaire Banker's Kin," *Desert News*, February 26, 1977.
2. Christopher Winans, *Malcolm Forbes: The Man Who Had Everything*, quoted in Steve Farrar, *Family Survival in the American Jungle* (Sisters, OR: Multnomah, 1991), 47–48; cited in "The Man Who Had Everything," *Bible.org*, http://bible.org/illustration/man-who-had-everything, accessed January 23, 2011.
3. Farrar, *Family Survival in the American Jungle*, 48.

LESSON THREE: TRIUMPH OVER TEMPTATION

1. Martin Luther, *The Letters of Martin Luther*, translated by Margaret A. Currie (London, Macmillan and Co., 1908), 221.
2. Jerry Della Femina, quoted in James Hewitt, ed., *Illustrations Unlimited* (Carol Stream, IL: Tyndale, 1988), 364.

LESSON FOUR: MIRROR, MIRROR, IN THE WORD

1. Jacob and Wilhelm Grimm, "Little Snow White," *Kinder- und Hausmärchen* (Berlin, 1857), translated by D. L. Ashliman, November 15, 2005, www.pitt.edu/~dash/grimm053.html.
2. "Man of the Glass," Infosearch, adapted from Peter Dale Wimbrow Sr., "The Guy in the Glass," *American Magazine*, 1934.
3. Nikhil Swaminathan, "Gender Jabber: Do Women Talk More than Men?" *Scientific American*, July 6, 2007, www.scientificamerican.com/article.cfm?id=women-talk-more-than-men.
4. "9/11 by the Numbers," *New York Magazine*, http://nymag.com/news/articles/wtc/1year/numbers.htm.

LESSON FIVE: CLASS WARFARE

1. Jill Briscoe, "I Don't Mean to Sound Prejudiced, but ..." *Today's Christian Woman*, May/June 1987, 32–35, quoted in Infosearch.
2. Emily Post, *Etiquette* (New York: Cosimo, 2007), 3.
3. "Catherine Booth," *Bible.org*, accessed February 20, 2012, http://bible.org/illustration/catherine-booth.

LESSON SIX: FLATLINE FAITH

1. John MacArthur, *The MacArthur New Testament Commentary: Matthew 8–15* (Chicago: Moody Publishers, 1987), 42.

2. John White, *The Fight: A Practical Handbook for Christian Living* (Downers Grove, IL: InterVarsity Press, 1976), 97–98.

Lesson Seven: Loose Lips Sink Ships

1. Jeannine Finton, "Titanic Science: Activity Guide," *Titanic Science*, 13, 30, www.titanic-science.com/TSci-ActivityGuideFinal.pdf.

Lesson Eight: The Moral of the Story Is …

1. Corrie ten Boom, *I Stand at the Door and Knock* (Grand Rapids, MI: Zondervan, 2008), 15.

Lesson Ten: What You Don't Know Can Hurt You

1. "Timothy McVeigh Profile," CNN, 2001, http://www.cnn.com/CNN/Programs/people/shows/mcveigh/profile.html.
2. Pam Belluck, "The McVeigh Execution," *New York Times*, June 12, 2001, http://www.nytimes.com/2001/06/12/us/mcveigh-execution-scene-calm-execution-site-silence-mcveigh-prove-unsettling-for.html?pagewanted=all&src=pm, accessed July 31, 2012.

Lesson Twelve: Powerful Prayer

1. Randolph C. Byrd, "Positive Therapeutic Effects of Intercessory Prayer in a Coronary Care Unit Population," *Southern Medical Journal*, 81.7, July 1988: 829.
2. Sir Thomas Browne, quoted in Edward McKendree Bounds, *Purpose in Prayer* (New York: Fleming H. Revell, 1920), 43–44.
3. Dietrich Bonhoeffer, *Life Together* (New York: Harper, 1954), 116.
4. John C. Wengatz, *Miracles in Black* (Nicholasville, KY: Schmul, 1987), page number unknown.
5. Abraham Lincoln, "Proclamation 97—Appointing a Day of National Humiliation, Fasting, and Prayer," March 30, 1863, The American Presidency Project, www.presidency.ucsb.edu/ws/index.php?pid=69891.

With Gratitude

nya—I am forever indebted to the inspiring saints who have boldly displayed their living ith to me and the world around them: Tamara Nuttle, who had the courage in high hool to share her faith with me at the risk of being labeled a "Jesus Freak." Dave and ebbie Gustaveson, who were willing to sacrifice property, plans, and their professions to come lifelong ministers with Youth With A Mission, leaving me an example to follow. stly, I dedicate this book in loving memory of my friend Patty Davis. She was the feistiest d most fervent prayer warrior ever to stand by my side. Her heart for the world, her ends, and her family motivated her to do good works that continue to shine like the stars.

nny—I dedicate this book to the memory of my grandparents. I am so grateful that they hibited living faith and passed it on to their children and grandchildren. On my maternal le: to "Mima," Lillian Maloy Whitlock, whose faith was the hallmark of her life and who ntly touched the heart of everyone who crossed her path, and to "Granddaddy," Frank hitlock, who never met a stranger and was always willing to lend a helping hand. On my ternal side: to "Mom," Beulah Pierce, who loved Bible study and prayed diligently for r family, and to "Pop," Chrys Pierce, who assisted anyone in need and whose dinnertime ayers we remember to this day.

About the Authors

Born in a small town on the shores of Lake Michigan, Lenya Heitzig moved to beach cities in California and Hawaii before settling into the mountainous terrain of Albuquerque, New Mexico, where she now resides. Whether majoring in fashion merchandising, or serving as a missionary with YWAM, or being a cancer survivor, Lenya thrives on adventure. As executive director of *she* Ministries of Albuquerque and coauthor of two Bible study series—the Pathway series published by Tyndale, and the Fresh Life series, published by David C Cook—she delights in seeing God's Word resulting in God's work in the lives of women. Her first book, *Pathway to God's Treasure: Ephesians*, received the Gold Medallion Award. She also contributed a number of devotionals to the *New Women's Devotional Bible* (Zondervan), which was a finalist in the 2007 Christian Book Awards. Her semi-autobiographical book, *Holy Moments* (Regal), enlightens readers to see God's hand of providence move miraculously in daily life. Her husband, Skip Heitzig, is senior pastor of fourteen-thousand-member congregation. Their son, Nathan, and his wife, Janaé, have two children, Seth Nathaniel and Kaydence Joy.

Penny Rose is a Gold Medallion Award–winning author. She is the coauthor of the Fresh Life Bible study series and was the general editor and a devotional writer for the *New Women's Devotional Bible* (Zondervan), a finalist for the Christian Book Award. She also contributed to *True Identity: The Bible for Women* (Zondervan). She wrote *A Garden of Friends* (Regal), as an ode to biblical friendship. Penny lives in Albuquerque, New Mexico with her husband, Kerry, a pastor at Calvary Albuquerque. They have two daughters, Erin Rose and Ryan Secor; a granddaughter, Charlotte Secor; a son, Kristian.